PRISON THEATR
THE GLOBAL CRISIS OF
INCARCERATION

Ashley E. Lucas is Associate Professor of Theatre & Drama, the Residential College, the Penny Stamps School of Art & Design, and English Language and Literature at the University of Michigan, USA, where she also serves as Director of the Prison Creative Arts Project. She and Jodie Lawston coedited the book *Razor Wire Women: Prisoners, Scholars, Artists, and Activists* (2011), and they cofounded a blog by the same name. Lucas wrote the play *Doin' Time: Through the Visiting Glass*, which she has performed as a one-woman show since 2004.

Also available in the Critical Companions series from Methuen Drama:

CRITICAL COMPANION TO NATIVE AMERICAN AND FIRST
NATIONS THEATRE AND PERFORMANCE: INDIGENOUS SPACES
Jaye T. Darby, Courtney Elkin Mohler, and Christy Stanlake

THE DRAMA AND THEATRE OF SARAH RUHL
Amy Muse

THE THEATRE OF AUGUST WILSON
Alan Nadel

THE THEATRE OF EUGENE O'NEILL: AMERICAN MODERNISM ON
THE WORLD STAGE
Kurt Eisen

THE THEATRE AND FILMS OF CONNOR MCPHERSON:
CONSPICUOUS COMMUNITIES
Eamonn Jordan

IRISH DRAMA AND THEATRE SINCE 1950
Patrick Lonergan

For a full listing, please visit www.bloomsbury.com/series/criticalcompanions/

PRISON THEATRE AND THE GLOBAL CRISIS OF INCARCERATION

Ashley E. Lucas

Series Editors: Patrick Lonergan and Kevin J. Wetmore, Jr.

methuen | drama

LONDON • NEW YORK • OXFORD • NEW DELHI • SYDNEY

METHUEN DRAMA
Bloomsbury Publishing Plc
50 Bedford Square, London, WC1B 3DP, UK
1385 Broadway, New York, NY 10018, USA

BLOOMSBURY, METHUEN DRAMA and the Methuen Drama logo are
trademarks of Bloomsbury Publishing Plc

First published in Great Britain 2021

Library of Congress Cataloging-in-Publication Data
Names: Lucas, Ashley, author.
Title: Prison theatre and the global crisis of incarceration / Ashley
Lucas. Description: New York : Methuen Drama, 2020. | Series: Critical companions |
Includes bibliographical references and index. | Summary: "Obscured behind concrete
and razor wire, the lives of the incarcerated remain hidden from public view.
Inside the walls, imprisoned people all over the world stage theatrical productions that
enable them to assert their humanity and capabilities. Prison Theatre and the
Global Crisis in Incarceration examines performances within prisons across the
globe, offering a uniquely international account and exploration of prison theatre.
By discussing a range of performance practices tied to incarceration, this book looks
at the ways in which arts practitioners and imprisoned people use theatre
as a means to build communities, attain professional skills, create social
change, and maintain hope. Ashley Lucas's writing offers a distinctive blend of
storytelling, performance analysis, travelogue, and personal experience as the child
of an incarcerated father. Distinct examples of theatre performed in prisons
are explored throughout the main text and also in a section of Critical Perspectives by international
scholars and practitioners considering the philosophical underpinnings of this work and its impact on
audiences and actors. The vivid descriptions of performances make this volume a terrific resource
for students, facilitators and teachers of prison theatre"– Provided by publisher. Identifiers:
LCCN 2020019120 (print) | LCCN 2020019121 (ebook) | ISBN 9781408185896 (paperback) |
ISBN 9781472508416 (hardback) | ISBN 9781472511706 (epub) | ISBN 9781408185919 (ebook)
Subjects: LCSH: Prison theater. | Criminals–Rehabilitation.
Classification: LCC HV8861 .L83 2020 (print) | LCC HV8861 (ebook) | DDC 365/.668–dc23
LC record available at https://lccn.loc.gov/2020019120
LC ebook record available at https://lccn.loc.gov/2020019121

ISBN: HB: 978-1-4725-0841-6
PB: 978-1-4081-8589-6
ePDF: 978-1-4081-8591-9
eBook: 978-1-4725-1170-6

Series: Critical Companions

Typeset by Deanta Global Publishing Services, Chennai, India

To find out more about our authors and books visit www.bloomsbury.com
and sign up for our newsletters

For all the prison theatre makers on both sides of the walls

and for those we lost along the way:

Buzz Alexander

Bushra Azzouz

Andrew Butler

Robert Cabot

Davie Devine

Jemma Edwards

Ryan Elliot

Tom Engel

David K. Hudson-Bey

Tim Hurley

Kenny

Nancy Loiselle

John Lonchar

Mike Maloney

Nomphumelelo Manyepelo

Sandy McLaughlan

Dick Meisler

Joyce Mvelase

Stephen Reid

raúlrsalinas

Timothy John Spytma

Andrea E. Wiggins

Agnes Wilcox

most of all

for Poppa

que en paz descansen

CONTENTS

Contents

ILLUSTRATIONS

FOREWORD

Heather Ann Thompson

There are few moments in history where the injustices visited on human beings seem utterly unfathomable. Still, we seek to understand those moments, those periods in our collective past in which the forces of rationality, and the ethos of compassion and empathy, suddenly evaporated and gave way, inexplicably but overwhelmingly, to suspicion and cold-heartedness. To understand those terrifying times in which the ugly became codified in law and then normalized in culture, we hope, will give us the wisdom we need to prevent their future occurrence.

And yet, today, we once again find ourselves in another one of those unfathomable moments in history.

Today in the United States, we imprison more human beings than any other country on the planet, and at a rate higher than at any other time in our country's past. Throughout American history, the number of people locked away in prisons has, in fact, remained relatively steady and unremarkable. That group so confined has always been disproportionately poor and nonwhite, but despite serious changes in the economy, the polity, and times of war, its size has remained fairly constant.[1] Beginning in the early 1970s, however, the number of people deemed "criminal" began steadily to rise. Whereas the prison population in this country had actually decreased by 16,524 between 1960 and 1970, in the subsequent four decades it exploded.[2] In 1972, the incarceration rate in the United States was 161 per 100,000, but by 2009, it had quintupled to a stunning rate of 767 per 100,000.[3] Today, a full 2.3 million people are locked away in this nation's "1,719 state prisons, 109 federal prisons, 1,772 juvenile correctional facilities, 3,163 local jails, and 80 Indian Country jails as well as in military prisons, immigration detention facilities, civil commitment centers, state psychiatric hospitals, and prisons in the U.S. territories."[4] Additionally, almost 7 million people live under some other form of correctional control.[5] Indicating just how punitive this moment is, nearly 53,000 children also live behind bars and, according to the Prison Policy Initiative, "nearly one in ten is held in an adult jail or prison."[6] Indeed, there are now more children serving life sentences than at any other time in our nation's past as well.

As a result of this punitive turn over the last five decades, today between 70 and 100 million Americans live with the mark of some sort of criminal record, and those Americans are, again, disproportionately poor and black or brown.[7]

The fact that the United States took such punitive turn not because of historically unprecedented crime rates, but rather because of political calculations and policy choices will deeply unsettle future generations as they look back on this unfathomable historic moment.[8] What will horrify them, however, is the staggering human costs of having made this policy choice.

Although the evidence is clear that mass incarceration has not made Americans safer, it has utterly destroyed entire communities, orphaned and significantly impoverished millions of children, and caused unimaginable trauma for those who have experienced it most firsthand.[9] While the collateral damage done to communities and people by mass incarceration can be discerned by taking even a cursory glance at this nation's most heavily incarcerated urban and rural neighborhoods, its impact on those on the inside is deliberately hidden away. Even though the overwhelming majority of prisons are public, and therefore paid for by the public and ostensibly, therefore, operated according to its wishes, the public is barred from entering prison to see how it in fact is being run and how those locked inside of it are faring.

As this extraordinary volume makes clear, however, no matter how thick or high a prison's wall, that wall can be breached by the magic of theatre. And, no matter how inhumane a prison's logics, be they prisons here in the United States or in other countries around the world, those logics are utterly undermined by the empathic power of performance.

Theatre behind bars has a long and rich history in this country and others, but it is in this particularly acute moment of mass incarceration that its own logics and its own power are truly revealed. *Prison Theatre and the Global Crisis of Incarceration* takes us into several nations' institutions of confinement via prison theatre in ways we have never before been taken. This is not just a study that shines important new light on the praxis of doing theatre behind bars, nor is it merely a powerful critical theoretical intervention in the field of theatre studies. This volume offers a whole new way of understanding theatre by marshaling the very storytelling method that theatre itself uses to engage its audience and to make it possible for that audience really to see, feel, and better understand.

Indeed, it is via storytelling and rich descriptive narrative that author Ashley Lucas is able not only to illuminate the complex experiences of doing prison theatre from the perspectives of those on inside and outside alike so powerfully but also to locate those myriad experiences in ways theoretically and contextually sophisticated. Ultimately, the stories told and experiences shared in this allow Lucas to argue that theatre, and the act of performance itself, has a role to play in society that is transformative in ways that few appreciate. Theatre does not just engage, train, or entertain; it renders those who participate in it human in ways that are unexpectedly, but wonderfully, subversive.

In fact, after reading Lucas's core chapters in this volume that explore prison theatre as both lived process and potential strategy in the United States and internationally, as well as the additional chapters authored by other experts on the theory and praxis of prison theatre, readers will understand theatre as far more than art and expression. They will see theatre as an intervention and a tool; one that can be accessed and employed to help move this nation past this most recent unfathomably unjust historic moment and maybe even to imagine a world without prisons at all. Few may doubt that prison theatre is life-changing for those on the inside who have the opportunity to experience it as well as for those on the outside who have the opportunity to join them in that experience. But, far more important, as the stories told and experiences shared in this volume make clear, prison theatre humanizes all of us and in doing so, gives us all hope for a more just future.

ACKNOWLEDGMENTS

I give foremost thanks to the incarcerated women, men, and children who welcomed me to their rehearsals and performances. I cannot list you all here, but each of you taught me something meaningful. My best wishes to you and your families.

Prison staff and administrators have also made significant contributions to this book, particularly Mary Berghuis, George Lombardi, Randy Geer, John Lonergan, Sherry Iles, and Tom O'Connor; we need more people like you who are brave enough to make humanizing changes to the system.

A Ford Foundation Postdoctoral Fellowship enabled me to begin my studies of prison theatre. The Ford Fellows and staff have helped me continuously. Koritha Mitchell, in particular, offered consistent encouragement as well as feedback on the book's introduction. The University of North Carolina at Chapel Hill's Institute for Arts and Humanities and the University of Michigan's Institute for the Humanities gave me faculty fellowships and thoughtful communities of fellow writers. My Michigan 2018 summer fellowship colleagues—Jeremy Chamberlin, Phil D'Anieri, Victor Fanucchi, David Gold, Peggy McCracken, Scott Spector, and Greta Uehling—convinced me that more than twelve people might read this book.

A fellowship at Hedgebrook enabled me to finish this manuscript at a particularly turbulent moment in my life. The peace and care of the place and its remarkable staff cannot be adequately repaid, but if you ever need me, I will be there for you and for my Hedgemates (Leslie Blanco, Drea Brown, Zeeva Bukai, Jacklyn Chan, Carla Du Pree, Dana Fitz Gale, Amber Flame, Jocelyn Johnson, Elaine Kim, Holly Morris, and Margarita Ramírez Loya) who gave me courage.

The University of Michigan (UM) provided me with generous research funding from a variety of sources, including the Office of Research; the School of Music, Theatre, and Dance; the Center for World Performance Studies; and the African Studies Center. UM's Brazil Initiative, Center for Global and Intercultural Studies, Center for Latin American and Caribbean Studies, Department of Theatre & Drama, and Residential College all helped to fund and organize my travel to Brazil for six years with my students. A Mellon Foundation Workshop on "Performance Arts and Political Action" enabled me to return to Johannesburg.

So many gracious people hosted me, fed me, took me to the theatre, and trusted me with the sensitive and beautiful work that they do inside prisons. Many of these people did not know me at all, and they took a significant risk because sensationalized and thoughtless writing about prison arts programs has often caused great harm. Though I cannot pay tribute to all who helped me along the way—some must remain anonymous—the following people enabled me to gain access to difficult spaces and introduced me to the theatre makers and performances that fill this book.

Those who welcomed me to the United Kingdom and Ireland include Phil Scraton, Tom Magill, Kirsten Kearney, Elly Goodman, Neil Packham, Jess Thorpe, Isabel McCue, Simon Ruding, Sarah Colvin, Aylwyn Walsh, Mark Bixby, Becky Warnock, Leonidas Cheliotis, Caoimhe McAvinchey, Christina Quinlan, Marie Louise O'Donnell, and Shelley Troupe.

In Canada, Kathleen Greenfield, Ingrid Hansen, and Peter Balkwill introduced me to their fanciful and fantastic work. The indefatigable Kate Rubin spent time with me in person and on the phone, tracked down photos and permissions, and ferried me to the prison. Sylvie Frigon connected me to a wide variety of artists working in prisons. Julia Ainsworth, Aleks Zajko, and Devora Neumark provided valuable insights.

In South Africa, Colette Gordon, Carol Brown, Clinton Osborne, Malika Ndlovu, Sinethemba Makanya, Sila Chatikobo, Laurie Gaum, and Lesley gave generously of their time and knowledge. Miranda Young-Jahangeer spent days with me and provided me with a host of invaluable resources.

The people I met in Australia and New Zealand could not have been warmer or more thoughtful: Deborah Beck, Mindy Sotiri, Sophia Marinos, Scott Rankin, Andrew Viney, Stuart Thorne, Sharon Hall, Moana Tipa, Miranda Harcourt, Stuart McKenzie, Molly Mullen, Robin Kelly, Rod Wills, Kelsi Cox, Leah Sanderson, Kat in Ararat, Jacquie Maginnis, Katie Langford, Michael Balfour, and Sarah Woodland. Jacqui Moyes introduced me to New Zealand's prisons and to the structural support for prison arts work there. Acacia Cochise and Michael Walsh adopted me for days and gave me the best possible crash course in New Zealand culture. Michelle Hall serendipitously appeared in Michigan and helped me make connections in Australia. Kharen Harper and Maud Clark shared their lives and work with me for several days and gave me a beautiful day with the women of Somebody's Daughter. Natasha Woods was the consummate guide to

Tasmania's prisons and later brought her family to visit mine in Michigan. Rob Pensalfini took me to a koala sanctuary to discuss Shakespeare in prisons. Gustavo Moraes and Pia Susaeta generously hosted me in Uruguay. *Espero que nuestros caminos se crucen de nuevo.* My colleagues in Brazil have become lifelong friends. *Gratidão profunda para Ana Achar, Carmela Soares Correa, Marina Henriques Coutinho, Miguel Vellinho, e Renato Icarahy. Naguissa Takemoto Viegas e Alé Melo da Luz, vocês trazem grande alegria para mim e meus alunos, enquanto cria um trabalho muito significativo. Edson Sodré, Sergio Costa, Luan de Almeida, e todo o mundo de Teatro na Prisão, todos vocês me ensinaram muito sobre o quanto podemos fazer juntos, mesmo quando temos poucos recursos. Natália Fiche, Viviane Narvaes, e Vicente Concilio, o que vocês fazem é o coração deste livro. Obrigada, Vivi, por ler rascunhos de meus capítulos e responder a todas as minhas perguntas. Por causa de todos vocês, parte da minha alma sempre viverá no Brasil.*

In my own country, my sincere gratitude extends to Heather Martin, Lisa Biggs, Niels Herold, Stephanie Gaskill, Mary Gould, Devon Johnston, Vincent Lloyd, Tiffany Ann Lopez, Alan Gomez, Rhodessa Jones, Idris Ackamore, Felicia Scaggs, Joseph Megel, Sherrin Fitzer, Alex Miller, Frannie Shepherd-Bates, Matthew Van Meter, Kyle Stefek, Curt Tofteland, James Sturdivant, Johnny Stallings, Nancy Scharbach, Howard Thoreson, Bushra Azzouz, Andy Larkin, Sharon Lemm, Diana Kardia, Christopher Limber, Rachel Tibbetts, Beth Charlebois, and Agnes Wilcox. Sara Warner and Erin Hurley supported the idea of this book before it existed. Dick Meisler and Tim O'Brien helped me interview people and record their stories.

Julita Ramírez and Jodie Lawston joined me in adventures that feature in this book. Andy Martínez's brilliance as a researcher, and warmth as a friend, fundamentally shaped this book. May we always travel this world together.

My PCAP family sustains me while doing work inside prisons every day. Buzz Alexander and Janie Paul have given decades of their lives to these labors and did me the honor of recruiting me. The PCAP staff Vanessa Mayesky, Graham Hamilton, Mary Heinen McPherson, Elaine Chen, Cozine Welch, Fernanda Pires, and Rikki Morrow-Spitzer make everything possible. Nora Krinitsky took the weight off my shoulders. Shaka Senghor helped me find the best way to teach. Andrea and Dave Scott always stand by me. Currently and formerly incarcerated members of the PCAP family have given me vital feedback on chapters of the book: Carlton Banks, Patrick Bates, Curtis Dawkins, Ricardo Ferrell, Mary Heinen McPherson,

Acknowledgments

Rik McDonough, Cozine Welch, and Martín Vargas. A host of student research assistants helped me: Hannah Agnew, Justin Gordon, Jonathan Mathews, Destiny McMillan, Stina Perkins, Lillian Zhou, Ali Friedman, Sergio Barrera, Anna Mester, and Silvina Yi. PCAP students, volunteers, and participants teach me all the time; their influence seeps through the pages of this book.

My graduate school advisers have remained a part of my life and family. Nadine George-Graves, Jorge Huerta, and Ana Celia Zentella continue to love and counsel me through every phase of my career. Marianne McDonald sponsored my performances in Ireland and got me into the prisons. Roberto Alvarez gave thoughtful feedback on multiple chapters of this book. George Lipsitz always reminds me that the struggle continues.

Kerry Myers and Jeffrey Dale Hilburn live in my heart and have supported me throughout this journey. Both contributed research to this project, and Dale has given thorough and moving responses to my chapters.

My extended family has loved and encouraged me throughout this process. Thanks to Aunt Sandy, the Naps, Christmans, Clarks, and Eckmans, especially to Leah, who went to the prisons in Brazil with me. Aunt Nancy, my second mother, traveled the world to see me perform in prisons and did not live to see this book published. My love and gratitude for her live on. My heart jumps with joy every time I lay eyes on the Woodland Creature and Justin.

Stefani and Alden were there when most needed; I could never have left if you had not come. My mother insisted that this book mattered, even at the height of a crisis in our family; her strength and love are the foundation of my life. Phil, my first and best editor, my partner in all things, my Cute Husband, saw me through all the struggles, large and small; we have so much more to love, live, and write together.

Poppa, may this book serve as a testament to your life and love. They never broke us.

PART I
PRISON THEATRE
STRATEGIES FOR A BETTER LIFE

INTRODUCTION
JOURNEYS IN PRISON THEATRE

The first performance I saw inside a prison caught me off guard. I had traveled to the Louisiana State Penitentiary—popularly known as Angola—to attend an event called Longtermers' Day in 2004. This celebration honored the lives of men who had served twenty-five years or more in prison, and families and visitors were invited to spend the day in the visiting area with over 200 men. I was twenty-five years old; every man around me, it occurred to me as I looked around the room, had been in prison at least as long as I had been alive. Angola has a wide variety of organizations run by incarcerated men, and this event had been put together by the Human Relations Club—a group whose mission is to care for the indigent and elderly and to bury in the prison cemetery those whose families cannot or will not claim their bodies. Though all of the longtermers had been told they could invite their loved ones to the event, I was among fewer than a dozen visitors that year and not related to anyone in the room. Many families could not make the journey to Angola, which sits in a Louisiana swamp over an hour's drive from Baton Rouge. Other longtermers had lost touch with their loved ones or outlived everyone they had known in the free world.

I spent the whole day inside the prison, chatting with the men and listening to several prison bands play. At one point, as we ate heaping plates of jambalaya, two men stood up and started yelling greetings to one another from across the tables. The rest of us soon fell quiet as these men claimed the front of the room as a stage and started a performance. Most folks around me knew what I did not—that the players before us were members of the Angola Drama Club. The scene that ensued involved two men standing on a street corner talking about the women they saw walking past them. They had plenty to say, and though the women they described were never seen by the audience, the actors' reactions told the story.

The scene was charming; the audience laughed so much and so loudly that I could hardly hear the dialogue, despite being seated close to the performers. The climax of the play arrived when a third actor—by far the largest man in the room—emerged from the back of the audience dressed in drag in a messy wig and a giant flowered dress. He lumbered through the audience swaying his hips, and when he reached the main characters in this skit, they lost all their fast talk and could not speak to the one "woman" who actually talked back to them.[1]

A group of men in the audience laughed so hard they actually fell out of their seats. Years later, when I started doing programming in other US prisons, I was cautioned at volunteer training never to lead a theatre exercise that involved participants lying on the floor, particularly in a group—it could be seen as a security threat, or suggest that someone had been attacked. I have no memory of prison staff being at Longtermers' Day, but they must have been present given the fact that outside visitors were mixed into the crowd. No one objected to the men laughing on the floor. Thus, though I did not know it at the time, I had watched an act of theatre shift the boundaries of what was acceptable or alarming in a prison context.

But then everything about my experience at Longtermers' Day seemed to alter, erode, or entirely undo, a boundary of some kind. All that I witnessed that day stood in stark contrast to what I had read and been told about Angola—the grim accounts of the Angola Three, who had each served more than a quarter century in solitary confinement; the stories about men in the general population who slept with phone books on their chests in case someone tried to stab them in the night. The men I met at Angola treated me with great dignity and respect. They took care of each other. The Human Relations Club had spent a whole year organizing this event to honor the fortitude and endurance of those who could survive decades of incarceration, and they celebrated with performances that required considerable talent and skill. Every piece of Longtermers' Day had been rehearsed and curated to ensure that those men and their guests could experience a few hours of distraction—a kind of reprieve from the extraordinary stress, boredom, and indignity of daily life in prison.

For years afterward, I found that I did not have the ability to make my friends and colleagues understand what Longtermers' Day meant to me. How could I explain to anyone in the free world that I had seen some of the best comedy of my life inside one of the most notorious prisons in the United States? How could I convey to others the fullness of such happiness and fun inside the same facility that holds Louisiana's death row? What are the ethics of attempting to tell such a story to people in the free world? How could I convince people to have discussions about these kinds of events instead of the crime stories that others in my life often demanded to the exclusion of any other narrative about people in prison? The play by the Angola Drama Club gave us all permission to share a kind of communal joy that is antithetical to the environment of the prison itself. Something was

4

going on there that I had never seen before; the practice of theatre made the prison into a different kind of space, one that relaxed and united the gathered people, rather than—as is the fundamental purpose of a carceral institution—enclosing and isolating them.

Free-world theatre makers have a great deal to learn from those in prison about what theatre is and can be—the ways it connects people, makes us more capable human beings, changes structural realities, and gives us reasons to endure, even in the face of great hardship. We also have much to learn from incarcerated audiences and the free-world people who are willing to sacrifice some small measure of their own freedom to work with and bear witness to performers in confinement. Rather than reproducing the current literature, which explains why professional theatre makers go into prisons, I attempt—and attempting is the best a person not living in a prison can do—to convey why incarcerated people think theatrical collaboration enriches their lives.

Part I of this book sets out to describe several meaningful strategies that imprisoned theatre makers are using to transform their lives and alter the conditions in which they live. These strategies include building communities, developing professional skills, creating social change, and maintaining hope as a means of survival. Most every theatre group I encountered was enacting all of these strategies on some level, but the troupes who serve as the major narrative vehicles for each chapter most vividly realized a particular modality for getting what they needed. Each of the next four chapters in this volume uses one or several theatre programs as central exemplars of a strategy for accomplishing something inside the prison. In Chapter 1, a group of men performing Shakespeare in a US prison use their love of theatre and one another to build communities that cross the lines drawn between free and incarcerated people, prison staff, families, and audiences. Chapter 2 describes how another group of imprisoned men in Canada develop a host of professional skills by running their own board of directors, hiring free-world theatre makers, and putting on a puppet play. The South African women addressed in Chapter 3 created a meaningful structural shift when they performed an original play about the deplorable hospice care inside the prison where they live and convinced the administration to make changes. Women in a Brazilian prison, introduced in Chapter 4, rewrote the ending of one of Shakespeare's tragedies as a way to maintain the hope they needed to endure everyday life inside the walls. The conclusion to Part I explains how these groups used theatre to reframe the boundaries of the prison—those that draw lines between the free and the captive—and made the rigid environment inside the walls temporarily more porous and elastic.

The second part of this book offers four critical case studies written by other scholars and prison theatre makers. The inclusion of other perspectives serves as a political commitment for me—to bring together multiple viewpoints in an attempt to illuminate the difficult question of what is happening with theatre inside the walls. Because prisons pose so many barriers to both research and human interaction, even people living and working inside them need much information from others in order to get an accurate sense of what occurs. The voices of the scholars and practitioners featured in Part II of this book serve as additional observers of the phenomena described in Part I and help to enliven the philosophical debates surrounding why and how people produce theatre inside the walls.

As a whole, this book calls upon us to consider how incarcerated people use theatre to make their struggles visible to one another, prison staff, and other audiences. This theatre also reveals how prisons shape all of our lives, whether we know it or not. Prison theatre makes plain the ways in which incarcerated people have greater complexity and depth than the stereotypes about those in prisons suggest, and in complicating the identities of those in prison, the theatre can make us question notions of whether any person is deserving of the things that the incarcerated endure and whether any of this makes us safer. (The most obvious answer to this last question is that most people do not feel safe when the state has total control of their lives, therefore no one feels safe in prison. Likewise, people in the free world are not safe if the state cannot be trusted to treat all of its subjects as full human beings.) We should never forget that all of our notions of freedom are built upon the backs of those who are not free. In the theatre we can join together—from both sides of the walls—to imagine a different way to live.

How Do We Know That People Make Theatre in Prisons?

By the time I arrived at Angola, I had studied theatre and performance extensively—for the duration of a bachelor's degree and three years of graduate school. No one had ever told me that people did theatre in prisons. In point of fact, historical documentation from all over the world reveals that people in prisons have been engaged with theatre for thousands of years. In the fifth century BCE, government officials in Athens would temporarily release those in their prisons so that they could attend plays and ceremonies as part of the City Dionysia Festival.[2] The ancient Romans devised a brutal variety of dramatic reenactments in which prisoners of war and those condemned for execution were forced to wear costumes and be executed in the manner of the mythological character they had been dressed to represent.[3] For a much later empire, theatre culture traveled as a colonial force alongside the idea of incarceration as the British set out to establish the only nation ever founded as a place to imprison people. In January 1788, a group of men convicted and sentenced in England arrived in the penal colony of Sydney Cove in what would become Australia; by November of that same year, they had begun staging plays.[4] Contemporary prison theatre programs have sprung up in facilities around the world in myriad ways. Much of the rest of this book tells those stories.

Undoubtedly, more prison theatre has existed than we can trace, given the array of nations and historical time periods that have incarcerated people. Such work must often have been, from ancient times, as spontaneous as a jam session, as secret as a cellmate's furtive impersonations of a testy guard. Everywhere and in every age, we find ways to perform for one another, but even when we look only at plays staged in prisons for a public of some kind, these events and people prove exceedingly difficult to track, historically or at present. Today, most prison theatre programs and those who run them keep few records and are hidden (and often censored) by the facilities in which they occur. More simply put, most of us who go into prisons to do this work put so much energy into making theatre in these difficult spaces that we have few resources left over to document or publicize what we are doing. Only the programs that endure for many years tend to have the impulse and ability to create websites, archives, program evaluations, videos, news stories, and blogs to record and share what they have done. Incarcerated people usually have even fewer written records of these programs because many prisons severely limit the amount of paperwork and photographs that a person can keep with them. At times their family members become the repositories of scripts, programs, photographs, and letters describing the theatre work, as incarcerated participants send home information for safe keeping. (One such case of a mother who adopted her son's whole theatre troupe will be discussed in detail in Chapter 1.) Therefore, nothing in this book should be read as an exhaustive catalog or complete history of prison theatre programs. Such an account could never be accurate because of the number of programs that emerge and quickly disappear without leaving much, if any, record of their existence. Rather, I focus on case studies drawn from the ten countries where I was able to travel during the six years that

I spent conducting focused research from 2013 to 2019, with the aim of gaining a better understanding of the complex function of theatre programs in the lives of incarcerated people.

Much of the highly incomplete record we do have of theatre in prisons, particularly in the twentieth and twenty-first centuries, was written by people, like me, who run programs inside prisons—theatre professionals, teachers, and activists volunteering in correctional facilities and, on rare but notable occasion, prison staff. Throughout the course of my research and my own work inside the walls, I learned a great deal about what theatre practitioners think is happening when we stage plays in prisons. Buzz Alexander, founder of the Prison Creative Arts Project in Michigan, USA, asserts that our work begins "whenever youth, adults, and students step forward together in institutions where there is much pain and little trust, to risk collaboration and creativity, to begin to laugh, imagine, and play, and to take ownership of their voices."[5] Jean Trounstine went inside a Massachusetts (USA) prison to teach Shakespeare because she wanted to give the women there hope.[6] Rob Pensalfini, artistic director of the Queensland Shakespeare Ensemble in Brisbane, Australia, expresses a desire to debunk "an underlying assumption that anything of value that happens in a prison must be concerned with bringing about changes in prisoners" and suggests alternative uses for this work, like "bringing about changes in prisons and in attitudes towards prisoners and imprisonment."[7] All of these motivations for making prison theatre rely on the assumption that prisons are dynamic spaces where growth, learning, and cultural shifts can be possible.

How This Book Describes Prison Theatre

The case studies described within the covers of this volume specifically focus on theatre as rehearsed and staged performance—whether scripted, devised, or improvised—in which actors (and often directors, stage managers, and technicians) present their work to an audience. The dynamics among directors and ensemble members during rehearsals, the process of learning various theatrical traditions and techniques, and the unique set of interactions between actors and audience members during a performance all take on added layers of meaning in the unnatural and highly regulated context of a prison.

What a theatre group can actually do inside a prison varies drastically from country to country and even prison to prison within the same state.

Within the United States, I have encountered facilities that prohibit any use of costumes, sets, or props, while the production of *The Winter's Tale* at an Oregon prison that I discuss in Chapter 1 outfitted their cast in wigs and a wardrobe borrowed from the Portland Opera and performed in front of a series of painted backdrops. In some facilities, theatre groups can meet for just an hour and a half each week, and in others, theatre professionals can spend all day inside the walls rehearsing. Some facilities allow only a select handful of incarcerated audience members to attend a performance, while others invite hundreds of members of the prison population to watch. Some prison systems forbid family members of imprisoned actors and the general public from attending the plays, while the William Head on Stage troupe in Canada sells tickets online for its productions. Certain facilities censor the scripts that can be performed, though Shakespeare's plays seldom face scrutiny, despite the Bard's tendency toward bawdy humor and violence on stage. Ultimately, the prison administration at each facility makes its own choices about what is permissible, and as a result, access to time, space, people, and resources can change drastically with a shift in personnel. Everything that can be accomplished inside the walls involves relationship building and collaboration among prison staff, incarcerated people, and outside volunteers. As a general rule from what I observed in my research, the more trust and openness that can be cultivated in a facility, the greater the benefits of the program for all involved and the higher the artistic quality of the work produced.

The work described in this book should not be confused with drama therapy, which is a very specific kind of artistic practice, ideally led by people with graduate degrees in psychology or psychiatry. Geese Theatre, which began its work in the United States in 1980 and in the United Kingdom in 1987, serves as the most well-known example of a prison theatre company that uses drama therapy techniques. Both John Bergman and Clark Baim, who founded the two chapters of Geese, have extensive training in psychodrama.[8] Their qualifications make them well suited to do work that actually uses theatre in the service of mental health treatment. However, the majority of us doing this work are not trained psychoanalysts and cannot be said to be responsibly providing any form of therapy.

Maud Clark, artistic director and CEO of Somebody's Daughter Theatre Company in Melbourne, Australia, strongly objects whenever someone likens prison arts work to therapy. She says that privileged people get to make art for art's sake, but when it is done by the poor, the marginalized, or those in prison, we call it therapy. Artistic practice of any kind can certainly have many emotional and psychological benefits for us all, but in this respect people in prison are not exceptional. I do not resist the work of arts therapy or contest the idea that art making is an inherently therapeutic process, but it becomes problematic when used as a measuring stick for success. (For more on this, see the section of Chapter 1 entitled "Toward a More Loving Prison.") Moreover, prisons cause many subsequent and repeated forms of trauma (i.e., family separation, witnessing and experiencing violence, being trapped and powerless) for which incarcerated people need therapy; it does not make sense to claim the prison as a site for therapeutic work.

Some advocates extol the virtues of theatre in prisons as a means to an end—a kind of communal shepherding of incarcerated people toward rehabilitation. Though arts practice of any kind always has the potential to enliven our humanity, to make us better than we were, people in prison do not have more to gain in this regard than the rest of us. We all could stand to work toward the goals of rehabilitation: personal growth, education, greater empathy, better decision-making, and an increased awareness of how our actions affect others. No one reaches a plateau of achievement or moral surety where we cease needing further introspection, questioning, and learning. Singling out incarcerated people as categorically necessitating these things more than the rest of us—more than, say, world leaders, professors, or indeed anyone who interacts with others—does not make sense. We all could stand to live better, and the process of theatre-making may indeed have a significant role to play in this for some people. The theatre can cultivate networks of support, empathy, and the belief that our lives and actions matter to others. If indeed this is what rehabilitation ultimately means, then people in prison form just one part of the spectrum of humanity who could use these lessons and behavioral changes.

We also cannot assume that all arts work done in prisons inherently improves the lives of the incarcerated. In Chapter 5 of this volume, Selina Busby describes an instance in which prison theatre programming led one incarcerated actor to enact physical violence upon another. In the introduction to his edited collection *The Arts of Imprisonment*, Leonidas Cheliotis describes a number of instances in which art making in prisons has actively harmed people, including a piece of theatre performed in 1944 by the inhabitants of a concentration camp, which the Nazis used to convince members of Red Cross that "Theresienstadt was a benign place."[9] Even though the majority of us who provide prison arts programming enter into the work with good intentions, we cannot assume that this work does no harm; we need to continually reevaluate the ethics of our engagement with a fundamentally coercive and punitive system.

Prisons as Spaces of Theatrical Potential

One of my colleagues in a university theatre department where I once taught told me that what I studied in prisons was not, in his estimation, "real theatre." He was quite convinced that nothing of any artistic integrity could be taking place inside a locked facility, but beyond that, his comment implied that incarcerated people did not constitute legitimate audiences. My former colleague's viewpoint may have come from the fact that so little mainstream reportage about prison theatre exists. How could he respect a thing he does not know—particularly while considering himself an expert on theatre in a broad sense?

Almost no one in the free world treats prison performances as worthy of the sort of review one would get from a professional theatre critic. The physical inaccessibility of prisons and the paucity of reporting on such performances make it difficult for many potential audience members from outside to learn of productions in time to gain the necessary security clearance for admission. Incarcerated audience members, many of whom have thoughtful and considered opinions of the theatre they have seen, have few public outlets to share their reactions with others.

The news stories that do appear about this work tend to marvel at the existence of theatre in prisons. I have yet to find a news outlet that sends its culture reporter or theatre critic to a prison more than once to review multiple plays produced by the same theatre company, as they would for an established local theatre outside the walls. In all theatrical traditions, you find some mix of glorious, passable, and totally inept practitioners and productions, and prison theatre is no exception. Popular news pieces on prison theatre tend not to analyze the production for its artistry, directing, acting, or production values but instead provide a profile of the program in question and sing the praises of its uses for rehabilitation or healing. This book does not come close to filling this significant gap in the writing about prison theatre but rather attempts to lay some of the groundwork for prison theatre to be taken seriously as a long-standing and vibrant art form and a subject of genuine interest for those who watch, critique, and enjoy theatre.

Prisons, like theatres, serve as what scholar Mary Louise Pratt calls "'contact zones,' social spaces where disparate cultures meet, clash, and grapple with each other, often in highly asymmetrical relations of domination and subordination—like colonialism, slavery, or their aftermaths."[10] The boundaries that prisons create between people seem obvious, but both the physical and cultural spaces of carceral institutions also, by definition, bring free and incarcerated people (workers, visitors, families, and residents) into contact. The prison also serves as a site of institutionalized power, as Pratt describes, reifying impossibly imbalanced relationships. As will be explained more thoroughly in Chapter 3, European colonization in Africa and other continents brought prisons as we know them today to parts of the world that previously did not have them. In doing so, the logic of the colonizer—the privileged outsider who claims to know what is best for the poor and the deviant—became enshrined in the carceral systems that now undergird nations all over the world, hence the global crisis of incarceration. Prisons now serve the world over to teach us carceral logics, like punishment, shame, social death, and institutionalized violence.

This social space of cultural contact and unequal power has the key elements of great theatre (high stakes, conflict, interesting characters). It also gives everyone in the facility a keen awareness that even when we are making theatre, the implications of what we do in that space together can have larger ramifications to improve or diminish the quality of life of incarcerated people. Such cultural shifts threaten the naturalized logic of the prison and can put theatre makers—both incarcerated and not— in precarious situations. Chloé Branders writes about her own theatre workshops with incarcerated people in Belgium in 2014, describing the tensions surrounding spontaneity in the midst of constant regulation and community participation in a place designed for mistrust: "In the particular context of prison, collective creation is as dangerous as conducting an investigation."[11]

In prison, both the folks who live inside the walls and those of us who visit or volunteer always have the sense that everything could be taken away at any moment. I have been turned away from prison because I wore the wrong clothing (even though the same outfit was fine last week), arrived during a lockdown, or encountered a staff member at the front desk who did not know how to find my valid security clearance in the facility's computer. I have been in theatre workshops in prisons that were abruptly interrupted and sometimes canceled for the day because we laughed too loud, because a staff person decided there were too many people in one room, or because a medical emergency elsewhere in the facility caused a lockdown. A group of my students once drove well over an hour through a blizzard to arrive at prison, went through a full pat down and security check, made a long walk across the prison yard in fierce wind and heavy snow, and then were turned away at the classroom building by the staff who said the weather was too bad to call the incarcerated men to theatre workshop. Another student of mine received a hug from a participant on the last day of their theatre workshop and was subsequently banned from volunteering at that prison. Some of the reasons for disrupting or canceling programs have legitimate roots in security and safety regulations; many merely reveal the arbitrary exercise of power that characterizes all prison life.

People living inside prisons face far more dire consequences in these situations than volunteers do. An incarcerated man who had been participating in the Prison Creative Arts Project's programming for years once was found to have saved a banana from his lunch and carried it back to his cell; because removal of any food from the chow hall is prohibited, he was banned from participation in any programming for an entire semester. When he filed a complaint about the severity of his punishment and asked to be allowed back into the workshop, he was instead transferred—perhaps punitively—to a different prison against his will.

These stressful circumstances can greatly intensify the experience of making theatre in prison. Because we know that our ability to congregate can be taken away from us at any time, each moment that we have together feels heightened and precious. In theatrical terms, we are truly present with one another, in the moment, and not contemplating what comes next. We focus exclusively on what is happening in that rehearsal. The distractions of the outside world melt away so that we can share our time together as fully as possible. This, of course, does not happen at every point of contact in a prison theatre program, but it occurs frequently enough to make the phenomenon palpable and notable.

This often also translates in performance into stage presence, which playwright Anna Deavere Smith describes as

> that quality that makes you feel as though you're standing right next to the actor, no matter where you're sitting in the theater. It's the feeling that you have that the performer is right in front of you, speaking to you and only you. . . . These moments have a kind of authenticity, because they reach the heart. . . . They speak to us because they are real in their effort to be together with a very large *you*, the *you* being all men and women.[12]

For incarcerated performers, particularly those who have excellent instincts about acting, this notion of presence takes on heightened stakes. Whether performing for an audience of incarcerated peers or outsiders, actors who live in confinement have a keen awareness of this opportunity to communicate to a group of people—a sense that whatever must be said and done today should be said and done intensely because this chance might not come again. This often, but not always, enables performances of extraordinary force and poignancy, even when the actors lack formal training. It also temporarily shifts the power dynamics inside the walls; prison theatre programs enable the incarcerated to become actors rather than those acted upon.

Why Do Incarcerated People Make Theatre?

Incarcerated people keep making theatre across thousands of years and in a great variety of nations. But why? Natalia Kuziakina notes the significance of the plays the inhabitants performed inside the Solovki prison camp in Russia in the 1920s and 1930s: "To most of the prisoners the theatre was more than simply a place of recreation or aesthetic delight: it was a place where one could return to one's former normal life as a free citizen."[13] Kuziakina is undoubtedly well intentioned, but I bristled when reading that last line. Theatre in prison certainly does more than entertain, but it neither makes people free nor gives them back their prior lives. Rather, as Chloé Branders argued at a conference on prison theatre at the University of Ottawa in 2016, we should get much more specific about the ways theatre does and does not make people free. Folks participating in theatre programs get certain kinds of liberties—interacting with volunteers, wearing different clothes, and spending time outdoors, to name just a few. It could help their cases for parole or give them meaningful ways to reconnect with their families. But we should never be casual or totalizing in saying that the theatre makes people free or helps them escape—emotionally or otherwise—when it does not actually release them from the walls that imprison them. That said, Kuziakina was onto something in questioning how the theatre makes the prison less prison-like.

The vast majority of incarcerated women and men I met in the course of my research had little to no relationship to theatre prior to their imprisonment. Many of them had never seen a play performed outside of a prison. Some had never seen a play until they performed in one themselves as part of a theatre program inside the walls. There were a few extraordinary exceptions to this rule. I met a woman in a prison outside Melbourne, Australia, who had done professional theatre in London's West End prior to her incarceration. A man in a workshop in a US prison had had a long career as a musical director for a variety of theatre companies. Another had been a technical director in the theatre and hopes to find a job in a university theatre department after his release. Other than these folks, and a handful of others, who held aspirations of returning to their former professions, the people I met doing theatre in prisons did not have a realistic sense of whether or how they could use their performing arts training in another setting. A few people, particularly those in the United States, hoped that they could have a career in film, hip hop, or motivational speaking after being released and believed that their involvement in a performing arts program in prison might help prepare them.

However, most of the people I met wanted to talk about what the theatre was doing in their lives at present, about how it helped them survive the daily torments of confinement. I realized in listening to them that people in prison are often using theatre as a strategy to accomplish something other than the staging of a play. Many of them held themselves to high artistic standards and sought to achieve the utmost level of skill that they could in rehearsals and performances, but what they gained in doing so transformed their experiences of life inside the walls. Like the men whose laughter sent them tumbling to the floor of the visiting room at Angola, incarcerated actors, stage managers, technicians, and audiences experience the theatre as a way to temporarily shift the power dynamics of the prison and to engage in a celebration of their lives.

A Note on Prison Terminology and the Use of Names

The words *prisoner*, *inmate*, and *convict* do not appear in my writing in this book except in quotations from other speakers or writers. I, like many activists, prefer what some call "people-centered language," privileging the humanity of *people who live in prisons* and eschewing the label of *prisoner* because it forefronts the idea of the prison itself as a person's defining characteristic. Political theorist Eduardo Galeano understood this all too well and eschewed labels that presuppose that people are incapable of growth: "*We are what we do, especially what we do to change what we are: our identity resides in action and struggle. Therefore, the revelation of what* we are implies the denunciation of those who stop us from being what we can become."[14] This dynamic sense of our ability to become something more or different than what we are today directly contradicts the idea of the prison itself, which serves as a holding tank, a barrier to growth, a force for containing not just people but also their potential. It exists to punish the person who committed the offense, and if that person grows into a different person—in that philosophically complex but recognizably truthful colloquialism—their growth frustrates the objectives of the system.

I use the terms *imprisoned person, the incarcerated,* and *people who live in prisons* because I wish to remind readers both of the humanity of those who live in confinement and of the ever-present and domineering force of the institution itself on the lives of those inside it. Though incarceration should never be the characteristic that defines a person, the state of being imprisoned does have a profound impact on a person's identity. Imprisoned person is as diverse and complex an identity category as any other that encompasses millions of people, yet the pervasive stereotypes and prejudices that color our perceptions of people serving time often flatten out these myriad individuals into a single terrifying and inaccurate image.

In this book, I often use first names, rather than last names, in narrating people's stories. Prison authorities often refer to incarcerated people only by their last names or their prison numbers, and some carceral systems will not allow scholars or journalists to publish the legal names of imprisoned people. Some of the incarcerated people in the chapters that follow chose their own pseudonyms. (Notes indicate when this is the case.) Some prison systems allowed me to use only first names of incarcerated people, and some folks in prison did not want to be named. Others insisted that their full names be printed. The academic tradition of using only last names to describe a recurring figure in a text felt like a reinforcement of prison ideology to some of the readers of early drafts of my chapters. In the pages that follow, I honor whatever requests individuals made about the use of their names, within the guidelines of what each prison permits.

My Positionality in This Work

This book grew out of a long series of journeys. The first of those took place long before I had any inkling that I would write a book on this or any subject, when I was fifteen years old—on Christmas Eve 1994, when my mother and I drove into a prison parking lot for the first time. My father had been convicted by a Texas court about a month prior and plunged into the depths of a system that we had no idea how to navigate. At that time, the Texas prisons threw all new admissions into what they call diagnostics—a thirty-day period during which a newly incarcerated person can have no contact of any kind with their loved ones. We did not even know where he was being held until he was allowed to write us a letter for the first time. My mother and I immediately flew to the airport nearest this prison and rented a car. (These details point to a degree of economic privilege not shared by many families of the incarcerated. They also point to a truth about how privilege and oppression can not only coexist but cooperate; sometimes you are allowed just enough opportunity to negotiate the terms of your devastation.) My father had no way of knowing that we were coming.

Prisons are seldom easy to reach or enter. Because of the size of the great state of Texas, my father was over 700 miles from home and over 80 miles from the nearest airport. My mother and I used the map that the rental car agency gave us to locate the prison. This was in the days before cell phones were common or GPS technology was readily available. We found our way down country roads with a paper map spread across the dashboard. As soon as we pulled up to the gate house at the edge of the prison parking lot, a guard searched our car and took away our map. We were told that our map—on which the prison did not even appear, and which would never have left our car—was contraband; it could help someone escape from prison. The officer showed no concern for the fact that we now had nothing to guide us back to town after our visit. Our map was never returned. This was my first lesson in how to understand a prison: there is no map to guide you through this experience, and even if there were, someone would take it away.

I learned much from my early encounters with the carceral state—that is to say, the systems, institutions, and social norms that enable and perpetuate an extraordinary level of state policing, supervision, and control in our lives. My father would ultimately spend twenty years and five months in prison, and my mother, sister, and I quickly realized that the forces that held him in that prison had much hold on our lives, too. Every resource we had was poured into trying to bring him home, put money on his prison account, pay for the outrageously priced collect phone calls, visit him, let him know that he was loved. I sent him so many letters that my neighborhood mail carrier once thanked me for supporting the US Postal Service. We had to learn new ways to survive financially, emotionally, intellectually. Though my father was released, some piece of me will always live inside a prison. I know too much about people in prison that I cannot forget.

In that sense, this book grows out of the perspective of a person shaped by incarceration from adolescence but who has never spent a night in prison. Many people hear the word *prisoner* and think *crime*. I hear that word and think *father*. Our family began this journey with an overwhelming sense that this should not be happening to us, that somehow fate would rescue us from the clutches of a system that neither understood nor cared about the complexity of my father as a human being or the circumstances under which he came to be convicted. The more people I came to know inside the walls, the more I realized how thoroughly unexceptional we were, how much of everyone's humanity and dignity were erased by a system that sought to draw a hard line between those who are free and those who are not.

My father was incarcerated when I began writing this book, was released in 2014, and lived in freedom for five and a half years before he passed away. Though he never participated in a theatre program inside the walls, his experiences of prison and life thereafter inform my understanding of what kinds of support systems benefit others in similar circumstances. He also informed my sense of how this book might or might not be useful to those still serving time and their surrounding communities. I would not have done this work without him, and my family connection to incarceration helped me to earn the trust of many of the people I met on both sides of the walls throughout my research process.

My involvement in prison theatre work as both a practitioner and a program director also influences how I perceive and understand the subject matter of this book. In the 2003–4 school year when I was a graduate student, I wrote an interview-based play about the families of the incarcerated called *Doin' Time: Through the Visiting Glass*. When I started performing this one-woman show, I began both to get invitations to perform inside prisons and to hear stories about other people doing theatre inside the walls. Only then did I realize that what I had seen at Longtermers' Day at Angola was not an anomaly but rather part of a larger phenomenon—that theatre programming was in fact happening inside many different prisons and in other countries.

In 2007, I met Buzz Alexander and Janie Paul, both professors at the University of Michigan who ran the Prison Creative Arts Project (PCAP). They invited me to perform *Doin' Time* in Ann Arbor and Detroit and to visit many of their weekly arts workshops in prisons. I decided to write a book about how this curricular program changed the lives of the university students leading these workshops. With the aid of a Ford Foundation

Postdoctoral Fellowship, I recorded over one hundred hours of conversation with PCAP staff, students, and faculty but ultimately abandoned this proposed book project. My research interests shifted away from facilitators of prison arts programs and toward those making theatre from inside the walls. In 2013, I accepted a position as a theatre professor and as the director of PCAP at the University of Michigan, as Alexander prepared to retire.

In the years since, being the director of PCAP has taught me a great deal about the daily machinations of administrating an arts program in a variety of carceral contexts. We offer weekly workshops inside facilities in the US federal prison system, the Michigan Department of Corrections, and a variety of youth facilities—each with their own set of rules and challenges. We also provide programming to those who have been released. Working with students, correctional administrators and staff, and those who live in each of these settings has helped me to understand how theatre makers on both sides of the walls navigate their creative engagement with one another in prisons.

These various facets of my identity have opened many doors for me—both literally and figuratively—in the process of conducting research for this book. My personal experiences with navigating family life in prison have helped some incarcerated people to open up to me about their lives and what the theatre means to them. At a number of points in my research process, people who saw me perform *Doin' Time* invited me either to visit their theatre program or to perform somewhere else, thereby expanding my contacts for further research. Often, performing a monologue inside a prison would enable me to start a conversation with a group about their own theatre practice. My status as the director of PCAP and a faculty member at the University of Michigan appears in several instances to have helped prison administrators to feel comfortable giving me access to the facilities that they run and even helped local theatre makers in Brazil to begin their own prison theatre program.[15]

Travel Writing

To go to a prison is to travel to a new destination, even if that prison sits in the center of the city where you live. Prisons often fail to show up on maps. This failure to acknowledge the presence of a building or place on official documents often indicates a willful obfuscation of the people and activities that take place inside it. Sometimes we do this for the highly privileged, as with the tombs (meeting houses) of secret societies on Yale University's campus, and sometimes we do it to hide the populations that authorities do not wish us to see or acknowledge, as with the enormous *favela* neighborhoods in many parts of Brazil. Both secret society tombs and *favelas* appear as unoccupied territory on many official maps. The spot where a prison should be often sits blank as well, the open space on the page belying the presence of hundreds or thousands of people inside.

When you do find a prison, the act of entering it displaces you from your prior reality. The landscape of the place, the single-gender environment, the rules of engagement, the uniformed staff and inhabitants, the conscription of movement, the sounds and smells all immediately indicate that you have left what you have known and entered into a new realm—one in which you have little control, whether you have come there to live, work, or volunteer. Rachel Marie-Crane Williams, who has spent much time making art with women in an Iowa prison, refers to this phenomenon as "traveling inside."[16]

I spend a substantial portion of my life en route to somewhere else. I had to travel to the world's prisons in an attempt to understand what was happening to my own family, to see the things my father could not show me and listen to others tell the sorts of stories he could not bear to tell his younger daughter. Often as I sit in cars or airplanes with the landscape rushing past me, I think of the stationary nature of life in prison. While I made my way to distant parts of the globe, my father stayed very still for twenty years. After being bounced around to a series of prisons in the first year or two of his confinement, he landed in a place surrounded by barbed wire and vast fields of cotton in the middle of nowhere West Texas. There he did the majority of his time in just one prison, going outside the fence just a handful of times in two decades so that he could receive medical treatment. The disjuncture between my body being swept away so quickly as to remain airborne while another part of me remained clamped to a fixed point in the red earth of Texas frequently left me feeling disoriented. It was the flip side of Johnny Cash's yearning lyric in the "Folsom Prison Blues," written from the perspective of a man who accepts his own confinement but feels tortured by the fact that free people keep on moving.

Travel often implies privilege, mobility, the ability to choose where you will go next. However, traveling to prisons complicates these notions significantly. The tension between the fixity of life inside prisons and the vast amount of movement required for most of us outside the walls to access incarcerated loved ones plagues both families and volunteer programs like the ones described in this book. The onus of travel—the time, distance, cost, exhaustion, and sometimes humiliation—involved in getting to the prison and through security to enter the gates always falls on the free person because those inside have no means to even attempt to meet us halfway. Incarcerated people cannot witness all the details of this struggle that outsiders make to enter prisons, but they imagine it and often feel it keenly, as they live in the supreme frustration of disempowerment, without the means to support their children and families or to ease the journeys of the volunteers who come to offer programming.

I started writing detailed accounts of my travels to my father as a way of explaining what I was doing. His physical absence from my daily life felt so enormous and profound that I needed a way to make sure that we would not lose track of one another. For about the first fifteen years of his time inside, the state of Texas allowed each incarcerated person one collect phone call every ninety days. These calls lasted five minutes each and were egregiously expensive—up to five times the cost of free-world long distance. We mostly refrained from communicating by phone because if some emergency befell him, my father would have no way to tell us if he had already used his call for that three-month period. Since the prison where he spent the majority of those twenty years was an eight-hour drive from our home, my mother and I could only manage to visit once a month while I was in high school. I saw him just three times a year after I left the state for college. We had no choice but to live our family life in letters. My need for my father was so great that I wrote him every day that the mail went out. He wrote me about twice a week, and in this manner, we shared more with one another than many people who live in the same home do.

When my research travels for this book began, I had a fresh source of content for my letters to my father. I detailed the events of each encounter I had with a prison theatre program in letters to him and emails to my mother and husband. Soon it became apparent that these narrative accounts of my travels were my best source of field notes from my research, and this material became the starting points for several of the chapters that follow. Narrative descriptions of place and culture, both in prisons and elsewhere in the countries that contain them, help set the stage for the theatre at the heart of this book. Each nation's cultures, carceral history, and performance traditions shape what kind of theatre people make in prisons and how audiences receive it. For all these reasons, this book often adopts the manner of a travelogue, alongside other research methodologies.

Methodology

I entered into this work wanting to know what people living in prisons thought about making theatre together yet knowing how difficult it is to have forthright conversations inside the walls. Issues of access and a lack of freedom of speech make prisons challenging places for ethnographers to work, as Loïc Wacquant has thoughtfully described.[17] All human interactions in a prison setting are framed by the structure of the facility and the ever-present sense of the panopticon. Even when no one in authority is actually listening or watching, you cannot ever attain a sense of privacy. Every place in the prison, including the bathrooms for incarcerated people, has been constructed to create sight lines rather than to prevent them. This means that people in prison often cannot speak directly or openly about the conditions of their lives; their speech becomes nearly as conscripted as their movements. Because of this, I have used a range of methodologies to gather information about prison theatre programs and vet the quality and accuracy of what I have found with as many relevant constituencies as I could.

I conducted research on the history of incarceration in the nations where I was studying prison theatre programs. I visited many museums and historical sites that documented carceral histories and also viewed and collected archival materials, such as videos, photographs, playbills, and other documents, from various prison theatre troupes. Theatre professionals, criminal justice advocates, and incarcerated people referred me to books and articles for further context, and some currently and formerly imprisoned theatre makers corresponded with me about their experiences after I had met them in my research travels.

My research took me to ten different countries to visit theatre programs in prisons: the United States, Canada, the United Kingdom, Ireland, South Africa, Australia, New Zealand, Brazil, Portugal, and Uruguay. Because the published literature on prison theatre has many significant gaps, I felt compelled to travel to as many countries as I could to meet with theatre practitioners and prison officials, access archives, and observe theatre workshops and performances. I began at home in the United States where I already had contacts with prison theatre makers, and those people introduced me to folks doing similar work in the United Kingdom, Ireland, Australia, and South Africa. The University of Michigan invited me to lead a study abroad program to do prison theatre work with my students in Brazil, and when my university's news service ran a story about the exchange program and released it to the press throughout Latin America, people in Uruguay invited me there to help them attempt to start a new theatre project in a prison. In this manner, the list of countries and programs that I studied grew haphazardly, through connections among practitioners and research that I did on my own about programs near others I was planning to visit. I went to the places where people were generous enough to help me gain security clearance and then let me observe and participate. I stopped traveling after six years of research, not because there was no more to see but because I realized I could go on for the rest of my life—and might well do that—and never see enough to write a comprehensive history of contemporary theatre in prisons.

The research methodologies used here are performance analysis, participant observation in theatre workshops inside prisons, formal and informal interviews with incarcerated practitioners and their collaborators, and archival research. I have been researching prison theatre in the United States since 2004 and in that time have met with prison theatre practitioners, conducted interviews, accessed archives, and seen rehearsals and performances in state and federal prisons and youth facilities in North Carolina, Wyoming, Michigan, California, Kentucky, New York, Illinois, Iowa, Ohio, Oregon, Louisiana, and Missouri. This cross section of programming in various geographic regions of the United States has given me a detailed sense of how place, culture, and differing regulations within state and federal prison systems in a single nation can have an enormous impact on what theatre makers can and cannot do within a locked facility. This also engages the creative subversion of prison doctrine and regulations in fascinating ways, showing the remarkable adaptive abilities of incarcerated people and those who collaborate with them.

A quick rundown of the timeline and nature of these trips: My international prison theatre research began informally in 2005, when I visited two women's prisons in Dublin and Limerick, Ireland, to give performances of *Doin' Time* and meet with prison theatre practitioners. I gave another such performance in a women's prison in Kitchener, Ontario, Canada, in 2011. In the summer of 2013, shortly after receiving a contract to write this book, I began intensive and focused research for this project with a journey to the United Kingdom and Ireland. In fall 2013, I took two short research trips to Canada to meet with theatre makers in Ottawa and Montreal and attended a puppet performance in a men's prison in British Columbia. In the summer of 2014, I traveled to South Africa for three weeks to Johannesburg, Pretoria, Durban, and Cape Town. I went in summer 2015 to conduct research in Melbourne, Sydney, Brisbane, Ballarat, and Ararat, Australia, as well as Auckland and Wellington, New Zealand. In 2017, I traveled to Uruguay to lead theatre workshops in prisons in Montevideo and Maldonado and to meet with government officials and theatre practitioners about starting more such programming. A symposium on performance in Johannesburg, South Africa, in June 2017 enabled me to return there to conduct further interviews with prison theatre practitioners. In November 2018, the Institute of Art at the Polish Academy of Sciences hosted a conference on theatre in prisons and introduced me to a group of scholars, practitioners, and prison staff members who had been a part of the Polish National Competition of Dramatic Art for Prison Inmates.[18] In September 2019, the EIRPAC conference on theatre in communities in Porto, Portugal, gave me access to a performance in a juvenile detention facility.

Each summer from 2013 to 2019, I have taken groups of University of Michigan students to Rio de Janeiro and Florianópolis, Brazil, as part of a study abroad program that I run in conjunction with my Theatre and Incarceration course. Students on this trip have all facilitated at least one ten-week theatre workshop in an adult prison, juvenile facility, or reentry community in Michigan prior to our travel. While we are in Brazil, we accompany faculty and students from the Universidade Federal do Estado do Rio de Janeiro (UniRio) and the Universidade do Estado de Santa Catarina (UDESC) into theatre workshops in six different prisons. Our exchange program has greatly enriched my research and my students' understandings of how theatre interacts with state power and criminal justice systems.

I have participated in sixteen national and international symposia and theatre festivals where prison arts work was discussed in Michigan, New York, New Jersey, Florida, Indiana, and Iowa (USA); Rio de Janeiro and Florianópolis (Brazil); Johannesburg (South Africa); Warsaw (Poland); Ottawa (Canada); and Porto (Portugal). At these events, prison theatre practitioners network with one another, share best practices, and imagine what the future of our work might look like. Much of my thinking about what we do and why has been shaped by the conversations held at such gatherings.

Outside of prisons, I conducted extensive interviews with professionals and volunteers who go into facilities to run or participate in these programs. In most of the prisons I visited, I had no means to conduct formal interviews, and often I could not take notes and could not even carry a notebook or pen with me. Only once in my years of research was it possible to make a video recording of an interview with the cast of a play inside the walls. I observed performances, workshops, and rehearsals; sometimes led theatre games or performed something as a means of introducing myself; and talked to as many people as I could, including incarcerated participants and audience members, staff, administrators, and family members and other free-world spectators who had come to see a play. After each visit to a prison, I would rush to the nearest place where I could sit and write down an outline of my observations of what happened that day. From those notes, I would write up more narrative field notes.

Because of the imprecise nature of this note-taking method, I have followed up with free-world practitioners via phone, email, and in-person conversations to see if their memories of events and conversations in prisons match mine. I have also asked currently and formerly incarcerated people to read drafts of chapters of this book and to give me feedback not just on the accuracy of what I have written but also on the way that I have characterized life in prison. These collaborators have been particularly helpful in letting me know whether my writing has adequately described the complex logics, cultures, and emotional resonances of the prison system and those who live inside it. Prior to publication, each of the chapters I wrote for this book was vetted by multiple people who spent time in prison.

The Human Cost of This Book: A Lesson in Institutional Power and Resilience

In postmodernity, we accept that to describe a thing is to change it; to describe prison, then, is an ethically fraught act, since tiny changes in any direction can weigh heavily on those targeted by the carceral system. The process of writing this book indirectly set off a series of events that markedly changed the life of my student Justin Gordon and many people who care about him. Justin became my research assistant in the summer of 2014 through a program at my university designed to give prospective transfer students some research experience and a sense of campus life over the summer. Justin chose me as a mentor because the description of this book project strongly appealed to him. So much so that the first time we had agreed to meet, he arrived an hour early because he was so eager to begin our work together. He alerted me early that first summer that he was serving a sentence on probation and wanted to better understand and support the many people from his community in Detroit who now live in Michigan prisons. Justin's contagious good humor, intellect, and dedication to the work quickly made him a darling of the PCAP community. He officially began his studies at Michigan in January 2015. He became a facilitator of theatre and creative writing workshops for formerly incarcerated people in Detroit, volunteered with our *Annual Exhibition of Art by Michigan Prisoners*, helped train new PCAP facilitators, and even worked as a teaching assistant in my classes. He served as an ambassador for our program and had a particular gift for making new people feel welcome, especially those recently released from prison.

In the summer of 2015, Justin researched the people and prison theatre companies that I would be meeting with in my travels to Australia and New Zealand. As I moved from city to city on the other side of the world, he emailed me dossiers on those I would observe and interview as well as articles written about prison theatre in those countries. In July, while I was abroad, Justin went to play basketball at one of the gymnasiums at our university. In the summer, students who are not enrolled in classes are supposed to buy a day pass for $7 to use the gym. Like over 300 other people that school year, Justin had gone into the gym without buying the pass. In fact, he likely did not need to buy a pass because he was receiving course credit that summer as my research assistant. The student worker at the desk—a young white woman—suspected that Justin—a young black man—was not a student and asked him for his school ID. He had no identification on him at the time, and when he refused to leave the gym, the student worker called the police. Meanwhile, Justin had gone out to his car to get $7 to buy the day pass, and when he walked back into the gym with money in hand, three armed police officers arrested him and handcuffed him in front of a crowd of students. He was taken to the local police station and released. No charges were ever pressed against him by anyone at the university.

Because Justin was serving a probation sentence, this incident set off a series of hearings that ultimately led him to spend three months in county jail for the crime of failing to report police contact to his probation officer. While serving his jail sentence, he sat (in shackles) through a two-day trial for the crime of "breaking and entering" the gym, despite the fact that nothing was broken and that he entered during business hours while the gym was open; a jury took less than five minutes of deliberation to acquit him. Then he returned to jail to serve the remainder of his sentence for the probation violation. His lawyer would hand me the paper towels on which Justin's homework assignments were written because the jail refused to provide him notebook paper. Justin had to complete at least one class that semester while in jail to avoid having his university scholarships rescinded. He also took a job in the jail's kitchen during those months as part of a program in which his labor earned him four days off his sentence. He called me from the jail, delighted to have found a way to move more quickly toward his release. A staff member at the jail told Justin that this program was called indentured servitude—a concept Justin connected with the history of US slavery only when he registered my horror on the phone that day.

Meanwhile, the university discovered that Justin had failed to check the box on his admissions application to declare that he had a criminal record. For this, he was threatened with expulsion and the loss of all of his course credits. A campaign mounted by more than thirty faculty, students, and staff members helped reduce this to a year's suspension. The university failed to see three months in county jail as sufficient punishment for Justin's transgressions and never acknowledged its hand in creating a campus climate in which armed police would be called to arrest a student for the crime of being black while playing basketball. In the years that followed his return to school, Justin could never again secure a room in university housing and was denied five different jobs on campus—all of which were offered to him enthusiastically by those who wanted to employ him and then summarily taken away from him by the Office of Human Resources because of his criminal record. In May 2018, Justin earned his bachelor's degree with honors and was the only student invited to speak at the English department's graduation ceremony. In November of that year, he completed his probationary sentence and is no longer under any official judicial supervision.

Justin has since become a poet, actor, and advocate for those with criminal records. He joins in the ongoing efforts on our campus to fight against the university's draconian policies of requiring employees to disclose felony charges, asking prospective students to check the box regarding prior criminal records, and running unnecessary background checks on both students and employees. His voice holds significant weight because of both his academic credentials as an alumnus of the university and his experiences as a persecuted member of our community. In spite of his extraordinary talent, Justin continues to receive job offers, which get rescinded as soon as someone runs a background check, even though he tells prospective employers about his record from the beginning of the application process. He hopes to have a career as a performer, filmmaker, and writer. I believe he will.

The promise of working on this book drew Justin to me and helped him gain admission to the University of Michigan, yet his presence on our campus as my research assistant ultimately condemned him to three months of jail time. He lived with me and my husband for a time in the months after his release from jail because he could not get university housing and could not otherwise afford to live in Ann Arbor; our neighbor called the police the first weekend that Justin stayed at our home because there was a black man going into our house at night. (Thankfully, that was resolved without further judicial consequences.) The fact remains that universities and neighborhoods with little crime are not safe places for everyone.

The legacies of settler colonialism and racism that plague Justin, the University of Michigan, and my neighborhood revealed themselves everywhere I traveled in the world. The poor, the black, the indigenous, the queer, and the uneducated have been murdered, fenced in, rounded up, and incarcerated in every country I visited. How can a book begin to not just shed light on this but undo the systemic forces that kill, assault, and confine generations of people? In particular, how can it do so when the system it seeks to critique is so insidious that writing the book can become a source of danger to those trapped within that system? The reality that, as Frank B. Wilderson III puts it, certain racialized bodies "magnetize bullets," while others do not, draws painful and threatening lines around this work.[19] My best attempts to honor Justin's intellect and life experience—indeed to keep him safe—put him in danger repeatedly. This book is meant to uplift, analyze, and make visible the extraordinary work of incarcerated theatre makers, yet I find myself terrified that I might write something that could be misinterpreted by the authorities, that would levy on others already living in confinement the kind of cost that Justin paid. I persist, with extreme apprehension, because knowledge, deployed well and thoughtfully, can give us gifts that cannot be taken away—education, solidarity, empathy, community, and a connection to our ancestors. The prison theatre makers described in this book also have much to teach us in both practical and ideological terms about how to negotiate institutional power, what we can accomplish with performance, and why we must not lose hope even in the face of the direst circumstances.

CHAPTER 1
THEATRE AS A STRATEGY FOR COMMUNITY BUILDING

The play's the thing
Wherein I'll catch the conscience of the king.

—*Hamlet*, 2.2.633–4

In late September 2014, I flew to Oregon, USA, to find out what a group of incarcerated men at the Two Rivers Correctional Facility had made out of Shakespeare's beautifully wrought play *The Winter's Tale*. The performance I was about to see was, in an important sense, secondary in the performers' minds to the process of its creation. Johnny Stallings, the founder and executive director of Open Hearts Open Minds (OHOM),[1] insists that the plays his group stages in Oregon prisons—including that weekend's presentation of *The Winter's Tale*—are not the most important product of their work. The plays give the group a pretext for their rehearsals and performances, which provide spaces for human connection, meaningful interaction, and community building.

Prisons are not meant to engender communities. The institutional rhetoric depicts each incarcerated person as someone responsible for her own bad choices, someone who exiled herself from decent people by breaking the social contract, someone who should not be trusted. However, theatre, like life, requires collaborations built on mutual respect, familiarity, shared investment, and even fondness for one another and the work at hand. The work of community building in prison gives people reasons to trust and support one another, to labor together for a more just and beautiful life, to tear down in some measure the categorical divisions that prisons create between people, to make vulnerability and openness signs of strength rather than weakness, and to enable appropriate and loving physical touch in a space where bodies are usually read as threats. Community building serves as a humanizing act, reminding us to be thoughtful in our interactions and to see each person in her full humanity rather than as a representation of a category like "criminal" or "guard."

Like the other prison theatre practitioners surveyed in this chapter, Stallings sees performances not as the culmination of labor but as the thing that enables the group to form a community in these terms and to spend time with one another and with audiences. In this way he and the other members of OHOM make theatre as a form of community building—a practice that this chapter will elucidate with particular attention to OHOM's work, while drawing in examples from other programs.

The Play Is the Pretext for the Thing: *The Winter's Tale* Produced by OHOM

Though seldom characterized in these terms, *The Winter's Tale* proves itself remarkably suited for performance in prison. King Leontes comes to suspect that his pregnant wife Hermione has betrayed him and is carrying another king's child. Despite protestations of innocence from his wife and others, Leontes orders his newborn daughter to be abandoned in the wilderness. Leontes's only other child, his son Mamillius, dies of an illness brought on by the false accusations against his mother. Hermione swoons and is carried away by her friend Paulina, who later reports Hermione's death. Leontes is overwhelmed with grief and regret.

A lord from the court has taken Leontes and Hermione's daughter Perdita to abandon her, and though the lord wishes to save the child, he is forced to flee without her, incidentally providing the occasion for Shakespeare's most famous stage direction, "*Exit, pursued by a bear.*"[2] Perdita is rescued by a shepherd and his son who raise her. Sixteen years and many plot twists later, Perdita resurfaces in her father's court and discovers that she is his daughter. Shortly thereafter, noblewoman Paulina brings out a statue of Queen Hermione, which then begins to move and speak. The queen was never dead but in hiding all these years. At last, the family is reunited. The play poignantly explores the fallibility of an authority figure pronouncing judgment and sentence, separation from and reunion with family members, and the extended passage of time while loved ones are held in isolation from one another—all themes that resonate very differently in the context of a prison than in other performance venues.

The Winter's Tale was performed in the visiting room at Two Rivers for two weekends in September 2014. The woman who sat next to me (whom I would come to know better later) at the closing night performance radiated joy, as did much of the audience. The prison authorities had permitted three professional photographers to be present that night, and the owners of Voodoo Doughnut—a popular eatery in Portland known for its oversized doughnuts with outrageously decadent toppings—had brought many dozens of boxes of doughnuts for the reception following the play. The prison staff had already started eating doughnuts before the play began. The room was high on anticipation, excitement, and sugar. In this way, too, the thrill of the event transcended what was on stage.

The production itself felt decadent in comparison to the sparse setting of the prison visiting room with its linoleum floors and plastic chairs. The cast included eighteen actors and two musicians (all of them incarcerated men, except for Stallings, who stepped in to play Leontes after another actor left the prison), wearing luxurious costumes and wigs borrowed from the Portland Opera. Backdrops with hand-painted landscapes hung from a small structure of plastic pipes, and the actors would pull across a new backdrop to change the scenes. The actors' performances, though uneven, were heartfelt and well-rehearsed. The cast committed fully to the world of the play, never hesitating or breaking character. The audience, even the children, laughed and cried emphatically at appropriate moments throughout the performance.

During the three-hour drive from Portland to the prison, I asked Stallings why he had chosen Shakespeare's scripts for five out of the six productions he had at that time directed in this prison. He replied that the Bard offers lots of parts for actors, all of them really good roles regardless of their size. Stallings also explained that since he lives so far from the prison, he can get there to rehearse no more than twice a week. At this rate, it takes him at least six months of rehearsals to stage a play, and Shakespeare's texts, more than others, prove themselves well worthy of holding his and the actors' attention for that length of time. Stallings also noted that prison officials do not censor the script when he proposes a play by Shakespeare. In fact, in my observation, Shakespeare might be the only playwright so renowned that prison administrators and staff in facilities around the world seldom insist that violence, sex, or profanity be edited out of the performance.[3] Stallings also finds Shakespeare appropriate material for incarcerated actors because the Bard's work has such enduring appeal for audiences: "the jokes have been good for four hundred years."[4] Stallings loves Shakespeare and the theatre itself, but he is most interested in the human interactions that the rehearsal process and performances facilitate.

Stallings, his collaborators, and the participants in this program mount productions of Shakespeare and study his works intensively. However, during my time with them, Stallings and the incarcerated actors, musicians, and stage hands made it clear that the rehearsal process was less about creating a play and more about providing a network of support to one another through the shared process of this artistic project. According to Stallings, many of the people who have attended the plays have told him that the postshow discussions impressed them more deeply than the play itself. After each question and answer session following a performance, the cast and audience are allowed to mingle, eat doughnuts, and talk about the play. The greatest payoff of this work lies not in the production itself but in the human connections formed among the cast in rehearsal and shared with families, friends, guests, and prison staff during the receptions after each performance. It turns out that the play is not the thing after all; the play merely serves as the pretext for group interaction and the breaking down of social and institutional barriers.

The History of Open Hearts Open Minds at Two Rivers Correctional Facility

OHOM, like most prison theatre programs, grew slowly over time because of one remarkable individual's commitment to the work. The process of overcoming all the hurdles of entering a prison, gaining the trust of participants, and establishing a space where a creative process can flourish cannot happen quickly, nor should it. Stallings's transformation from concerned citizen with no contact with incarcerated people to executive director of a prison arts organization outlines a trajectory taken by many of the theatre makers I met who now volunteer in prisons. Curiosity about something connected to the world of the prison or the people inside it draws them to an initial point of contact. Then the extraordinary men or women living in that prison motivate the volunteer to return repeatedly, until entering the prison to encounter those people becomes a major focus of the theatre maker's life and work.

When the Oregon Department of Corrections began talking of building a prison near his rural home in 2004, Stallings decided to take a tour of Two Rivers Correctional Facility in the small town of Umatilla to see what a prison was like. He found the staff at the prison to be "friendly and intelligent people" and the place itself "a kind of social service agency."[5] It occurred to him that a prison would be an interesting place to perform his one-man version of *King Lear*, and administrators at the facility agreed.

Stallings performed the show twice in one day for different groups of incarcerated men and held discussions with the audience each time. The men in the prison defied Stallings's stereotypes about criminality, and he found their commentary on his work to be interesting and thoughtful. They asked him to come back and perform again.

About six months later, Stallings premiered another of his one-man performances, a show about meditation called *Silence*, at Two Rivers, prompting even better discussions among its audiences. Stallings recalls:

> One of the guys said that it reminded him of ancient Athens where they would sit around with Socrates in the public square and talk about big questions. I said: "Yeah, this is great! But you could do this without me. You could just get together with each other." One of the guys said: "I hate to break your bubble, but we can't get together. More than six people can't be together at one time." (They eat at tables of six.) He went on to say: "We can't do this unless someone comes in from the outside—someone like you."[6]

Prohibitions on incarcerated people congregating with one another, outside of religious activities, exist in many facilities around the world. Such regulations are often meant to curb gang activity and political organizing against the prison, but they also prevent other community-building activities, such as peer-led classes and tutoring, support groups, and collaborative projects. Even if outside volunteers have little or no expertise in a given activity or field of knowledge, they create opportunities for incarcerated men and women to assemble and learn from one another.

Six months later, after performing a third solo play based on *Hamlet* at the prison, Stallings decided that he would like to facilitate a dialogue group at Two Rivers and found generous financial support from the Jerry and Donna Smith Family Foundation to pay for his time and the three-hour commute each way to and from the prison. He proposed that the group would meet once a week and spend about three weeks discussing each of sixteen topics, including love, freedom, happiness, and silence.

In 2008, the men in the dialogue group wanted to try their hand at theatre, so Stallings doubled his trips to the prison and began spending six hours a week with the men, rehearsing an abridged version of *Hamlet*. Ten actors, none of whom had prior theatre experience, each played multiple roles—four of them playing the title character at different points in the play. This would be the first of five Shakespearian plays that the men at

Two Rivers would do over the next six years. They also did a production of *Twelve Angry Men* in 2012.

In 2007, Stallings founded the nonprofit OHOM with the mission "to nurture inner transformation through dialogue, silence, education and the arts, in order to promote peace, love and understanding."[7] Stallings serves as the organization's executive director and continues to visit Two Rivers once a month, though a handful of co-facilitators are now working with him to keep the dialogue group and play rehearsals running without Stallings having to make the long commute so often. He also leads a weekly dialogue group with music exercises at the Columbia River Correctional Facility in Portland. The level of commitment that Stallings has made consistently for more than a decade has laid a foundation of trust and reliability that has enabled the program at Two Rivers to flourish.

Community Formation within the Cast of *The Winter's Tale*

Though they clearly love performing, the cast of *The Winter's Tale* repeatedly insisted that their work in the theatre was primarily about forging bonds with other people. In the alienating and divisive world of the prison, these men found solidarity and kinship with one another through the process of creating plays together. They often referred to themselves as "a family"[8] and spoke openly about this among themselves as well as in front of members of the facility's staff and me, though we had just met.

The morning after the closing performance of the show, I was allowed to reenter the prison with Stallings, his partner Nancy Scharbach—who was in charge of costumes, props, and sets for the play—filmmaker and OHOM advisory board member Bushra Azzouz, her husband Andy Larkin, and Stallings's friend Howard Thoresen, who flies to Oregon from New York every year to see the latest play at Two Rivers. We spent over two hours in a room with the cast and a member of the correctional staff, debriefing about the play while Azzouz filmed our conversation. In my research travels to prisons throughout the world, no other prison granted me so much access to speak with a group of incarcerated theatre makers outside of a workshop or rehearsal or to film our interactions. The support that the Two Rivers facility offers this program clearly has an impact on the ability of the men to interact with one another both during and outside of the rehearsal process.

The cast of *The Winter's Tale* and the other Shakespeare productions at Two Rivers needed one another's support in part because they always use male actors to play the female roles, as Shakespeare's own company did. Various prison theatre companies navigate the question of cross-gender casting in different ways. Shakespeare Behind Bars in Kentucky and Massachusetts (USA),[9] Shakespeare in Prison in Michigan (USA), Somebody's Daughter in Victoria (Australia), Acting Out in Illinois (USA), Prison Performing Arts in Missouri (USA), and Teatro na Prisão in Rio de Janeiro (Brazil) have all successfully used cross-gender casting with incarcerated actors. The drama programs at Mountjoy Prison in Dublin (Ireland)[10] and William Head on Stage in British Columbia (Canada) tend to use professional actors of the opposite gender to play the roles that the incarcerated company could not accommodate without cross-gender casting. The risks of cross-gender casting, particularly in men's prisons, can be significant. A director of a prison theatre company who did not wish to be named told me that when she was directing a production of *Hamlet* in a men's prison in the United States, she had cast men in the women's roles. Outside of rehearsal, incarcerated men who were not a part of the theatre program beat the actor in the role of the Player Queen so badly that the actor missed several weeks of rehearsals. Apparently, the notion of a man playing a woman so violated the gender norms of that prison that the men in the general population felt the need to take a violent stand against this actor and, by extension, the theatre group. After this incident, the theatre company ceased cross-gender casting for many years.[11]

By all accounts, the OHOM group at Two Rivers has never experienced significant discrimination or harassment for using men to play women's roles. In fact, when I asked the cast of *The Winter's Tale* how they had felt when they first discovered they would be playing women, James Stewart, who played Emilia, answered that he had been, "really nervous about playing the part of a woman because I didn't know if my voice would be low enough or sound girlish or whatever. And then trying to make myself do the movements of a woman. It was a challenge."[12] Not one of the eight other men in the cast who addressed this question in our conversation expressed the slightest bit of concern that a member of the cast would be in physical danger or experience harassment from the prison population for playing a woman. Jack Baird, who had never played a female part in any of the group's plays, remarked,

> I always admired the courage that the guys have shown that have played those [female] roles that have pretty much said, "Forget about what anybody thinks. We're going to do this, and we're going to do it the best that we possibly can." Those people I've always had a huge amount of respect for, especially doing it in a prison.[13]

A culture of respect surrounding prison theatre programming, particularly around issues of performances connected to gender or sexuality, does not tend to emerge on its own without deliberate cultivation and active commitment from the theatre group's participants. Curt Tofteland claims, "For the guys in Shakespeare Behind Bars, it's a great honor to be able to play women's roles."[14] The men in the group have done the serious work of actors to study and inhabit female characters, and Tofteland sees them as finding this opportunity to relate meaningfully to women as a privilege in an environment that keeps them forcibly separated from most members of the opposite sex.

The Winter's Tale cast raised the necessities of the ensemble above their own interests because of their investment in one another as a community. As they discussed taking on women's roles, they spoke of being needed, having "commitment," and taking part in a "team."[15] The sense that someone else needs you and that you have a unique role to play in a community can be hard to come by in prison and counteracts the institutional culture that reduces each incarcerated person to a number in a prison uniform.

They also had a lot of fun in the process, and this had significant implications for making the members of the cast feel connected and comfortable with one another. Lonnie Glinski (who played Mopsa and Cleomenes) said,

> I didn't suffer any stigma from playing a woman, I think. We all have parts, and they're all vital to the play. . . . However, I did get a lot of mileage out of it. People thought they could harass me by saying, "Well, you're wearing a dress." [I replied,] "I am not wearing a dress! I wear a skirt!"[16]

In this moment, Glinski shows that he does not take himself too seriously and also recognizes that his risk-taking in playing a female character is "vital" to the success of the group.

The Robbed That Smiles, Steals Something from the Thief: The Joy in Prison Theatre

The silliness, joy, and laughter that infuse the processes of rehearsal and performance entice new members to join prison theatre groups and help participants to feel warmly connected to one another. Everyday life in prison involves so many risks that asking people who live in such an environment to make themselves more vulnerable can seem not only counterintuitive but downright malicious. Yet, openness and vulnerability bring us closer to one another and enable bonding and the kinds of community formation that can provide individuals with protection, emotionally and physically. (In prison, those without a visible community can become targets of violence.) Theatre practice in prisons requires emotive and intellectual risk-taking. It asks people who cannot escape the constant presence of others to outwardly demonstrate a wide range of feelings. We theatre folk open ourselves to the potential for both mockery and admiration when we use our bodies and voices to represent new worlds and characters. The fact that creating a performance also involves play and laughter encourages people to do the hard work of opening up to others. With joy in such short supply in prisons (and sometimes also in the world outside), the opportunity to have a gloriously good time on a regular basis motivates people to care about one another and consistently return to the group.

My students at the Prison Creative Arts Project (PCAP) facilitate weekly theatre workshops in adult and youth correctional facilities, and my perennial instruction to them as they enter these spaces of confinement each week is to *bring the joy*. Whether or not any of us who make theatre in prisons succeed in creating great art, an essential piece of the work is to enable moments of fun, happiness, and laughter in places where people often struggle to get through the day. The greatest contraband a person can sneak into a prison is joy. My students consistently report that they find immense pleasure in this work as well. They often say that going to prison is the best part of their week. None of them enjoy prisons, but the workshop participants they meet there give more of themselves and engage one another as a supportive community far more than people we meet outside the walls.

A healthy theatre ensemble engenders a supportive environment that values each group member for their strengths and finds ways to highlight what each person does best. Prisons as institutions tend to work hard to make sure individuals never lose sight of their status as confined people, undeserving of recognition. When we succeed in finding joy together in prison—the kind that comes from a genuine celebration of life and not from asserting our superiority over others—we take back some power from the dehumanizing force of the prison. In Shakespeare's words, "The robbed that smiles, steals something from the thief."[17] Any day that an incarcerated person experiences happiness in prison, they reassert their humanity and the sense that the place in which they live cannot fully define them.

The cast of *The Winter's Tale* laughed often during our discussion on the morning after closing night of the play. (They also wept openly. More on that later.) Eight different men shared memories about other members of the cast helping them to learn their lines or feel comfortable speaking in public. Often these tales involved humor, usually in the form of the men trying to distract one another in order to test their castmates' ability to stay in character. One such moment involved a man surprising the actor playing the Old Shepherd as he was on the prison's basketball court reciting lines. Another actor lay down on the ground in a fetal position behind the Shepherd and pretended to be the infant Perdita so that when the Shepherd turned around to find the baby, he actually discovered a grown man making baby faces.[18] The theatre engenders many such moments of joy, silliness, and collaboration inside the prison and gives participants a reason and courage to model positive friendship and interactions in public.

The men in *The Winter's Tale* shared this sense of fun with their audiences during their performances and in the magical times before and after the play when they could interact freely with outsiders. During the discussion with the cast, Joshua Friar (Young Shepherd) recounted this story about another actor's young grandchildren who came to see the play:

> When they first came in, there was a stack of cookies. (*laughter*) about this tall (*gestures 18 inches high*) that had come off our food carts, and I approached their mom. And I said, "Is this okay?" and she said yes. I said, "I have a job for you to do. We have this stack of cookies that need to disappear. (*laughter*) And I need your help with this." And their eyes got . . . big . . . and they all picked one cookie up, and I says [*sic*], "What kind of kids are you?" I said, "Go get all of them!" (*laughter*) They . . . got them all. And they were all happy, and then your granddaughter came up to me at the end of the play. And she goes, "You know that job you had us do? We got it done." (*laughter*)[19]

Friar essentially engaged his friend's grandchildren in a role-playing game, making the gift of cookies into a call for assistance. Though at face value this may sound like routine behavior, it bears the added significance of happening in a prison, where the resident population has very limited access to children, particularly when they are not part of one's own family. Under most other circumstances, the prison authorities and the girls' mother and grandfather would likely have prevented the children from having any contact with other incarcerated men. The joy of this moment of connection before the play—and those that followed the performance, which will be discussed later—can only take place because of the cast's demonstration of themselves as a cohesive and trustworthy group.

Prison Theatre and the Formation of Group Identity

In order for such collective cohesion to happen, each member of the group had to make active choices both to participate and to invest in the rest of the people in the cast. Joseph Opyd, who played the teenage Perdita in *The Winter's Tale,* described the experience of being in the play as having "helped me to mold my character. It helps me to see who I want to be, you know. I especially like this group of guys, you know. Every one of you means something so special to me. All of you do."[20] This level of openness and sincere regard for the other men in the group flies in the face of the vast majority of popular and sensationalized representations of the social interactions of men in prison. It also emphasizes the fact that people who live inside the walls can and do have meaningful, nonviolent, noncoercive, nurturing, and even tender relationships with one another.

The opportunity to create theatre in prison gives incarcerated people the chance to reimagine themselves, individually and as a group. All theatre enables this process, but it takes on additional layers of meaning in prison, which by its very nature works to flatten out individual identities and demands conformity in most aspects of daily life. Niels Herold describes the experience of witnessing incarcerated actors asserting themselves on stage, "The richness of these extraordinary prison productions lies . . . in the profound delight we can feel the inmates discovering in their efforts to give the plays and themselves another life."[21] All plays certainly receive life whenever they are embodied anew, but the question of "another life" for incarcerated actors is not as simple.

The theatre—particularly when well produced—can momentarily lift performers and audiences out of the present setting and into a different and shared experience. This does not, however, free people from incarceration. The gift of being able to cease thinking about imprisonment for a moment has profound implications, but it does not ultimately remove individuals from state control, change their legal status, or even enable them to use the restroom without asking permission. The theatre can promote free thinking and empathy, but it is not, in fact, liberation.

Jack Baird (Autolycus and the First Lord) acknowledges this while also emphasizing the magnitude of his theatre experiences on his life:

> I'm an inmate in an American prison, and . . . as luck would have it, I happen to be in a prison where I'm actually able to . . . perform in a play and get to express myself to other people that don't live in prison. . . . There's not one day that goes by that I don't tell somebody how lucky I am for the things that I do have, and one of them is this group of guys. . . . The fact that we can do things here at this prison that no other inmate can do in the state of Oregon. . . . That's huge to me. That's huge to my family. . . . It's a life changing thing on so many levels that . . . it's really hard to take it in some days.[22]

This experience has not removed him from confinement, but it has significantly improved the quality of his life and, by extension, his family's. Baird sees his connections to the rest of the cast and their collective ability to communicate with people who do not live in prison as exceptional in the environment of the prison. Of course, the people from the world outside prison with whom the cast has the most contact are the theatre makers who come into the prison to rehearse and produce the plays.

As one of the men who met Stallings after one of his early solo performances at Two Rivers mentioned, the presence of volunteers in the prison makes it possible for the incarcerated men to congregate and collaborate. Without the presence of non-incarcerated theatre makers, the group cannot exist. This holds true in most prisons in the United States and in carceral systems in many other parts of the world as well. After the closing of *The Winter's Tale*, cast member Philip Florek reflected on his interactions with others in the theatre troupe,

> I'm just excited that I got to meet everybody here and more positive people in prison than I knew existed . . . and then everybody that came in and has volunteered their time or just came to watch, it's just amazing to me that people would actually care that much about a prisoner.[23]

The cast had many kind and specific words of praise for Stallings and the other volunteers with OHOM, but Florek's comment here reflects the abjection and abandonment that many people in prison feel. It strikes him as remarkable that another person would care about the humanity of imprisoned people rather than seeing them simply as an embodiment of criminality. The project of creating a performance together gives volunteers and incarcerated people alike the ability to connect with one another about something other than prison. I rediscovered this when I visited the Shakespeare Behind Bars program in Michigan.

Shakespeare Behind Bars in Michigan: "Please, Would You Please Do *Macbeth*?"

Curt L. Tofteland tells me that prisons offer the best places in the world to gain a better understanding of humanity. All of the work that he does with prison theatre stems from the question, "What does it mean to be human?" Tofteland has found meaningful answers to this question in Shakespeare's texts and in his interactions with incarcerated people.[24] He started going into Kentucky prisons in 1995 and began a process of exploring art, theatre, original writing, and Shakespeare's writings with incarcerated men and women.[25] This work developed into Shakespeare Behind Bars (SBB)—one of the best-known prison theatre programs in the United States. Their eponymous documentary film follows the creation of a 2003 production of *The Tempest* with men inside Luther Luckett Correctional Complex in LaGrange, Kentucky.[26] In 2008, Tofteland moved to Michigan and began a new set of SBB programs in that state in 2011, while the Kentucky programming continues under Artistic Director Matt Wallace.[27]

On a bright morning in late June 2014, I drove from my home in Ann Arbor to visit Tofteland and the men in SBB at Earnest C. Brooks Correctional Facility in Muskegon Heights, Michigan. Tofteland and his co-facilitator Edward Hartline took me to a classroom in the prison where some of the men from the group had already taken up their places in the circle of chairs. As they entered, Tofteland and Hartline walked around the room shaking hands with every man in the circle before they chose their own seats. I did the same and settled myself next to a man named James Sturdivant, who had previously been published in the *Michigan Review of Prisoner Creative Writing*—the literary journal edited by my husband Phil Christman at PCAP. As we chatted about writing, other men entered the room and shook everyone's hands before sitting down. Everyone warmly acknowledged me in the moment of the handshake, and no one seemed to mind my presence or express much curiosity about me, though I had not yet been introduced to the group. Warden Mary Berghuis walked into the room and joined the circle as well.[28] The men welcomed her without reservation and did not seem the least bit concerned that the most powerful person in the prison had taken a part in their group.

Small conversations formed all over the circle, and as we all talked to our neighbors, I began to wonder when and how the workshop would start. This could easily have been morning coffee hour at a local diner if we had not been in prison and were allowed refreshments. What did any of this have to do with Shakespeare? Quite a few of the men carried a hardback copy of the Royal Shakespeare Company edition of *The Complete Works of Shakespeare*, but otherwise nothing about the energy of the group suggested that we might soon do something performative.

Gradually, one conversation in the room began to seem more urgent than the others. Tofteland spoke across the circle to a man who seemed distressed. The rest of the room fell silent, as this man told us about his children. Their mother would soon be moving out of state to live with another man, and the children would go with her. This father mourned the fact that this would essentially mean that he would not have any contact with his children. The only way that they communicated now was through phone calls when his mother would watch the children. When they moved away, those calls would stop. He also worried about whether the new man would be kind to his children.

Other men in the circle began responding to things the concerned father said. They told stories about their own children's responses to difficult situations. One man said that his son had come to visit recently and claimed to remember the day that his father was arrested. The father responded that his son could not possibly remember that day because the child had been a toddler when it happened. The son remembered crouching under a table while police officers burst into the house, threw his father on the floor, and handcuffed him. The father listened in astonishment as his son recalled specific things that had been said and done that terrible day. Ultimately, this man wanted the other concerned father to know that his child had survived this trauma and still grew into a well-adjusted young man. The first father could have hope that his children would be able to face whatever they might encounter.

Another man jumped into the conversation. He told the concerned father that everyone in that circle trusted him to do the right thing by his children. They knew him well and believed him to be a good father. He said, "We should keep talking about this situation, but first, please, would you please do *Macbeth*?" For a moment, I thought I must have misheard him.

Could he really be asking this worried father to perform Shakespeare in the middle of this conversation? Before I could delve further into my own doubt, the father, still seated in his chair, began reciting:

> To-morrow, and to-morrow, and to-morrow,
> Creeps in this petty pace from day to day
> To the last syllable of recorded time,
> And all our yesterdays have lighted fools
> The way to dusty death. Out, out, brief candle!
> Life's but a walking shadow, a poor player
> That struts and frets his hour upon the stage
> And then is heard no more: it is a tale
> Told by an idiot, full of sound and fury,
> Signifying nothing.[29]

He stumbled over a line, and the rest of the men in the group, without hesitation and as a chorus, fed him the correct words. The father repeated the line the group had given him and continued to the end. We applauded, and he immediately commenced speaking about his children again.

I have heard this monologue performed many times, but never has it struck me with such poignancy and depth. Macbeth says these words after being told that his wife has died, and this father in a Michigan prison imbued the words with the sorrow of his confinement, the futility he felt with the passage of time, the profound barriers between him and his children who grew and changed every day without him being able to bear witness to their lives. I wept silently and tried to brush my tears away without being noticed. The conversation proceeded in this manner for at least fifteen minutes longer—heartfelt stories about people's children interrupted by Shakespearian monologues.

When the conversation had wound down sufficiently, Tofteland changed the tone of the day by introducing me. I thanked the men for their generosity and told them that my father had just been released one month earlier, after serving twenty years and five months in a Texas prison. I described the one-woman play I perform about the families of incarcerated people. The unplanned synergy between their chosen topic of the day and my life and work struck us all. I performed three monologues from my play, and we talked more about our families and how performance brings us into the same room and enables us to have conversations we otherwise could not have had.

Shakespeare Behind Bars: The Circle as a Place to Practice Humanity

SBB participants and facilitators always sit in a circle and often articulate their group identity in these terms. The circle, built on trust and safety, serves as a place where members can be remarkably open and vulnerable without harm. Tofteland sees this work as good for all people but particularly vital to those in prison because the environment "pushes everything toward non-trust." He says all members of the circle, including himself, come there to "practice being human." (This aligns well with Harold Bloom's notion that Shakespeare played an essential role in our literary understandings of humanity as we know it.[30]) Because trust and openness prove difficult for many adults, not just incarcerated ones, the emotional skills learned in the circle must be practiced there and in the world beyond—be that the prison yard or the world outside the razor wire.

As I witnessed, SBB's circles identify storytelling as their primary mode of exchange. Tofteland begins each new group with Richard II's tower monologue and encourages the men to analyze it in ways that personalize the Bard's words and emotions:

> I have been studying how I may compare
> This prison where I live unto the world:
> And for because the world is populous
> And here is not a creature but myself,
> I cannot do it; yet I'll hammer it out.[31]

The monologue continues for another fifty-nine lines in which Richard grapples with his identity and the value of his own life. Tofteland says that the people in SBB's circles intuitively feel the heart of these words— the power of Richard coming to understand his incarceration through unpacking his life. Someone in the circle invariably asks whether Shakespeare did time. Tofteland replies that we cannot know with any certainty whether or not the Bard did,[32] but he had a greater capacity than most to draw upon his dramatic imagination to fill in the gaps in his own life experiences. In Tofteland's words, "Shakespeare makes each character fully human."[33] We could learn a great deal from the care and attention given to all of the characters in Shakespeare. In his writing, no character appears to be less real or complex simply because they have fewer things to say. If criminal justice proceedings treated each person as someone more than the value of their worst actions, we would live in a very different world.

Each SBB circle spends a lengthy period of time analyzing monologues. Tofteland says they talk about each one in "great great great depth" before moving on to another. Tofteland finds this process so important that he felt reluctant about even having performances at all in the early years of SBB. He wanted to linger in the work that the incarcerated men were doing with their process of rehearsing monologues, scenes, and sonnets from Shakespeare and discussing the connections between the texts and their own lives. Tofteland feared at that time that "the pursuit of performance would distract the participants from the pursuit of personal truth by creating an end game of product rather than the ongoing process of deep personal exploration of the material." After beginning with Richard's tower speech, Tofteland chooses other monologues that feel like they address the concerns of each particular group. He describes this process as "Shakespeare giving language to the feelings we all have." When I began to write this chapter four years after my visit to the SBB circle, I asked Tofteland to explain to me what had been happening when the man at Brooks Correctional had transformed Macbeth's words as he spoke about his children. Tofteland said that the man had been using "Shakespeare to get at the drama."[34]

The whole circle knew that this man held a particularly close connection to Macbeth's monologue because they had discussed the work together at great length. The other men in the circle knew that this man was using Shakespeare's words to unpack his own emotions, and when someone else requested a recitation of *Macbeth*, the man had permission to express something profound and complicated about his own life without having to find the right words on his own. Even as a complete outsider with no prior context for this use of Shakespeare, I implicitly felt and understood what happened in this moment. That was why it moved me to such a remarkable degree. This untrained actor had seamlessly accomplished what I have watched theatre professionals attempt throughout a lifetime of study; he lived and spoke the present moment of his emotions as embodied in the poetry of the playwright's words.

Perhaps more significantly, this moment exemplified the supportive community of the SBB circle. Shakespeare provided the occasion and some of the language for these men to share their experiences as fathers—a rare opportunity in an environment where people must fight for privacy and seldom want others in the prison to know anything about their families.

Tofteland claims that this process of storytelling and practicing humanity opens people up, giving them the "courage to apologize and say, 'I love you'" to folks in the circle, as well as others on the prison yard or in their own families.[35] The sense of community begins in the circle and extends outward, even including the staff at the prison.

Theatre as a Means to Build Connections with Prison Staff

Prison theatre programs cannot function without some form of partnership with the people who run the institution. Indeed, no one can get inside the prison at all without the cooperation of the staff and approval of the administration. Buzz Alexander, cofounder of PCAP, describes the tension between the mission of an arts organization and a prison:

> On the whole PCAP believes in creativity and growth. On the whole the prison believes in containment and security, though those who either pay lip service to growth or who entirely believe in it make it possible for us to be there. And PCAP and the prison are both right: unless they are stifled, human beings have a propensity and a right to become more fully human, and prison is volatile and needs discipline, clear policies, strict demarcations. The question is how to accommodate the two languages.[36]

Tofteland, too, has written of navigating this terrain while running SBB in Kentucky. He emphasizes the need to cultivate strong relationships with prison staff and administrators at every level inside the prison.[37] The existing literature on prison arts programming reinforces what Alexander and Tofteland advise.[38] It also describes at length the extraordinary challenges that volunteers face in attempting to build and maintain positive relationships with staff.[39]

Paul Heritage, a British theatre practitioner and scholar who did prison theatre work in Brazil from 1992 to 2005,[40] provides dramatic examples of the extraordinary failures and successes of prison officials and theatre makers working together.[41] He, too, found that when prison administrations and incarcerated populations work together, they do less harm to one another, physically and psychologically. However, the lasting cultural impact of theatre programs on prison staff has not previously been well documented.

In his autobiography, *The Governor: The Life and Times of the Man Who Ran Mountjoy*, prison warden (or prison governor, as they say in Ireland) John Lonergan describes the impact of theatre on the men who lived and worked at this facility in Dublin during his tenure there:

> One night during the run [of the show], I met Paul [an incarcerated actor] after a performance and he told me the play changed his life: "I have been coming in here for years and nobody ever asked me how I was, but yesterday up on my landing the class officer asked me how I was getting on and said, 'You are brilliant in that play.' Nobody ever told me I was brilliant before. And another officer asked me, 'Can I do anything for you?' Jaysus, no one ever asked me before whether they could do anything for me."[42]

The staff at Mountjoy see the growth in Paul, but they also demonstrate their own development as officers more interested in cultivating an environment of mutual respect in the prison.

As mentioned earlier, Warden Mary Berghuis sat in the circle with us throughout my entire visit to SBB at Brooks Correctional. She knew the group's customs and shook hands with everyone in the room. None of the men hesitated or seemed inhibited by her presence as they shared much personal information about themselves and their families. Warden Berghuis did not speak during the conversation but often made eye contact with speakers and nodded encouragingly. She listened to my monologues as I performed them and seemed sympathetic to the characters of family members who had difficulty gaining access to their incarcerated loved ones. She walked with me and the SBB facilitators as we left the prison and told me how much SBB does to help the men in that prison. Throughout her time as warden at both Brooks and neighboring West Shoreline Correctional, she consistently promoted SBB and enabled the program to have special privileges, such as access to hardback copies of *The Complete Works of Shakespeare* and allowing the men to wear SBB tee shirts and wristbands on the yard as a sign of their involvement in the program.[43] Her enthusiastic support of SBB gave Warden Berghuis the opportunity to show these men that she wanted them to learn and grow, and it enabled the men to demonstrate to her and one another their commitment to this project, thus increasing a broader sense of community inside the prison. She also believes that this work cultivates a better environment throughout the prison, asking me after reading an early draft of this chapter, "Which prison is safer and more secure: one where the prisoners hate the warden and staff, or one where they are treated fairly and humanely? I don't think the later reflects a softness on security but strengthens it."[44]

Across the country in Oregon, the cast of *The Winter's Tale* reported marked shifts in staff behavior because of OHOM's presence at Two Rivers Correctional. Raymond Alderman (Camillo) recounts:

> I've had staff members ask what our next production was going to be, and I mean it's amazing . . . seeing . . . the change in a lot of the staff's attitudes about it. . . . My first play four years ago . . . they would kinda snicker and ask, "Who are you playing? Are you playing a girl?" But now it's like they literally ask you, "So what's the play about? What part are you playing?" And there's been staff that have actually gone out and read the plays because we're doing them. . . . I'm happy that it's changed . . . a lot of the staff.[45]

The sense of this more positive approach toward men in the theatre group appears to be increasing over time, as Alderman observes: "This year I think we've had more staff come to the play and actually watch it, instead of just coming in and looking around for a couple of minutes and then leaving. More staff actually staying for the whole play and being interested in it. So, it just shows that this place is changing a lot every year."[46] These long-term impacts on the staff's engagement with the incarcerated men suggest a minor shift in the culture of the prison.

Because I was present as a researcher, the prison's Public Information Officer Sherry Iles joined the cast of *The Winter's Tale* for our entire discussion. As in the conversation that the men at SBB had in front of Warden Berghuis, the men of OHOM displayed remarkable vulnerability and did not seem to mind Ms. Iles's presence in the room. She even briefly joined in the conversation:

> You guys are fabulous, and I don't know much about theatre. But to be able to put on a performance like that and bring everything to life with just yourselves—I mean, you don't have a lot to work with—is amazing. So, I'm looking forward to the future, too, and maybe you guys writing your own play and directing it and performing it. I think that would be amazing.[47]

The bright future that Ms. Iles anticipates here includes herself. She wants to bear witness to their work and enjoy it. The ability for staff and incarcerated people to share joy and a positive emotional investment in what will happen in the prison helps to build a common culture inside the walls.

As the men in OHOM deepen and expand their interest in performance, some of the staff have also become theatre goers for the first time. Two of the members of *The Winter's Tale* cast, Rocky Hutchinson—who stage managed the play and acted the role of a satyr—and Joshua Underhill (Antigonus) work together in their prison jobs, and a staff member who supervises them received her first introduction to live theatre through OHOM's performances at Two Rivers. She became such an enthusiast that she now travels to see professional plays in other cities. Hutchinson delights in his supervisor's newfound love of theatre: "Now she goes to [plays] on the street.[48] She spent like, what, something like $1,500 to go to see *Oz*. She's like, 'It's all your guys' fault! [*sic*]."[49] By design, prisons encourage those who live and work within them to focus on changing the behavior of the incarcerated, but we tend to assume that those socializing forces do not travel in the opposite direction, from imprisoned people to those employed to guard them and organize their days. By inciting prison staff to become readers and audience members of theatre, the incarcerated men of OHOM have attained a marked level of influence as culture makers inside Two Rivers. Through their performances, they have changed their environment and many of the people in it, including staff and audiences of incarcerated men and visitors from the outside world.

Building Community with Audiences from Both Sides of the Walls

The theatre offers audiences moments of feeling part of something greater than ourselves. Theatre scholar Jill Dolan argues that "Audiences form temporary communities, sites of public discourse that . . . can model new investments in and interactions with variously constituted public spheres."[50] When audience members and theatre makers can share in a form of emotional engagement through the medium of performance, they turn toward what Dolan calls "utopia in performance"—that shared, live experience of imagining a better world together in the theatre. This turn can disrupt many of the ideological and structural barriers that separate those who live and work in prisons as well as those who visit from outside the walls.[51] Even as closed, guarded, and divided spaces, prisons have their own publics. The opportunity to form a community—even one as fleeting as the audience for a play—can give incarcerated people a rare moment of feeling part of an engaging, positive, and vibrant social interaction, especially when visitors from outside the prison take part.

A theatrical event in prison has the potential to make an extraordinary impact on the people living and working inside the prison and whomever else has been allowed to enter the space for the performance. Architecturally and ideologically, prisons divide people in myriad ways. Incarcerated people seldom have the ability to congregate in a large group for an organized activity other than eating a meal or having a religious service. In the United States, as in many other parts of the world, the majority of incarcerated people have never seen a play performed live.[52]

Many of the professional theatre makers I have known say that audiences in prison make performances in all other contexts feel less rich and meaningful. People in prison, particularly those who have been there for many years, pay extraordinary attention to anything new that enters their world. A friend who traveled with me when I was doing my one-woman play in a prison in Wyoming said that she watched the audience throughout my performance. She was struck by their singular focus throughout the entirety of the play and said that it seemed "their souls were in their eyes" as they watched. I have witnessed this phenomenon of the extraordinary attentiveness of prison audiences everywhere I have gone in my research travels. Even audiences of free-world guests who have come to a prison to see a play seem to adopt a significant measure of this hypersensitive observation. The prison environment keeps everyone alert, even when no obvious threat presents itself, and when a theatrical performance interrupts the sense of one's being inside a prison, the focus appears not to diminish but to shift to the theatrical event.

According to the men in *The Winter's Tale,* the community of incarcerated spectators at OHOM's performances have carried their experiences into the rest of their lives in the prison. Jason Beito (Paulina) says:

> The greatest thing about this . . . has just been . . . not only what we've gotten out of it as inmates participating in this program, but what it has done in the inmate community over the five, six years we've been doing these plays, performing them—how it's grown each year, how our inmate audiences have gotten larger, how more people have been more accepting of it and wanting to attend it and . . . wanting to be more involved. "How do I get involved in this? What do I do to sign up?" . . . You wouldn't think that in a place like this Shakespeare would be . . . something that so many people look forward to seeing.[53]

Having something to look forward to matters more in prison than it does in other places. This has most famously been demonstrated in theatre in the numerous productions of Samuel Beckett's *Waiting for Godot* in prisons around the world, particularly with the landmark performance directed by Herbert Blau in San Quentin prison in California in 1957.[54] The play's characters wait and wait for the absent Godot to appear—a state of being to which incarcerated actors and audiences can poignantly relate. As scholar Lance Duerfahrd has noted, "He who never appears (Godot) nevertheless keeps bringing his promise to arrive to Lüttringhausen, San Quentin, Kumla, and Raiford prisons [where the play has been performed]."[55] *Godot* keeps getting produced inside the walls because this essential fact of prison life—the state of time in prolonged limbo—never changes.

Incarcerated people spend an inordinate proportion of their lives inside the walls waiting, often without having anything promising on the horizon, so the promise of OHOM performing a new play each year at Two Rivers has given many men there something exciting to anticipate for months on end. Stage manager Rocky Hutchinson describes this phenomenon: "There's a lot of people in the whole prison that . . . are like . . . 'When is you guys' next play?' . . . It has become a culture. It's spread like wildfire kinda, and it's great because, you know, we don't have a whole lot. It's something very special, and I'm so proud to be able to be a part of it."[56] Each performance of an OHOM play lasts less than two hours, but the culture of joyful expectation created inside the prison lasts throughout the year.

Nathan Harris (Polixenes) wanted to devise a system for hanging onto his memories of performing *The Winter's Tale*:

> My whole hook is to make it 364 days and remember a little bit about every visitor of the two public performances, and it's a lot of people. It's easy to forget because there are so many neat things about each individual person and the guys that I'm with. And so, to formulate something to make it last a whole year is my goal. . . . To meet so many different people and to use it in my personal life really makes a difference in who I become.[57]

Harris connects his individual growth with what he can glean from these rare and precious interactions with people from the free world. If he can manage to remember these people, he can carry the joy of these performance days into the long stretch of monotonous prison life that awaits him.

Richard Brumbach, who played the Old Shepherd, told the discussion group on the day after closing night that he had the sense that the incarcerated actors and audiences had shared something profound during *The Winter's Tale* performances: "You know, part of what I realized this morning that we had inmates after the inmate performances tell us that for a little while they felt like they were no longer in prison. (*long pause as he gets choked up and weeps*) Last night [with the audience of visitors] I didn't feel like I was in prison."[58] Brumbach experiences not only a few hours of forgetting about the forces that confine him; he knows that he helped others to experience the same phenomenon. Indeed, his own sense of transcending his life inside the prison could not have been possible without the collective participation of the other actors and the audience. No one goes inside the walls without a specific reason, and OHOM's performances give those in prison and those who visit an occasion not just to see one another but also to celebrate the joy and momentary well-being of all those present.

The force of prison theatre as a catalyst for caring resurfaced in the ways in which people talked about this work everywhere I went in my research travels. It serves as a palpable hallmark of the experience of seeing theatre inside the walls. Howard Thoresen, who flies every year from New York to Oregon to see each new play at Two Rivers, told the cast of *The Winter's Tale* about how OHOM's work has influenced his perception of free-world theatre about prisons:

> There's an English company that did a production of *Macbeth* that I saw in New York with all women, and the frame that they put on it was that it was being produced in a women's prison. . . . It was excellent, but I wrote to them because I had just been here [to Two Rivers] and seen *King Lear*. And I went back to New York and saw this, and I said, "It's a great production. The acting was great, but you've got it all wrong." Because they tried to create an atmosphere where the audience felt like they were in prison. You felt, you know, guards around telling us to shut up and all this kind of stuff. I said, "When you go to a play in prison, you're in heaven! (*laughs*) It's a wonderful experience. It's so beautiful. It's so enlightening."[59]

In no other context have I heard someone say that an experience in prison felt like "heaven," yet many who see theatre in prisons will describe the performance as a time full of wonder, excitement, and joy. Much of this comes from the sense that such a rigid place of confinement can be transformed, that the actors, prison staff, and audiences together have created a period of shared grace, when the institutional boundaries that divide people can be laid aside temporarily in the service of our common humanity. These feelings resonate all the more palpably when prisons allow the actors' families to attend the plays, as Two Rivers does.

Using the Play (and the Reception That Follows) to Strengthen and Reunify Families

The families of the incarcerated seldom have opportunities to celebrate the achievements of their imprisoned loved ones, much less in a shared forum with others. In fact, people on both sides of the walls whose lives are shaped by incarceration routinely endure the presumption that people who commit crimes do not love their families enough to deserve to spend time with them. Rachel Kushner's novel *The Mars Room* offers a dramatic but believable rendering of this sentiment. A prison staff member calls Romy Hall, the incarcerated protagonist of the novel, into an administrative office to tell her that a car accident has taken her mother's life and sent her son to the hospital. Romy panics and tries to grab the piece of paper the officer is holding in order to learn more about what has happened to her family members. One staff member restrains Romy on the floor, while another tells her, "If you want to be a parent, you don't end up in prison. Plain and simple."[60] The families of the incarcerated hear this sentiment routinely yet live a far more complex version of the truth. As I sat in the lobby of a prison waiting to get to see my own father, I once met a mother visiting her son who told me, "I'm not proud of him, but he's mine. You can't help belonging to one another when you're family."[61] Prisons and criminal justice systems do irreparable harm to many families and bring about the ends of many marriages and other relationships; however, a great many of us keep loving one another across the walls and often have no way to explain this to other people.

Performances of plays in prison open up rare moments of recognition, when the actors can be honored for their talents and months of hard work. Families then have stories to carry out into their own communities about the good and beautiful thing that their loved one has done. It gives families narratives with which to combat the persistent cultural assumption that people in prison can only be imagined or discussed in terms of the crime that sent them away. The majority of the audience on closing night of *The*

Winter's Tale appeared to be members of the actors' families, and they brought a heightened level of joy and excitement to the space.

The day after closing night of *The Winter's Tale*, I asked the men in the cast to introduce themselves by saying how they were feeling that day. Many of them began by sharing about what it meant for their families to see them perform. Joshua Friar (Young Shepherd) said, "They're all good plays, but last night I had my family here and everyone else's families. So, it was definitely the highlight of my entire time."[62] Whether he was referencing his "entire time" in the theatre group or in prison, Friar points to the way in which having this heightened experience of joy with his family counteracts what might be the greatest continual torture of incarceration: the inability to share your daily life with the people you love most. David Gilmore, one of the musicians for the play, expressed similar sentiments:

> Last night was the first time that one of my children was able to be here. So that—I'm just completely full of that, and in fact I'll momentarily hopefully be called into a visit to spend some more time with my son. And that—it means so much to be able to share something like this with my family and with everybody else's families that come and friends [sic].[63]

Performances of plays in prisons also give estranged family members occasions to reunite in ways that can feel more accessible than a regular visit. The possibility of visiting someone in prison after a long period of silence can feel daunting—the peculiar fear of not knowing what to say to a person you have driven hours to see. A performance can help start new conversations, set visitors at ease, and give everyone present the chance to mingle as a group. It may give some guests more incentive to make the long drive to a rural prison, like Two Rivers. At the start of our conversation with the group, Stallings asked the cast how many of them had had someone who had never previously visited them in prison come to see the play. Four men raised their hands. Jason Beito (Paulina) told a particularly striking story in this vein:

> Last year my son got to come to the play. . . . We had never had any contact at all in our life [sic]. . . . But he came to the play last year, and that was a very important thing being able to have him there. . . . It was a real big positive thing, and I think John [Stallings] was looking forward to it about as much as I was because I remember my son

came in, and I remember John's just over there, just, "Oh, gosh! I'm gonna get to meet him!" And a lot of people were asking me, "Your son's coming, right?" There was a lot of support for everybody when people find out that somebody's getting to see one of their family members for the first time—getting to share something like this. David having his son come last night, that was a really nice thing. I know what he felt last night, what he was feeling from my experience last year with that. . . . It's a very precious and sacred thing.[64]

The reunion between Beito and his son becomes a collective experience for the whole theatre troupe. The photographers and videographers who record the OHOM performances and receptions capture many images of families commingled. These photos and videos not only give the actors and their families a way to preserve these memories; they also give others who could not attend the play a glimpse of the event, as do the news stories that reporters publish about prison theatre.

In one case, an article from the *Huffington Post* about Shakespeare in Prison (SIP)—not to be confused with Tofteland's Shakespeare Behind Bars program on the other side of Michigan—helped to reunite an incarcerated woman in Michigan with her aunt and uncle who had not spoken to her since her arrest.[65] Frannie Shepherd-Bates directs SIP, a program affiliated with the Detroit Public Theatre in Michigan. As she tells the story:

[The aunt and uncle] said that it made them happy and proud that [their niece] was doing something so positive with her time and asked her to tell them more about it. At the end of the call, they asked if they could come and visit her. And I believe those visits became regular. It was definitely a huge confidence boost for her, and, while she'd already been enjoying her time in the group, I think that's what made her fully commit to it—for years.[66]

Arts and educational programming in prisons helps families to have something to discuss other than the prison itself. It also makes life inside the walls feel less intimidating and more approachable to those of us on the outside who are attempting to understand our loved one's lives in prison. Shepherd-Bates has seen this with other members of SIP as well:

Participants have explicitly shared that their families—often parents and/or children—have seen this as such a point of pride that it's altered the way in which they interact. Several people's children have joined drama clubs and/or read lines with their parents over the phone. Others have had family members who were distant suddenly begin calling more frequently and sending them books specifically about Shakespeare and acting. There's a guy we're working with now who says this is the first thing he's felt passionate about in a time even longer than his incarceration (which has been more than ten years, mostly spent in solitary), and he feels now that acting is what he was meant to do—and that passion has resulted in his sister being regularly in contact and sending him more than a dozen plays and books about acting. . . . His relatives have also been all over our social media and website sharing publicly how thrilled they are about what he's doing in SIP.[67]

Shepherd-Bates says the news media about SIP gets shared on Twitter by the public information officer from the Michigan Department of Corrections as well.[68] This creates a moment in which families of the incarcerated and prison officials have a point of common interest and pride.

In a similar vein, Richard Brumbach, the Old Shepherd from *The Winter's Tale*, reported that his daughter and granddaughters had never seen a play before this one at Two Rivers; after that night, they intended to start going to the theatre in the outside world.[69] These stories demonstrate that theatre in prisons has the ability to change people's behavior beyond the walls and to help keep families actively engaged with one another even when a prison separates them.

The Family in the Same Prison But Still Apart

The theatre, of course, does not eliminate any of the structural barriers that prisons place in between family members, but it can offer opportunities for reconnection, even in the most difficult of circumstances. In at least one instance, it may have also disrupted a much-needed family reunion. This episode in my research travels haunts me as no other. It involves a theatre workshop that I led with my collaborator Andrew (Andy) Martínez in Uruguay, where we encountered a married couple and their children all living in the same prison.

On May 25, 2017, when Andy and I visited Cárcel de Las Rosas (Prison of the Roses) in the small town of Maldonado, Uruguay, the facility housed at least 800 incarcerated people—both men and women—when it had been built to hold only 620.[70] (As a side note, during the same trip to Uruguay, we saw another prison at the other end of the spectrum—with extraordinarily progressive policies and much better living conditions. No individual prison should be read as characteristic of all prisons in a given nation because conditions vary widely in facilities within any country.) The inhabitants of Las Rosas live in crumbling buildings with ten or twelve people packed into bunk beds squeezed into narrow *barrancas* (barracks) with an open bathroom at the end of the room. The *barrancas* we saw had only one small window, about ten inches across, with metal bars on it. The window gave the incarcerated women inside a slight view into the dark hallway, but they had no way to see outdoors. They had no ventilation or access to sunlight. Everything we could see was filthy and much of it wet.

We arrived in a particularly rainy season, and water seeped down the interior cement walls in many buildings in the prison. Pools of water covered the floor in many hallways and the corners of rooms. The sky, heavily darkened by storm clouds, offered very little natural light, and many parts of Las Rosas have no electricity. Stray cats roamed the prison and had defecated in many of the hallways. We passed what the staff at Las Rosas called a woodworking shop. The room did have some stacks of wood, but no tools or implements for woodworking were visible. An incarcerated man stood barefoot in about two inches of standing water that covered the floor. Splinters and debris swirled around his ankles as he fed pieces of wood into a little stove, which offered the only light in the room. Other educational spaces had padlocks on their doors and had not been in use for months or years because of lack of funding for program supplies. The classroom that had been set up for culinary classes could not be used because the prison could not afford food to use in the lessons.

Incarcerated people living in particularly bleak conditions have significant gains to make from arts programming. Though such activities seldom cause structural change in a prison, they can help those inside the walls survive each week by giving them the kind of joy and hope that the men in *The Winter's Tale* describe. No performing arts programming had been offered at Las Rosas prior to our visit. Local volunteers Pia Susaeta and Gustavo Moraes have ambitious plans to offer high-quality theatre workshops at Las Rosas. They are fundraising to pay professional theatre makers to teach the incarcerated men and women to act, make sets and costumes, stage manage, and run the technical aspects of a play. As part of their efforts to get this program started, Susaeta and Moraes invited me and Andy to give a lecture/theatre workshop at Las Rosas.

The prison staff took us into a wide cement room that had no electricity and no light fixtures. The two windows—big square holes with iron bars and no glass—let in the sound of the unceasing rain but hardly any light. As we stood there looking at the room and wondering how we might lead a theatre workshop in the dark, some of the incarcerated men came and hooked up a big light of the sort used at construction sites, hanging it from the bars on a window. It made an uncomfortably bright spotlight. Then the men brought in another light that was up on a stand and put it in the corner of the room. The electrical extension cords that connected these lights to an unseen power source snaked dangerously through standing water and the rain outdoors.

Three incarcerated men and nine women came into the room for the theatre workshop. One woman arrived with a double stroller with twin infants in it—a boy and a girl. Shortly thereafter a man arrived, swept the babies into his arms, and covered them with kisses. All of the other people in the room seemed to be giving the young couple and their children the space to reconnect with one another. Because the time had arrived for our lecture, Andy and I began our talk and followed it with a series of theatre games. The family stuck together throughout the activities, passing the babies back and forth and exchanging small gestures of tenderness. The woman and man both seemed to enjoy the theatre workshop but also looked at each other and the children with a kind of longing that made me wish we could dismiss them from the workshop to spend time together. The theatre games we played gave them permission to hold hands and physically interact with one another. The presence of such small infants also gave them the opportunity to sit out from the activities at certain moments to tend to the children.

We spent less than two hours in the workshop. In that time the group laughed, played together, and had a moving discussion about how prisons divide our families, prompted by some of the things I had shared about my father and my play about the families of the incarcerated. Quite a few men and women spoke of their own families, and some cried while doing so. The young couple paid close attention to the conversation but did not speak. Many other members of the workshop expressed exuberant thanks for the workshop and pleaded with us to return in future. Andy and I said that we would love to return but honestly could not say when that might happen. Moraes described his plans to introduce other theatre work at Las Rosas. We exchanged many hugs and a few more tears as a group before we parted.

When our time together ended, the young couple hugged each other as if they did not want to let go. The man relinquished the babies and bade farewell to the woman with great anguish. The father exited the room in one direction, and the mother and children left in a different one.

After the workshop, a member of the prison staff explained to us about how the mixed prison—one with both men and women in it—functions in Uruguay. Men and women live in separate, locked wings of the prison, but all educational and recreational programming is open to both genders. They eat separately and only come together under the supervision of educators and volunteers. Children born inside this prison can stay with their mothers until they are one year old. Four infants, including the two we met, were living in the prison at the time of our workshop. Older children raised in the prison eat what their mothers eat and have only the same programming and recreational activities that their mothers do. Mothers with babies have slightly better housing than the other women. If they have family in the free world, mothers can choose to send their children home to live with relatives. At the age of one the children must leave the prison. If they have no relatives who can take them, a government agency places the children in a home until a parent or guardian becomes ready to reclaim them. In this sense, incarcerated parents in Uruguay have far greater parental rights than those in my own country, who tend to lose legal access to their children quickly if their families cannot immediately take custody of the children.

The young couple, both of whom appeared to be in their twenties, had been married for some years prior to their incarceration. We were told they were prosecuted together for the same crime and both ended up in Las Rosas. The woman was pregnant at the time of their arrest and conviction and delivered the twins while incarcerated. They have three other children who live with the woman's parents somewhere away from the prison, and she and the babies live together on the women's side of Las Rosas. The father lives on the men's side and gets one visit with his wife and children every fifteen days, usually as part of an educational or cultural program that involves other people. Our theatre workshop counted as one of those visits. Since the babies were reported to be six months old, this would have been, at most, the twelfth time that this man had seen his children.

Our theatre workshop, by sheer happenstance, gave this family the opportunity to spend time together but also kept them active enough that it may have distracted them from the more important activity of reconnecting with one another. Had we understood the young family's history or visiting restrictions prior to the workshop, Andy and I would have designed our activities differently to give them more focused time together. I cannot recall this detail with certainty, but I fear that during one theatre game that involved putting participants into small groups, I may have separated the young parents from one another for one activity. If I did, I cost them precious time together when their family time could be measured in minutes every month.

With no clear sense of what other kinds of programs have offered the occasions for the young family's visits inside Las Rosas, we can only wonder whether our workshop gave them more or less contact and opportunity for reconnection than their other moments together. Did the theatre interrupt them more than it gave them an occasion to come together? Was our workshop more of an opportunity for physical touch and emotional connection than the other sorts of activities that constitute their visits? Could a long-term theatre program successfully implemented at Las Rosas not only give this family more access to one another but also enlist the other incarcerated men and women to deepen their relationships with one another as an extended family? The experiences of the cast of *The Winter's Tale* suggest that this might be possible.

A Tale of Two Sheep: Building New and Extended Families through Prison Theatre

Jeffrey Sanders acquired a new family while serving a life sentence with no possibility of parole. He has been in prison since 1997. Over the many years of his incarceration, he has resisted the notion that the prison defines his identity: "I will die in prison. They told me this. I am not an inmate. I am not going to fall into that. . . . I feel by putting myself in a category as an inmate, I feel like my grandfather four times over in slavery. I just hate it. I hate being an inmate. I am not an inmate. I am a human being."[71] During the postshow discussion on closing night, he told the audience that despite his life sentence, he was already free. The play helped him to become that by giving him a venue to publicly assert his humanity and also connecting him to people in the outside world.

Sanders played two roles in *The Winter's Tale*: Dion (one of the Lords of Sicilia) and a sheep. Shakespeare did not actually write it into the script that the shepherds in this play should have live sheep played by other actors, but the addition of two grown men in sheep costumes definitely added an extra layer of charm and humor to the Two Rivers production (Figure 1.1). The

Figure 1.1 Chester Gunter and Jeffrey Sanders as sheep.
Photo credit: Claire Stock.

children who came to the closing night performance loved the sheep. They giggled and pointed whenever the sheep appeared on stage. Chester Gunter played the other sheep, and his two young granddaughters wanted their picture taken with him and Sanders in their sheep costumes. At some point during the reception, one of the granddaughters started crying. Sanders recounts:

> I told her it was going to be okay. And she just looked at me and says, "Thank you." [Figure 1.2] This man (*pointing to himself*) was to have them precious moments to be able to really understand that we are all human. It's very easy to lose sight of that, and that's what comes along with saying, "I'm an inmate" because then you start to be subtracting yourself from your natural being.[72]

The play and the reception that followed offered Sanders the rare opportunity to interact with children, who are only ever seen in the prison visiting room. In Sanders's telling of this story, the little girl says only two words to him, and that small interaction carries the weight of reassuring him of his humanity. Gunter took this one step farther, not only expressing his kinship with the other members of the theatre group but also aligning them with his biological family: "We are a family, you

Figure 1.2 Jeffrey Sanders with Chester Gunter's granddaughter.
Photo credit: Claire Stock.

know. . . . My granddaughter wanted me to tell you she loved you. You know that we get as much out of the audience as they get, but what I get from each and every one of you guys is priceless. We are a family."[73] Gunter outlines here a circle of caring. Sanders comforts Gunter's granddaughter. She in turn tells her grandfather that she loves the other men in the cast. Gunter then expresses gratitude to the whole theatre troupe for being his family. This may sound like a fleeting or temporary phenomenon that exists only in the immediate aftermath of a play: all involved would be filled with positive feelings that would diminish over time. However, the OHOM theatre group started at Two Rivers enduringly perceives itself as a family, even after members gain their freedom or transfer to other prisons. Ironically, one of the people who keeps the family together lives nearly 600 miles away in Utah.

Momma Sharon, Manna from Heaven, and the Gifts of an Expanding Family

In 2013, Sharon Lemm and her sister Andrea Wiggins decided to drive twelve hours from their home in northeastern Utah to Umatilla, Oregon. Lemm's son Joseph Opyd was serving time at Two Rivers and was appearing in the OHOM production of *King Lear*. Lemm had never before entered a prison, though her son had begun his sentence two years earlier. When she went into Two Rivers, she experienced such profound fear that she said her "knees were shaking, and I could hardly breathe." She watched the play and loved it. She realized "that none of the men act like prisoners, just nice young guys." By the end of the show, she believed that "none of the men deserved to be there."[74] During the postshow reception, she asked each man in the cast to sign her program and write down their prison identification numbers if they would not mind her writing to them. All eighteen members of the cast provided their numbers.

Lemm wrote a group letter to the whole cast and mailed it to them along with stacks of pictures from the performance that she downloaded from the OHOM website and printed. Many members of the cast started writing back to her, and Lemm's sister began writing to the men as well. OHOM actor Raymond Alderman soon dubbed them Momma Sharon and Aunt Andrea, and the names stuck.

Every time a new man joins the OHOM dialogue group or theatre troupe, he gets added to Momma Sharon's list. She keeps an alphabetized document on her computer with each man's name, prison number, birthday, and release date. When someone transfers to a different prison or get released, Momma Sharon updates his address and keeps sending correspondence. The only men whose names end up leaving the list are the few who fail to keep in touch with her after their release. Her list has grown to include thirty-five men, and she anticipates that it will keep expanding every year. She sends five or six group letters with photographs per year to them all. Each man also receives a card from her on Christmas, Valentine's Day, and his birthday. One man had never before received a birthday card, and he told Momma Sharon that he carried her card with him for a whole month and showed it to everyone he met.

All in all, Momma Sharon sends roughly 280 pieces of correspondence to OHOM men each year. She waits until her favorite photography printing service has a sale and orders around 300 photos at a time so that she can include multiple images in each letter. This cost combined with postage proves financially challenging for her, and she does not know how much longer she can keep it up. For now, she says, "I have the will to do it, and God makes the way." Her reward for her efforts comes in the mail from the men. She calls their letters "manna from Heaven."[75]

Momma Sharon and Aunt Andrea sat in the front row of the closing night performance of *The Winter's Tale*. I had the serendipitous good fortune to sit next to Momma Sharon, and I complimented her on the sparkly cardigan that she wore to the play. She told me that the year before, she had seen folks who were dressed up and she thought she ought to do that as well because these performances were such special occasions. Momma Sharon and Aunt Andrea laughed and cried during the play. They could not have been more excited to be there, and this constituted a huge shift from their striking fear of entering the same prison for the first time just one year earlier.

During the postshow discussion on closing night of *The Winter's Tale*, several men in the cast thanked Momma Sharon and Aunt Andrea for being their family. At the reception thereafter, Jeffrey Sanders took pictures with Momma Sharon and Aunt Andrea and their biological son and nephew Joe Opyd. Sanders said while they posed together, "[Joe's] mother looked at me, and she was like, 'This is our adopted son!' She looked at me, and I looked at her. And I just laughed. . . . She says [to the person taking the picture], 'I'm talking about the little short one. Can't you see the family resemblance?'" (Figure 1.3).[76] Sanders, an African American, looks nothing like Momma Sharon or her family, who are white. He also stands nearly two feet taller than her and Aunt Andrea. None of that matters to Momma Sharon. She sees Sanders and registers that they belong to one another as family.

Figure 1.3 Aunt Andrea, Jeffrey Sanders, and Momma Sharon.
Photo credit: Claire Stock.

James Stewart (Emilia) describes the performances as the site where such family recognition can take place:

> It's a mutual gift that we get because what we give is our practice and our dedication and our love for this art. And what the audience brings to us is also love—to us because, like your mom, Joe, writes to us and sends us pictures and tries to incorporate us into her family. . . . I don't get visits. This is the only time I get to see people outside, and so this means so much to me even to be able to do it, to spend time with people and feel like I am still a person. So that's their gift to me [*sic*].[77]

Momma Sharon told me that one of the actors she met at an OHOM performance had had absolutely no contact with the outside world—no letters, phone calls, or visits—in sixteen years. She gave him the first hug he had had in all that time and adopted him into her family. This man has since been transferred to another prison several hours from Two Rivers, and Momma Sharon and Aunt Andrea add several more hours of driving to their already long journeys so that they can visit him after they stop at Two Rivers to visit Joe.[78]

At the time that *The Winter's Tale* was staged, Stallings had decided to stop producing plays at Two Rivers and just continue the dialogue group because he could no longer sustain the frequency of his long trips to the prison. Soon after closing night, a host of new volunteers joined OHOM and made it possible to continue the tradition of staging a play annually at Two Rivers. However, on closing night of *The Winter's Tale*, the cast and their families thought this might be the last play at the prison. In a group letter that she sent to the cast two months later, Momma Sharon wrote,

> My emotions were running pretty rampant at the play, knowing this might be the last opportunity for me to get to see several of you ever again. I was feeling quite badly for that, hoping that something would work out, because I could hardly stand to leave with that knowledge of not getting to see some of you ever again. . . . But now, I am better so when I get to see you again, I will probably hug you even harder next time.[79]

This remarkable level of attachment to the group evolved in a single year, largely through correspondence. Clearly, Momma Sharon's correspondence with the men has never been merely an act of charity—a case of her helping the less fortunate in prison. The men have given as much to her as she has given to them.

Momma Sharon's biological son confirmed this in the discussion that we had with the cast on the day after closing night (Figure 1.4). Joe arrived late to this conversation because he had been in a visit with his mother and aunt that morning. As he began speaking to the group, he was visibly moved:

> I'm going to start crying . . . because I have so much love for all of you, and communicating with my mom, that was never something that I had ever intended . . . she just liked you guys. She said, "Hey, do you think that I could write 'em?" And then you guys started writing to her and talking to her, and . . . her and my aunt just changed. Their lives had been kind of empty . . . you guys just sending them these letters and pouring your hearts out to them and accepting them. They are on cloud nine, and it's meant the world to me to see their lives filled with this excitement and love and this new vigor for life. They're not the same. . . . They're getting older, and you can see it. And their bodies are broken, and they make this effort to come out to see not only me but to see you guys.[80]

Momma Sharon and Aunt Andrea have both experienced health problems in recent years, and Aunt Andrea had been too ill to attend the last several

Figure 1.4 Aunt Andrea, Joe Opyd, and Momma Sharon.
Photo credit: Claire Stock.

plays at Two Rivers; the group dedicated their 2018 production of *Macbeth* to her. Momma Sharon says, "To [my sister's] delight she could not believe anything so special as that would be for her."[81] Momma Sharon says that the OHOM group sustained both her and her sister through these difficult times. She wrote as much in a letter to Jack Baird, who played two different lords in *The Winter's Tale*:

> My health continues to improve day by day. It sure has been a slow process but I am grateful for every good or a better day. I appreciate your prayers, kindness and love. You have no idea how much those generous things you gave helped me. They especially carried me through on bad days. I am like a kid in a candy store when I get those phone calls from friends and letters. They are like manna from heaven for me.[82]

Aunt Andrea passed away in 2018, and the men of OHOM mourned her along with Momma Sharon and Joe, who took comfort in their outpouring of love. Momma Sharon writes of her sister: "She loved many of the inmate actors at [Two Rivers]. I know they loved her, too. She was so funny when they wondered why she was looking at them. She identified them as 'eye candy' telling them 'I can look, because I am not dead yet.'" Aunt Andrea had a "huge crush" on a member of the company named Casey Wood and admired his long hair. He received word of Aunt Andrea's passing around the time of his release from prison, cut off his braid, sent it to Momma Sharon, and asked her to bury it with her sister.[83]

Momma Sharon also attributes the care and thoughtfulness of the men of OHOM with enabling her to worry less about her son Joe. Nancy Scharbach, costumer and set designer for *The Winter's Tale*, cried as she told Joe in our group discussion, "I saw your mom after the show, and she expressed to me how much easier it is to leave knowing that you are here with all of these guys."[84] In a letter to Joshua Underhill (Antigonus), Momma Sharon wrote:

> Many times I wish I lived closer so I could visit with my Joseph more often. . . . One thing for sure is how much I appreciate you and value your friendship with him. It helps soften my heartache with knowing he is not alone and has many friends, like you. My words could never say to you how much that means to me.[85]

The sense that a kind, thoughtful, and caring person walks beside your loved one in prison eases the everyday trauma of uncertainty in which the families of incarcerated people live. Momma Sharon's gratitude shows the men of OHOM that they have something significant to contribute to this relationship—that they do not passively receive her love but can offer her something in return.

Momma Sharon also takes seriously the job of mothering each member of her chosen family. She thinks the men feel comfortable with her because she does not judge them. She knows about the crimes that some of them have committed, but she never asks about the things that sent these men to prison. Occasionally, she finds out their crimes by accident when using the Oregon Department of Corrections website to find out their birthdays (so that she can make sure that no one goes without a birthday card). These men have already been convicted and are being punished for their wrongs. She says, "It's not our place to forgive them because God will do that."[86] Momma Sharon focuses instead on helping her "Big Boy Friends"[87] to make better choices and live ethically and responsibly. In a letter to Rocky Hutchinson (Young Shepherd), she offers advice to help him through time that he spent in solitary confinement:

> One would think that being in the hole [solitary confinement] is punishment enough for making a bad decision but the consequences that follow are ridiculous when you are not given a chance to prove your worthiness again. . . . Don't give up and keep trying. . . . Also you are trying to set a better example for your son. It is very important to be and stay honorable.[88]

Momma Sharon expresses a desire to see our notions of justice shift toward the cultivation of virtue and away from punishment without opportunities for growth and change. She critiques the prison's response to Rocky's behavior but does not say that there should not have been consequences for his "bad decision"; rather, she argues that the authorities' response to his misdeed should include an opportunity for remorse and the encouragement of his growth. She reminds him that his actions have an impact on others outside the prison, particularly his son. This suggests that all of us influence one another when we participate in a community and that our actions should model our own values and those we wish to instill in others.

Momma Sharon, Aunt Andrea, and the men of OHOM have become a network of support for one another. Their complex and interwoven relationships offer them each comfort, reassurance, and a sense that someone else cares about what happens to them from day to day. Each of the participants in this improvised family knows without a doubt that someone loves them. Momma Sharon's openness and generosity of spirit make sure of this. She often closes her letters to the group with a benediction, as she did in this 2016 missive: "God bless you and keep you. Always remember you are loved, cared for and remembered in my thoughts and prayers. Love always, Momma Sharon."[89] How differently might each person in prison behave if she or he knew that they were loved unconditionally? How much might it change the environment of every prison if all of our actions, policy decisions, and security measures were created and implemented with love?

Toward a More Loving Prison

Nothing has the potential to transform our prisons and our notions of justice and public safety as radically as love. Tom O'Connor has been trying to convince prison officials all over the world of this. O'Connor, a former monk and attorney who has worked in Religious Services for the Oregon Department of Corrections, runs a consulting firm that helps criminal justice agencies across the United States and internationally to "create a more compassionate, just and effective criminal justice system at lower cost."[90] When he speaks to prison officials, he asks them to consider not only whether their policies are effective but also whether they are loving— seeking the good of each individual so far as is possible.[91] In asking prison authorities to factor love into their decisions, he is not necessarily referring to emotion or affect; rather, he offers something similar to Tofteland's notion that SBB helps people practice their humanity. When we love someone, in O'Connor's definition, we offer up our own humanity and encourage that person to reciprocate.

Such disinterested, not necessarily reciprocal vulnerability has implications for prison policy. O'Connor does not argue that security standards should be lowered (ignoring people's safety would also, presumably, be a failure of love). However, he encourages those who run prisons to actively consider whether their policies and procedures are loving. We want our families, communities, schools, and hospitals to be places of compassion. Why not our prisons? We commonly justify prison procedures in terms of an appeal to an abstractly defined and imagined "common good"; O'Connor suggests that officials ask what is best for incarcerated people, not merely what is allowable. We must seek the positive good of the people we imprison, rather than simply asking what we are *allowed* to do to them under one or another system of ethics. He sees loving forms of programming in prisons as key to the kind of shift he would like to see.[92]

Randy Geer, a retired Administrator of Inmate Services for the Oregon Department of Corrections, agrees with O'Connor and extends his point to argue that the failure of love can itself pose security issues. Group activities in prison encourage a more respectful and safer environment because incarcerated people become invested in maintaining a stable, nonviolent community, Geer stated in my conversations with him. Without the kind of bonding that happens among incarcerated people through arts, educational, and sports programming, prison authorities would have a much harder time maintaining control and preventing low-level violence.[93]

Geer argues that love can transform the lives of prison staff as well: "It's hard on people to always operate from a position of fear. . . . If a good day at your job is when nothing bad happens, the bar is set too low. However, if the bar is set that a good day is when you see someone wrestle with something new for the first time and make progress, the work means so much more." He feels that the staff experiences a better quality of life at work when they see the incarcerated as people that staff can mentor and help: "If you start with the assumption that the inmates are worthy of love and respect, it makes the work easier and more rewarding." He believes that, "if people could love and be loved openly in prison, you'd see even more fundamental change in a hurry."[94] Stallings reinforces this notion, while also acknowledging that at present the culture of US prisons refuses to openly accept the idea of love; it has to be smuggled inside the walls: "Love sneaks into prisons among the volunteers. There will be a fair number of really warm-hearted people. It happens without announcing itself."[95] Love does fly under the radar within the closed classroom spaces of prison programming, but in theatrical performances for the larger prison population, staff, and outside visitors, it announces itself in a way that can draw audiences into this newly constituted, and often temporary, loving environment.

Many funding agencies and prison systems want to pigeonhole prison arts programming by instrumentalizing it as a tool to prevent recidivism. The humanities scholar and the artist in me bristle at the idea that our work has to be utilitarian, that it cannot be urgent, needed, and worthwhile unless it accomplishes someone else's goal. The creation of beauty, art, joy, community, or love matters in itself, apart from the kinds of social effects measurable in statistics; it does the work of making us more empathetic and humane. More significantly, the structural discrimination that sends disproportionate numbers of the poor, the illiterate, the indigenous, people of color, and queer people to prison does not end when they return to freedom. If your criminal record, poverty, and lack of support systems cause you to be homeless, jobless, starving, or in a dangerous place, you have a significant likelihood of returning to crime and incarceration. All the theatre in the world cannot prevent that unless other kinds of supports in the free world work in concert with programming inside the walls. However, there is some evidence that the community that prison theatre creates in one place has spillover effects when people go home. O'Connor has found not only that volunteers provided the equivalent of $13 million a year in prison programming (without expense to the state)[96] but that the more often a woman or man attended arts-related, educational, spiritual, or religious programming, the less recidivism they had over a follow-up period of thirteen years.[97] The research O'Connor and his colleagues have done on the subject suggests that this kind of love in prisons actually makes us safer by reducing recidivism.

Prison Theatre as an Act of Love

The concept that incarcerated people can love others and that others love them disrupts the very idea of the prison. Prisons, by design, hold the people we deliberately exile, the ones who cause harm, the people we do not want to contemplate. When we recognize those people in their full humanity, as complex beings capable of love—not just sexual desire and objectification, but the myriad and subtle kinds of human solidarity and altruism that surround us every day—it becomes harder to say that all they deserve in life is punishment. Love encompasses and enables family relationships, friendships, the kindnesses we do one another on a daily basis, admiration and respect for people and things we cherish, the willingness to put others' needs above our own, and so much more; it should not be reduced to a singular or fixed reference or a set of sexual acts. If someone who did something terrible (or many terrible things) can simultaneously be a loving person, then perhaps we should be cultivating the loving side of that person instead of reducing them to the worst thing they ever did and insisting that they are capable of nothing else.

Because theatre is a collaborative activity, theatre makers find themselves involved in every kind of love. This fact has high stakes for prison theatre makers who operate in a place where people have been deemed unworthy of love. When I asked Stallings if he took any particular approach to directing the incarcerated OHOM cast members, he simply replied that his approach to directing (and to life) is: "Love the heck out of everyone!"[98] The culture of theatre practitioners tends to encourage warmth or even outright physical affection with one another because acting and directing can demand such emotional vulnerability of the participants. This contrasts starkly with the boundary-laden, security-focused environment of the prison in which touch is strictly monitored and often forbidden. Rob Pensalfini, author of the book *Prison Shakespeare*, observed many prison theatre "practitioners who routinely hug maximum security prisoners (except where this is prohibited by prison rules), discuss personal matters in their own lives as a way of modeling vulnerability, or even (as I have observed on several occasions) telling prisoners that they love them."[99] I saw this in many of my visits to prison theatre programs as well and routinely noticed that in the programs where respectful physical and emotional openness were allowed by the prison authorities, the participants and facilitators appeared to be more comfortable.

On the whole such programs were producing performances of a higher artistic quality, in my opinion, than those in which touch and the sharing of one's personal experiences had been prevented. The level of trust—great or small—that the prison authorities place in its volunteers and those who live inside the prison translates artistically into how much openness or cautiousness incarcerated actors must embody on stage. All incarcerated actors walk a fine line between exploring the characters they portray and also monitoring and respecting the rules of the prison, and those who work under the harshest rules (particularly those governing touch and the ability to speak openly about one's feelings) must work harder to balance their artistic craft with the prison environment.

Even among theatre troupes—either in prison or in the free world—OHOM is a remarkably loving organization. Their very name would give many prison systems pause. Stallings refers to his life inside and outside the prison as the "Nonstop Love-In." Stallings's long-standing and strong relationships with prison administrators and staff—as well as the fact that he is a man volunteering at a men's prison—do much to ameliorate concerns about the emotional investment being made by the OHOM group. Pensalfini notes in his commentary on expressions of love betwixt theatre makers and incarcerated participants: "The practitioners that speak in this way are typically mature men speaking to other men. A middle-aged married man saying 'I love you' to a male prisoner would certainly ring differently than a woman of any age saying the same thing."[100] Indeed, Stallings's warmth with the actors never felt in any way untoward or inappropriate in my observation, and apparently the prison staff, after years of familiarity with Stallings and the theatre group, did not object.

Most importantly, the incarcerated actors not only seemed comfortable with Stallings's emotional embrace of them; they took great joy in receiving and returning that love. Stallings opened our conversation on the morning after closing night by saying, "It's another beautiful day. I'm very happy to be in the circle with all of you. I love you, and so I'm happy to be here."[101] The other men in the circle immediately chimed in to add to the chorus of joy. William Huffman—who played Mariner, Lady, and a shepherdess— smiled sheepishly as he said, "I have not been around anybody at any time in my prison stay where people were genuinely happy. I mean everybody. It felt almost like Christmas morning to me—the vibe in the air."[102] Timothy Hinkhouse—who played Jailer, Guard, a shepherdess, and a satyr—spoke next: "I'm actually filled with gratitude and contentment because last night was really starting out to be an emotionally traumatic situation for me, which ended in just elation and happiness. Being a part of this was something that helped me grow as a person."[103] The conversation continued in this vein with testimonial after testimonial of the magnitude of the emotional impact of being in this play. Hinkhouse had never before performed in a play, and he told the audience during the postshow discussion that he joined the OHOM theatre group because he had heard about the Voodoo Doughnuts at the receptions. The idea of performing had intimidated him, but the warmth and love of the group had enabled him to face his fears and then be swept up into the many positive and community-oriented experiences of the process.

Many of the men spoke with astounding vulnerability and used the word "love" frequently. Joe Opyd—Momma Sharon's son—felt particularly moved by the closing night performance and reception: "Seeing the audience, you know, pour their hearts into it . . . seeing them get emotional and crying. I mean, I started to get all teared up myself. . . . To see people maybe that were apprehensive at first just to—Hearts start to open, you know. That's just a beautiful thing to me, just to see. . . . It's not an experience that I would exchange for anything."[104] Opyd describes a kind of love feedback loop. He reads the audience as active participants in the play, giving back to the actors as they perform and reflecting the openness that the incarcerated men have worked so hard to achieve. Stallings responded to this with an affirmation: "Everybody in this room gave a gift to all of the people who came. . . . It's a beautiful two-way thing because they're giving you a lot of love, too. And I assume that's nourishing, nurturing."[105] The members of the circle continued to teach one another about what good can come of love and vulnerability. It felt like the incarcerated men in the room needed to catalog all of their positive feelings and wring every bit of love out of that room because they knew that soon they would be back to waiting another six months for rehearsals for a new play to begin, another year for the exuberant joy of the performances and receptions.

Chester Gunter (the sheep with granddaughters) most forcefully exemplified the urgent need to say all of these beautiful things out loud, while they had the sacred space of this time together to reflect about the play:

> We can't go anywhere [else] and feel the love that we feel with one another here, literally. . . . Bushra, Nancy, Johnny, there's truly no words that can explain what you mean to us, you know. The love that I have for you. I'd give my life for you, you know, and I know everybody else here would do it. I love you. . . . You know, if I died right now, I would die the happiest man in the world without a doubt.[106]

When people in the free world say, "I'd give my life for you," I tend to think they are hyperbolizing as a way to indicate the strength of their feelings, but in the context of prison, the expression strikes me as more literal. Particularly in men's facilities, incarcerated people live with the perpetual knowledge that real and sudden, life-threatening violence could erupt on any given day. Even in facilities where this seldom happens, imprisoned men have been acculturated to expect that such things could plausibly occur and that they must maintain a watchful vigilance to prevent it. When Gunter says that he or any other man in that group would lay down his life for the OHOM volunteers, I take him very literally. Many other men in the circle nodded as Gunter spoke. He had clearly named the stakes of this group's attachment to one another when he said, "We can't go anywhere and feel the love that we feel with one another here, literally." For Gunter, and likely at least some of the other men, that place of love is worth his very life.

Stallings's immediate response to this boldfaced declaration was, "But live!" The group erupted in laughter. Gunter replied cheerfully, "Yeah. Obviously. I'm ready for the next play."[107] Love gives us even more motivation to live than to die for one another. In prisons that allow it, the theatre offers incarcerated people the opportunity for expressions of love that are seldom sanctioned anywhere else in one's life in confinement, particularly in regard to physical contact and touch.

Appropriate Physical Touch and Why Prisons Need More of It

How much access an incarcerated person in the United States has to one's family and other visitors varies significantly depending on one's location. Each state in the United States has its own separate prison system, and the federal government has yet another set of prisons, as does the Immigration and Customs Enforcement. Each of these fifty-two distinct carceral systems has its own rules and procedures, as well as its own social norms for staff and incarcerated people. Within any given prison system, each individual facility also has a distinct culture and marked differentiations in procedures and norms for everyday practices in the prison, like visiting. Unfortunately, many carceral systems in the United States are moving away from allowing any physical contact at all. The county jails in Michigan, for instance, allow visits only through video monitors. Visitors still have to travel to the jail to see their loved ones, but they never get past the lobby. They take seats in front of a row of video monitors with telephone receivers, and when visiting hour begins, the screen lights up with a video feed of their incarcerated loved one who is sitting in a day room, elsewhere in the same building, talking on a similar device. This dystopian version of communication, void of touch and even proximity, will likely continue to spread throughout the United States in years to come because it supposedly requires less monitoring from prison staff and is therefore considered to be cheaper than other kinds of visits. Video visits prove particularly devastating for families with children who need physical touch in order to stay engaged with the incarcerated members of their families whom they are struggling to get to know better. (If video visits could be possible remotely from the personal computers or phones of families in their own homes, such a service would be enormously helpful *as an addition to, not a replacement of* contact visits at the prison.)

For now, the more common options for visiting in prisons throughout the United States involve either someone talking to their loved ones on a telephone through a pane of soundproof glass or a contact visit in which a family gets to sit together at a table with no divider between them. Contact visits usually only permit guests to hug and kiss their incarcerated loved ones once at the beginning of the visit and again just before they leave. For many families, like mine, these visiting rules and the difficulties of journeying to the far-flung locations of many prisons cause you to be able to count on your fingers the number of times you might kiss and hug your incarcerated loved one in a year.

Two Rivers Correctional Facility gives families more access to one another than many other prisons in the United States. While it does maintain the rule of one kiss and hug at the beginning and end of each contact visit, Two Rivers, like most prisons in Oregon, also has annual family picnics, which have far more permissive rules about physical touch. A family can sit together on a blanket outdoors for the better part of a day, sharing food and enjoying one another's company. Children can sit on their father's laps, and spouses can hold hands and put their arms around one another. They can behave more like a family for one glorious day of the year.

Performances provide a remarkable opportunity for the men and their families to have a different kind of access to one another than they do in regular prison visits or even picnics. The OHOM performances take place in the visiting room—the only space in most prisons where family members can be reunited for a brief time—and the entire audience shares in the performance. Everyone has witnessed the same cultural event and has built a collective relationship to it, as people throughout the audience saw one another laughing and crying, pointing at things, reacting to the story being told. Then, instead of having to divide into clusters where each family must be isolated from another—as in regular visits—the whole audience eats doughnuts and mingles.

On closing night of *The Winter's Tale*, Momma Sharon and Aunt Andrea made contact with every man in the cast and had them sign their programs. I had, at this point, never met any of the actors, yet I was able to spend time with many of them, offer my sincere congratulations on the performance, and ask questions about the play. Everyone hugged everyone else. Prison staff were always in the room, but I never saw them intervene in anyone's conversation or physical touch until the appointed hour when we all had to leave the visiting room. The incarcerated men were asked to line up on one end of the room, and the rest of us did the same on the other end. We walked out of different doors in two lines, and once again, as before we entered that space, we could be distinguished by our legal status: free or not free. During the performance and reception, those distinctions had been blurred significantly enough that our bodies and their proximity to one another had not been policed as they would have been on any other occasion in a US prison.

In our group conversation the next day, Stallings explained how this extraordinary physical liberty during the postshow receptions had begun:

> Before we did our first play . . . we were told it was good that the Department of Corrections gave us permission to do a play in the first place. . . . They said, "Okay. Now after the play is over, there is to be no contact . . . between the audience and the inmates." . . . And anyway, the play ended, and everybody just went (*gestures, bringing hands together, fingers interlaced*). You know, it happened so fast, and . . . none of [the staff] wanted to say, "Wait! Wait! No, you can't do that!" So, it became a precedent . . . because I think that the people in the Oregon Department of Corrections who have come into the room and watched it, whether in positions of high authority or not very high authority, have seen that the hug is love. It's just a simple expression of human beings expressing love for each other and that there's nothing inappropriate or sexually, you know, wrong about it . . . Ultimately, unless there's a little humanity, a little love, everything would just go down so dark that it would be unbearable.[108]

To some degree, Stallings must be right. At least up to this point in the history of OHOM's performances, those in power have done nothing to limit or stop the verbal and physical expressions of love that happen at these receptions. The staff I saw at *The Winter's Tale* closing reception were not engaged in mingling with the audience and actors, but they were eating doughnuts alongside us as they watched everything that was happening. The staff did not appear to be relaxed or less than fully vigilant, but they did not actively discipline anyone either. There was a sense of mutual respect between them and everyone in the room.

Stallings theorizes that the space of the visiting room itself makes these things possible because ordinary rules of the prison allow physical touch in that setting. Actor Jason Beito felt that the prison authorities would be reluctant to attempt to interrupt the receptions, "Because love is a force of nature. It's a universal force, and it's just something so much bigger than any one of us or all of us put together. And so, when something just takes over like that, that is so powerful and so much grander than any of us. No one's going to be able to stop it."[109] Chester Gunter felt that it had more to do with the plays changing staff culture in the prison: "I really appreciate [the DOC] allowing us to have them hugs because really if they wanted to stop that, they could do whatever they wanted. But you know, talking about breaking barriers, everybody's working together. . . . Each year they're . . . opening up to us."[110] Joshua Friar thought that it behooved the staff not to try to intervene: "And I picture like an eight-foot-tall, 400-pound guard against Joe's mom (*laughter*), five foot nothing, and I'd feel bad for the guard." Someone else adds, "'Cause he will hug her!"[111] This comic rejoinder might have been a way of saying that Momma Sharon would barrel past an obstacle of any size because of the force of her love for the cast; it might also mean that her love would encompass everything in its path, including the prison staff.

Something about the culture of love has definitely transformed the visiting room of Two Rivers on the nights of OHOM's performances for outside visitors. (The dynamics of physical touch are undoubtedly very different at the shows for incarcerated audiences.) Randy Geer, the retired Oregon prison administrator, reminded me that, "generally in prisons, you're talking about an environment in which all forms of touch are discouraged. [Incarcerated people] can't touch each other, staff, or their guests. It's a terrible kind of punishment for people."[112] Stallings and Momma Sharon each told me about different men who had gone for years without anyone hugging them until someone else's mother unexpectedly embraced them at an OHOM reception.[113] After years of not having contact with the outside world, Jeffrey Sanders actually feared interacting with the public at performances of his first play:

Last year in *King Lear*, I was so terrified. I sat in a corner, and Mr. Underhill's guest, she spoke. I cried that night. I was in a corner, and I was not going to move. I wasn't gonna move because I was gonna forget my lines, or somebody was gonna watch me, or I don't know what. . . . And Josh kept saying, "Watch. Somebody's going to give you a hug!" (*laughter*) And I was like, "Oh, my God! Please do not talk to me. Whoever you are, stay away from me." And then she came down, and she's like, "Why are you back here in a corner?" And I was like, "Okay. What's your name?" And that brought me out of my shell for this type of setting.[114]

Being able to talk to a kind stranger helped Sanders get through his first performance and the evening itself. He became the person who would be able to comfort a crying child the next year at another such reception.

Joshua Friar saw that the experience of watching an OHOM play helped humanize him enough to make an estranged visitor willing to hug him again:

> I was fortunate to have a family member show up that had never seen me in—and really didn't want to see me in—prison. . . . We had a meeting in visiting. . . . She wasn't going to hug me, and I made a comment about our food trays here or something like that, and her comment was, "Well, of course, you're a criminal." . . . And at the end of the play, she was in tears . . . she kind of went for a hug and then shook my hand, and then I said, "Well, can I get a hug?" And she did, and she was crying on the way out.[115]

The idea of prison and of Friar as "a criminal" had transformed this woman's view of how she saw a member of her own family, and somehow the play radically changed her perception of Friar and perhaps also of the kind of person who lives inside the walls. When she embraced him, she gave and received the gift of reconnection with someone who had been lost to her.

Prisons have the ability to foster or utterly prevent the kinds of community building that this chapter describes. Theatre makers—both the incarcerated ones and their free-world partners—do the vast majority of the labor involved in such processes, but those who govern the facility and enforce the rules have immense power in terms of the amount and nature of the meaningful connections that can be made inside the prison walls. When prison administrators encourage staff to mentor incarcerated people and invest in their well-being, the environment becomes safer and more enjoyable for everyone. If outside guests can be allowed to witness performances inside the walls, they will be transformed by the process and carry new understandings of the criminal justice system into the free world. When theatre can help reunite and strengthen families, people on both sides of the walls benefit enormously. Appropriate yet permissive boundaries for declarations of love and physical touch reassert the humanity of everyone involved and make the prison environment more permeable for a brief time. The theatre naturally sets these processes in motion, if only the keepers of the keys will let them unfold.

CHAPTER 2
THEATRE AS A STRATEGY FOR PROFESSIONALIZATION

I was totally gobsmacked at the talent of many of the prisoners, but I shouldn't have been: music, drama, visual arts, and all of the creative aspects of life are neglected in disadvantaged areas, and families cannot afford to pay for their children to attend private classes. This means that poor people's talents are untapped, not that they don't have any. Still, it was a revelation that men who had so little going for them could have such skills.

—John Lonergan, former warden of Mountjoy Prison in Dublin, Ireland[1]

The most physically beautiful prison I have ever seen also holds one of the oldest continually running prison theatre companies in the world. William Head Institution in British Columbia serves as a minimum security, federal, prerelease facility for men in the Correctional Service of Canada. The prison sits on a remarkable piece of land—on the coast of an island south of Vancouver. Surrounded by an ancient forest of Douglas firs and arbutus trees, William Head Institution occupies the territory once inhabited by Coast Salish and Scia'new First Nations peoples, Spanish colonizers, Chinese laborers, Scottish sheep farmers, and a quarantine station for sufferers of smallpox. In 2015, the incarcerated residents of William Head researched and devised a play about this long history, which they called *Here: A Captive Odyssey.*[2] This fascinating and informative play gives just a single scene to one of the more exceptional events that sets this place apart from the rest of Canada and the world: the founding of a successful professional theatre company run almost exclusively by incarcerated men.

In 1975, as postsecondary educational programming gained traction in Canada's federal prisons, a group of men imprisoned in Matsqui Institution in Abbotsford, British Columbia, founded a troupe called Institutional Theatre Productions, which lasted until a prison riot in 1981 shut down the program. Many members of that group transferred to William Head where they restarted the theatre company and formed an alliance with a college program from the University of Victoria. The university program ended in 1984, but the William Head on Stage (WHoS) theatre company remained and has operated autonomously ever since, under the leadership of an incarcerated board of directors.[3]

The prison theatre companies described in this chapter illustrate how various groups have cultivated the development of professional skills and performances among incarcerated participants. Such abilities include highly technical trades (like lighting design and puppet making), administrative capacities (like budgeting and delegating), and interpersonal skills (like time management and appropriate responses to challenges). The WHoS' original devised puppet play *Fractured Fables* and the development of *Hip Hop Hamlet* by the Prison Performing Arts company in Missouri, USA, serve as the guiding narratives of this chapter, offering two remarkable models for professionalization in prison theatre.

Fractured Fables: The Prison Puppet Project: My First Visit to the WHoS (or the WHoS on First)

Audience members from the free world can pay $25 (Canadian) on the internet to purchase a ticket to a WHoS production.[4] In October 2013, I purchased two and took my friend Julita Ramírez to see *Fractured Fables: The Prison Puppet Project*—an original play devised by WHoS. We nearly panicked driving up to the prison when it occurred to me that I had never entered Julita's name anywhere online during my ticket purchase. She had driven up from Seattle to meet me, and I was certain that she was about to get turned away from the prison because without her name, they could not possibly have run a background check to grant her security clearance to enter the facility. We arrived, showed the tickets we had printed at home, and were admitted to the prison after a quick verification of our passports. The ease of our entry astounded me. Such a thing has never happened to me in a prison anywhere in the world before or since. I am told that security has increased a bit since my first visit to William Head and that audience members are now searched by drug-sniffing dogs prior to entry.

After passing through a metal detector, we and other audience members got into a van, which took us down a road inside the prison and to the door of the theatre. The lobby area was full of arts and crafts, and a few incarcerated men greeted us and told us about the art and the literary magazine that they had made and were selling. When the doors to the theatre opened, incarcerated ushers led us to our seats and instructed us that once the play started we were not to get up or cross the lines taped on the floor around the audience. Other than the presence of a few uniformed officers at the back of the room and the admonition about not leaving our seats, I would never have known that I was in a prison and not any other professional theatre space. High-quality lighting equipment hung from the ceiling, pointed at a curtained stage, and before the performance began, all of the lights went out—another first for me. In all the prisons I have ever visited elsewhere, darkness is read as a security threat. Many memoirs written by those imprisoned around the world describe the torture of constant lights in their faces. The men in my father's prison used to tie socks together to make blindfolds to help them sleep at night. At William Head, the security team had posted officers unobtrusively along the edges of the audience, and the set and blocking of the production had been carefully designed to ensure that no part of the audience would ever be out of the officers' sight. So there I sat in the darkened theatre waiting for the lights to come up on the first act.

Over the course of the next hour, we watched one of the best performances I have seen in my life—in or out of a prison.

Strange and fascinating tales unfolded. A large seal puppet drifted majestically through the audience and became an odd-looking baby who grew into a man (Figure 2.1) and then in old age returned to being a seal and swam away again. A chorus of ostriches argue with one another and then have a lively and hilarious dance number (Figure 2.2). A man loses his eyeball, which then grows a kind of consciousness and has adventures of its own (Figure 2.3). In between these puppet scenes and many more, actors gave short monologues in which they told fables—some from their own lives and others that had started autobiographically but morphed into the fantastical.

The acting, puppetry, and music all felt seamless and whole, deeply connected to one another and grounded in a sense of emotional reality, though the plot and characters pushed all boundaries of belief. Very little of the play had spoken dialogue. Most of the action involved puppetry set to music played by a live band. The puppetry itself ranged from very small and intimate creatures to shadow puppets to birds the size of the actors who played them to giant animals that required multiple puppeteers to operate them. Theatre professionals often study for years on end to acquire the many different skills required to manufacture and convincingly manipulate this

Figure 2.1 Seal as an old man with shadow puppetry in background.
Photo credit: Jam Hamidi.

Figure 2.2 Bird puppets in *Fractured Fables*.
Photo credit: Jam Hamidi.

Figure 2.3 Eyeball with bird and bug.
Photo credit: Jam Hamidi.

broad range of puppets. The performance proved dazzling and surprising from start to finish—the audience almost too breathlessly delighted to be able to ask articulate questions during the fifteen-minute discussion that the actors were granted before having to leave the stage and any further interactions with us.

The production involved intricate collaboration between a startlingly large cast and crew—twenty-seven incarcerated men in all—plus a team of professionals hired from outside the prison and paid with government-funded arts grants. This included two directors, a professional actor, a lighting designer, set designer, musical director, a puppet doctor (who stayed backstage fixing puppets when they broke), and even a consultation with a puppet expert who had once worked with Henson Productions. In the weeks leading up to the performances, the theatre professionals and incarcerated men rehearsed six days a week. "And on the seventh day they made puppets!" Peter Balkwill, one of the directors, joked when I spoke with him about the production. In fact, puppet making took place concurrently with the development of the play; Balkwill and codirector Ingrid Hansen have written that they maintained "four active creative sites" during rehearsals: "men building puppets with Carole Klemm; musician Katrina Kadoski leading the inmate band; one director shaping puppet scenes, and the other director holed up in the WHoS company office, a former basketball storage closet, dissecting monologues with the actors."[5] The prison administrators at William Head have done something extraordinary in enabling a theatre company to have access to this much time and space for rehearsals, not to mention the materials used in puppet making, including chicken wire and other things that would ordinarily be very difficult to get into many other prisons.[6]

These resources and the high degree of autonomy that WHoS maintains enable them to do professional quality work and, in the process, to professionalize imprisoned theatre makers to a degree rare not only among arts programs but also among prison programs of any kind. WHoS also gives better theatre training to its actors, musicians, administrators, stage managers, and technicians than the vast majority of community theatres I have encountered in the free world. Seeing *Fractured Fables* made me want to know how and why the men at William Head had honed their skills to this level and developed such a high degree of professionalism across their more than thirty years as a producing company.

Startlingly Good: Quality Productions as Key for Sustainability and Shifting Prison Culture

Because William Head is a prerelease facility, most of the men housed there will serve less than three years of their sentences in this institution. In light of this, WHoS requires a consistent stream of new members as well as careful planning to provide mentorship for them and continuity for the theatre company. The quality of their performances and the scarcity of theatre programming in Canadian prisons have helped to establish WHoS' reputation far and wide.

Several of the men I met in WHoS had heard about the group while serving time in other prisons. A man named Alan and his family knew of the company prior to his incarceration; his wife and mother encouraged him to join WHoS immediately upon being sent to William Head so that he could do something meaningful with his talents as a singer and guitar player.[7] Another man named M.F. said that he "moved into a WHoS house" where all of those around him already participated in the theatre company. (The residents at William Head live in small houses with five men in each.) M.F. saw a video of *The Crossroads: A Prison Cabaret*—WHoS' original devised play from 2018 and the first to be filmed—and marveled at how professional it was and how different the men he knew were on stage than in their regular lives in prison. The feeling he had watching the video made him want to be part of something that could enable people to transform in that way.

Dylan, a formerly incarcerated WHoS participant, felt that his interactions with theatre professionals trained him to think and behave differently:

> That's the big thing for me, WHoS broke down barriers and prison attitudes, stuff like that, because being in and out of prison all the time for the past twenty years, it's like it seeps this negativity and judgmental things that aren't congruent with becoming a productive member of society [sic]. . . . So being a part of WHoS was breaking that down because you have outside people coming in, you got to address them a certain way and you can't be disrespectful [because] you have people that are compassionate, and caring coming in to give their time.[8]

The work of creating performances together gives incarcerated theatre participants awareness of a different social order in the world outside prison—particularly in the context of professional interactions. The fact that gainfully employed theatre makers welcome imprisoned participants into their workplace culture illustrates that people in prison can adapt and learn specific skills. This can result in performances so imaginative and well-performed that prison theatre companies can develop local and national reputations for excellence.

Hip Hop Hamlet at Prison Performing Arts in St. Louis, Missouri

I had been meaning to get to St. Louis, to go to see the Prison Performing Arts (PPA) company years before I managed to visit them. When I heard that their founder Agnes Wilcox planned to direct a hip hop theatre adaptation of *Hamlet* as her swan song before retirement, I knew I had to see it. On February 26, 2015, I and several dozen other visitors from the free world entered the Northeast Correctional Center (NECC) in Bowling Green, Missouri. One hopeful audience member was turned away at the gate. Her name had been on the list for the matinee that afternoon but not for the evening performance we were about to see. Despite the fact that she had passed the necessary background check and gained approval for entry to the facility, she fell victim to the arbitrary exercise of power at the prison and would not get to see *Hip Hop Hamlet*. It was closing night of a three-day run. As I made my way to my seat, I thought of the woman who was turned away, driving the hour and a half back to St. Louis by herself and wondered how many more people who wanted to see this work and support these men had missed this fleeting opportunity.

The seating had been placed on either side of a narrow stage running down the middle of the room, so that everyone watched the action like a tennis match with a good view of the other half of the audience. Since the lights never dimmed or went down, part of the joy of the show emerged in seeing how much fun everyone else was having. We had come to watch one of the greatest tragedies in theatre history, yet the play had been transformed into a comedy—not in the Shakespearian sense that the characters all get married in the end but a play full of comic dialogue and situations designed to elicit laughter. In her curtain speech before the start of the show, smiling broadly, Agnes Wilcox prepared us for this: "All we ask of you is that you laugh at our jokes. We wrote a very funny play, and if you don't laugh, we're just going to have to go home unhappy."[9]

No one went home unhappy. In fact, I have never seen an audience so joyful after watching the tragedy of *Hamlet*. The performance was as Agnes had promised—very funny from start to finish. At the top of the show, Hamlet enters and answers a call on his cell phone, saying, "Who's there?"— recognizably a nod to the opening of the original Shakespeare. From there, it takes off into a roll call of characters announcing themselves in rhyming couplets to a prerecorded hip hop beat:

I'm Claudius and here's the situation:
I'm the new head honcho of the corporation.
So I killed my brother, one little flaw,
Now I'm the boss—mwa, ha, ha, ha, ha![10]

As the characters introduce themselves, they also lay out the conceits of this adaptation. The script will always rhyme and be spoken in tempo. The actors will often directly address the audience. The plot basically remains faithful to Shakespeare, but the adaptation reconfigures not only the poetry of the text but also the setting and feel of the characters. Claudius murdered his brother to gain control not of Denmark but of a business called Elsinore

Enterprises. Laertes is captain of the Yale University fencing team and will soon go to law school. The Player King and his troupe have been transformed into Jerry Springer, his producers, and guests—a seemingly bizarre shift in the script but one that resonated particularly well in the cultural moment of reality television.

The all-male cast played the female roles in loose dresses but did not attempt to physically transform into women. The actors playing Ophelia and Gertrude moved and looked like men, yet their characters functioned meaningfully throughout the play as women to be taken seriously—not as men in drag or parodies of womanhood. Ophelia, played by Scott Brown with obvious sideburns and a meaty man's body (Figure 2.4), had the sensibility of a petulant teenager, reading *Seventeen* magazine, sulking, and expressing shock at Hamlet's treatment of her. David X. Turner took over the role of Gertrude only two weeks before the production when the actor originally cast as the ill-fated queen landed in solitary confinement and was forbidden to rejoin the show.[11] Turner had a muscular intensity and did not shave his mustache or cover his bald head for the role (Figure 2.5). His Gertrude commanded the audience and the other actors in a way that imbued the part with new meaning for me. This queen was no pawn in Claudius or Hamlet's games. She made bold choices and took agency as

Figure 2.4 Mark Sevier as Laertes and Scott Brown as Ophelia. Photo credit: Steve Tharp for PPA.

Figure 2.5 David X. Turner as Gertrude.
Photo credit: Steve Tharp for PPA.

much as her circumstances permitted. Yet, she was tender and loving, greatly pained by watching her only son descend into madness.

As an audience member, I never lost sight of the fact that the key women's roles were being played by two of the larger men in the cast, but this also did not distract me from what the characters did and said on stage. These casting choices felt not just like a nod to the all-male ensembles of Shakespeare's day but deliberate references to the hypermasculinity of the prison in which we sat. Theatre scholar Daniel Banks attributes this kind of social transformation and cultural resignification to the nature of hip hop performance, which he describes as "immediate, necessary, always changing, and consistent in its struggle for recognition."[12] These female characters were distinctly not versions of the Ophelia and Gertrude I had previously known, yet they fit seamlessly into the world of this play. They pushed me to think more about what *Hamlet* might mean to those who could not go home after this performance.

Gertrude meets her untimely demise because she cannot bear the tension of watching her son and Laertes duel, in this version with guns. As Osric slowly counts out the seconds before the men can turn and shoot—"One-one-thousand, two-one-thousand, three"—Gertrude snatches up the poisoned tumbler of Crown Royal that Claudius poured for Hamlet:

GERTRUDE

Too long!
I need a drink. Oh, this smells strong . . .

CLAUDIUS

> Give me that drink. You'll get too tipsy . . .

GERTRUDE

> I may be a woman, but I can handle my whisky.

> *She drinks.*[13]

Though she needed no physical movement to challenge him in this moment, Gertrude's body and voice clearly indicate that she could beat this Claudius to a bloody pulp if she chose, and he proves neither brave nor fast enough to prevent her from drinking the poisoned cup. In this case, her clear authority has undermined her and inadvertently caused her death. Yet, she shows vulnerability in her last breath. Hamlet recognizes that something terrible has befallen his mother, calling out, "Mom, what's wrong?" Claudius tries to deflect, but both Hamlet and Gertrude ignore him. Her last words, "Oh, Hamlet! Something's not right!" felt painful and poignant.

Hamlet cannot help her and meets his own death at the end of Laertes's gun, though he expires slowly enough to kill both Laertes and Claudius and last through another thirty-six lines of dialogue. Hamlet appeared to die and revive several times to great comic effect:

HORATIO

> You still haven't died?

> What more could you possibly have to say?

HAMLET

> Increase your annual donation to PPA!

> *Hamlet dies.*[14]

The force of the play's humor startled me, reclaiming Shakespeare for those who might be intimidated by his language or cultural distance. These men had also reinscribed the prison as a place of laughter and celebration. Wilcox saw this as a deliberate move on the part of PPA's leadership and the men in the cast and crew. When we met the next day, she commented on the attitude of carceral institutions, "Prisons assume that art in any form runs counter to order. It's an indulgence [incarcerated people] don't deserve. Fun is prohibited." The cast of *Hip Hop Hamlet* reclaimed some of their agency and an abundance of joy in their work on this production, which was made possible because of the years of relationship building and hard work put in by the incarcerated participants, PPA's administrators, and prison officials.

The Genesis of PPA and *Hip Hop Hamlet*

PPA has always had the mission of creating professional quality performances. Christopher Limber, who succeeded Wilcox as the artistic director of PPA in 2016, says, "PPA's foundational goal is creating a deep, resonant artistic experience for the participants and the audience—for this is what makes a difference in their lives and in the prison culture on many levels."[15] Founded in 1999, PPA came into existence as a side project of the New Theatre in St. Louis where Wilcox served as the artistic director. As the work in prisons became Wilcox's primary focus, PPA became an independent company with her at its helm.[16] PPA's leadership has always had an impressive array of professional theatre credentials. Wilcox earned her MFA in Directing from New York University and had taught there as well as at the Eugene O'Neill Theatre Center and Washington University in St. Louis. Limber holds a BFA in Acting from the State University of New York at Purchase and has worked for nearly four decades as a professional actor, director, playwright, dramaturg, poet, composer, and lyricist. Both Wilcox and Limber have brought their professional standards of work into prisons.[17] The results have garnered the company widespread recognition, especially after National Public Radio's *This American Life* program ran an episode called "Act V" about PPA in 2002, which has been repeatedly aired in the years since its release. The reporters Ira Glass and Jack Hitt play up the tensions between the public's low expectations of people in prison and the excellence of the incarcerated men's acting in PPA's production of the final act of *Hamlet*.[18]

Like his father's ghost, Hamlet has insistently haunted the folks at PPA. Wilcox began the company by directing all of *Hamlet*—one act every six months—with the men at NECC from December 1999 to 2002.[19] Though they have also produced many other plays in the intervening years, PPA returned to the troubled prince of Denmark in 2014 for a fifty-five minute abridgement of the whole play called *Trippingly Hamlet*, adapted by Limber, which Wilcox directed at NECC.[20] Over the course of a decade and a half, PPA had repeatedly brought Hamlet to live in this Midwestern prison with the men who played him and his contemporaries. They were well-primed to the difficult task of bringing the troubled Dane to life in contemporary language and rhythm.

Elizabeth Charlebois, an associate professor of English who specializes in Shakespeare studies at St. Mary's College of Maryland, had spent months in St. Louis while on sabbatical in 2007 and 2008 to serve as the

Scholar in Residence and dramaturg for PPA's productions of *Richard III* and *A Midsummer Night's Dream*. In May 2013, she saw a hip hop theatre production called *Othello: The Remix* at the Chicago Shakespeare Theatre, where it had traveled after having been commissioned by and performed at Shakespeare's Globe Theatre in London. She immediately had the idea to invite the playwright/performers, who call themselves the Q Brothers, to help the men at NECC to create a hip hop adaptation of *Hamlet*. It seemed the perfect way to close out Wilcox's time with PPA before her retirement, and soon the staff at PPA and the Q Brothers joined forces to develop *Hip Hop Hamlet*.[21]

The men at NECC were harder to convince. Charlebois had assumed that men in prison would feel comfortable with the genre of hip hop and get excited about the prospect of adapting Shakespeare into a familiar form. However, all but three or four of the men in the initial group working on *Hip Hop Hamlet* resisted the idea:

> In particular, some of the white actors who had worked with Agnes Wilcox on other productions clearly felt that the choice to do a hip-hop adaptation was an accommodation to black inmates. Their black counterparts didn't seem that enthused about it either, some resenting the expectation that they would or should be knowledgeable or competent in the genre in ways that they weren't.[22]

The prison administration also seemed wary of the notion of hip hop. Though they had never previously censored a Shakespearian production at the facility, the NECC staff removed several references to murder and drugs in *Hip Hop Hamlet*, despite the fact that these things occur in the original text.[23] Perhaps most damaging to the production, administrators forbade the incarcerated actors to have access to the beats provided by the Q Brothers that underscored the production.[24] This meant that the men had to write and learn to speak their lines to a rhythm to which they could not listen while composing or memorizing the words. They could only practice with the beats at the official PPA rehearsals, but because of the tight timeline for the production schedule, the vast majority of their writing and memorization happened on their own in the housing units.

At times in the performance that I attended, a few of the actors spoke curiously off tempo with the play's score. This fascinated me because most of their jokes and acting choices landed exceedingly well, even if they failed to keep time to the music. The parallel tracks of the writing/acting that did not always jive with the hip hop beat felt symbolic of something deeper in the play's development process. A disjuncture arose between the assumption that incarcerated people have expertise in hip hop and the realities faced by this particular cast. This set up structural difficulties, which the cast and crew worked valiantly and collaboratively to overcome. In particular, their complex and challenging script development work brought the actors, stage managers, Wilcox, and Charlebois (and to some extent the Q Brothers) into an interconnected working relationship that demanded a high level of skill from all of them.

Breaking It Down: Transforming *Hamlet* into Hip Hop

Wilcox, Charlebois, and the cast at NECC had only six months to study the original text of *Hamlet*, learn about hip hop theatre, adapt the text into their own words, and rehearse.[25] PPA hired the Q Brothers to come to Missouri three times to do devising workshops with the men at NECC, and on one of their visits they also worked with incarcerated women at Women's Eastern Reception, Diagnostic and Correctional Center (WERDCC) in the town of Vandalia. (The women at Vandalia mounted a revival of *Hip Hop Hamlet* in 2018, as will be described later.) At NECC, the Q Brothers performed scenes from *Othello: The Remix*, explained their process for adapting Shakespeare into hip hop, and helped the men shape specific scenes of *Hip Hop Hamlet*. Though the Q Brothers did much to shape the cast and crew's understanding of this style of performance, they did not actually write any of the play. They supplied the original beats that underscore the show and gave feedback on the script as it was developed. Ultimately, the enormous task of script writing fell to the men at NECC with Charlebois and Wilcox to guide them. None of them had any prior experience with hip hop theatre, and they had much to learn together. [26]

Charlebois divided the cast into ten groups based on the housing units where they lived and assigned them homework, divvying up sections of *Hamlet* to be translated into hip hop poetry. She handed out worksheets that asked the men to paraphrase what was happening and what had changed in each scene, the attributes of the characters involved, and the central questions being asked. Only after doing all of this were the men to get into the business of paraphrasing Shakespeare in their own language and then shaping this text into rhyming couplets.[27] This process required the men to practice the serious literary skills of close reading and script analysis and then to radically shift gears and become translators, playwrights, and poets. All the while, they collaborated with the two or three other men in their housing units as they did their homework and then faced the much larger challenge of integrating the work of the small groups into a cohesive script to be used by the entire cast. Charlebois and Wilcox did much of the editing of the hip hop scenes into a complete script, but Charlebois credits the men with all of the major choices that characterize *Hip Hop Hamlet*: "The main idea—the conceit of Elsinore Enterprises, the use of the Jerry Springer show as a contemporary 'Mousetrap,' even the idea of doing To be or Not to be as a group number— were all generated by the prison writer-actors."[28] When the script of *Hip Hop Hamlet* is published, it will name and credit all of the men who worked on the production "in collaboration with" Wilcox and Charlebois.[29] This formal acknowledgment of the immense work that each man, along with Wilcox and Charlebois, did on this production, not only as actors but also as writers, lends them not only a widely accepted free-world credential and, perhaps more significantly, also a sense of professional legitimacy seldom extended to those in prison. We rarely find ways to meaningfully and publicly acknowledge collaboration in the arts, and the extent to which Wilcox and Charlebois formally recognized the central role that the writer/actors at NECC played in the creative process is a distinctive and defining feature of *Hip Hop Hamlet*.

Revival Remix: The Women at Vandalia Stage *Hip Hop Hamlet*

PPA has found efficient and artistically rich ways to make as much as they can out of the major investment they made in *Hip Hop Hamlet*. In September 2018, Limber directed a new production of the play with women in WERDCC, describing it as "PPA's commitment to further develop and utilize an original piece." He notes that this process is "a key element of Prison Arts work—finding material that resonates and reinventing it with several prison groups. It's very cost effective and time-saving."[30] Daniel Banks calls this, "Another one of Hip Hop's revolutionary practices . . . versioning and renaming—taking ownership of a deprivileged situation through an act of self-determination."[31] The women at Vandalia reclaimed not just *Hamlet*, originally performed only by men in Shakespeare's day, but also *Hip Hop Hamlet*, created by and for male actors.

PPA sometimes shows videos of its productions in the other prisons where it works so that the groups inside can see what their counterparts are doing in other facilities. After watching the video of the closing night performance of *Hip Hop Hamlet* at NECC, the women at Vandalia voted to remount the production, saying "emphatically" to Limber, "We can do it better than they did."[32]

Limber directed the production that opened three and a half years after the men had performed. The women's development process involved five months of studying *Hamlet,* watching filmed versions of the play, and rehearsals. They used the Q Brothers' beats and the same script that the men at NECC had developed with Wilcox and Charlebois and credited all of them in the program for the show. The women performed with a larger cast, including a chorus of narrators, and they had a more fully realized set with painted backdrops.[33]

Limber says that the women did not share the men's unfamiliarity with or hesitation to perform hip hop music and dance, and unlike the men, they had access to the Q Brothers' beats outside of official rehearsals. As a result, their performance lived more deeply in the hip hop rhythms that undergird the text. In this sense the women's production felt more fully rendered as hip hop theatre than the men's did.[34] Janiece Moore (who played Claudius) and Laura Hulsey (who played Ophelia) also took on the roles of choreographers for the production, and they added quite a few dance numbers and extra moments of hip hop movement, including a dance scene

Figure 2.6 Laura Hulsey as Ophelia and dancers in Ophelia's death scene. Photo credit: Lisa Mandell.

to dramatize Ophelia's drowning. Ophelia scatters flowers around the stage. Then four dancers with panels of blue fabric join her. Ophelia, wearing a necklace of bones, dances to instrumental music mixed with the sound of moving water (Figure 2.6). She sometimes dances with the water and then fights against it until it pulls her offstage against her will. Moments like this one and the other storytelling work of dance in the production exemplified the ways in which the women made the play their own.

Mentorship, Mutual Growth, and the Development of Technical Skills at WHoS

In highly functioning prison theatre programs, like both PPA and WHoS, mentorship takes many forms and emerges in unexpected places. WHoS company members found myriad ways to use the skills they had already acquired—prior to or during their incarceration—in the service of the theatre because professionals from outside helped them to use their preexisting abilities in a new context. Some company members with backgrounds in carpentry have helped to design and build sets, while those who had completed an electrician's certification worked on lighting and others who learned sewing made costumes.[35] In WHoS productions, none of these technical or design roles prove to be simple. Thana Ridha, who wrote a master's thesis about WHoS, describes the costumes in one production as having "sequins, beading, textured layers, as well as personalized masks and headpieces—all of which were done by the men."[36] Professional designers in all of these fields have been hired by the WHoS board of directors to train the company members to learn and implement these skills. Lighting designer Poe Limkul from Thailand has worked in professional theatres around the world and on seven productions at WHoS. When visiting William Head, she not only focuses on the show at hand but holds a series of mentoring workshops for company members interested in lighting design.

Katrina Kadoski, the musical director for *Fractured Fables*, worked with a group of five men who had never before touched musical instruments. Over the course of the seven weeks of rehearsal, she taught them to play multiple instruments (including guitar, banjo, and a large variety of percussion instruments) and to compose music. The original score for the production was written and played by this group of men. As an audience member, I was deeply convinced that the band had been playing together for years and were recruited for the performances because their talents were known within the prison. When the men in the band revealed in the postshow discussion that they had learned to play music in the course of rehearsing for this production, the audience audibly gasped.

Lifer Lou, one of the men who played guitar for *Fractured Fables*, had gotten involved with the troupe as an actor on a previous show and remained a part of WHoS ever since, participating in eight productions. He has diversified his skill sets by working on multiple productions and getting involved in the administration of the company:

> I love everything about it. Thus far, I have worked in every part of the show from working sound, building the set, contributing ideas to scripts, managing the business finances as a board member and advisor to the board. . . . I have also taken on prominent roles as an actor, singer, and guitar player.[37]

Lifer Lou has had the experience of both acquiring a high level of skill very quickly (playing guitar fluidly in performance after a few weeks of lessons) and developing a broad range of abilities over the course of seven years with the company. He served as the musical director for the WHoS' 2019 production *The Emerald City Project*, leading other men in learning the skills that he has acquired through this program. Lifer Lou writes, "I still cannot believe what I have accomplished. None of this would have been possible if I was not in a prison that allowed for these programs to thrive."[38] This manifests not only in how the authorities grant permission for theatre professionals to enter the facility but also in the fact that the men at William Head are allowed to congregate and organize group activities among themselves at a level uncommon in many other prisons.

Mentoring at WHoS comes not only from the outsiders who enter the prison but also from within the troupe. Balkwill and Hansen write of "watch[ing] inmates who are 'old hats' at the theatre company counsel the newbies, and talk them down from the ledge when stage fright set in."[39] Jones, one of the company members, describes his role at WHoS as a people wrangler. At least four other men told me that they had joined WHoS because Jones encouraged them. He says he trusts people and that because of that, others trust him—a gift that can be in short supply in prison. After being a puppeteer in *Fractured Fables*, a company member named Ben wrote,

> By being involved with WHoS, I am able to stop harbouring greed, hatred, grumpiness, self-pity, and other counter-productive contents

and put in grace, kindness, patience, and compassion, and reflect a wonderful nature. They gave me the trust I needed to put one foot in front of the other, gratitude for being in their care, peacefulness about my destiny, trusting that someday I will be home.[40]

Mentorship within the group serves not just as an avenue toward personal growth and skill building but also as a means to perpetuate the theatre company itself.

As with all aspects of prison theatre, professionals have much to learn from incarcerated artists, whose lack of formal training or traditional experience with the craft often engenders a startling and provocative kind of creativity. Peter Balkwill writes about the process of developing *Fractured Fables* with the men of WHoS:

It became clear that none of these individuals had any experience with puppets. Hilarious I thought, this is going to be an honest collaborative creation process because we all truly needed to rely on each other to find the missing pieces, create the bridges and fill the gaps. I knew I would learn and grow a ton from this engagement.[41]

Theatre professionals going to work in prisons need more than just their craft and knowledge to collaborate well in such a setting. Kate Rubin, who has directed four plays for WHoS and performed in several others, has been involved with this group in various capacities since 2003, and she has watched many other theatre makers journey inside William Head to try their hand at this work. Rubin asserts that simply being a good director, designer, stage manager, or actor is not enough. Successful collaborators must have either direct knowledge of or intuitive sensitivity to the continuous struggles and restrictions that incarcerated people face on a daily basis. Otherwise, they can too easily become tyrants rather than directors and fail to understand the emotional and intellectual harm that can be caused by adding an extra layer of authoritarianism to an exceedingly difficult environment.[42]

The fact that Peter Balkwill and Ingrid Hansen arrived at William Head ready to "learn and grow a ton" enabled them to adapt to the environment and provide the level of mentoring required for such a technically challenging play to emerge. This sense of mutual discovery rather than a hierarchical form of mentorship produced remarkable results in *Fractured Fables*. The strangeness, whimsy, and technical precision in the storytelling and puppetry made the work feel personal, oddly relatable, and riveting to watch. Balkwill and Hansen seemed to want to cultivate a sense of ownership in the members of WHoS, throughout the entire process:

> At the prison, any materials the outside artists wanted to bring in needed security clearance—a process that takes at least two days. Often we did not know what materials would be needed until we were elbow-deep in paper-mache. So the inmate builders would rustle up a piece of Something from Somewhere and make it work, and in some instances would find results better than those previously theorized.[43]

Balkwill and Hansen encouraged the men to make their own artistic choices, and the rigid constraints of the prison environment had previously taught the men to be resourceful and creative—a skill that they might not have known they had or could apply in a professional setting.

WHoS Board of Directors: Theatre Company Management from Inside the Walls

From the start of any new production at WHoS, the men on the board of directors decide which theatre professionals they want to hire, what kind of budget and fundraising they will need, and whether they would like to devise a new play or mount a previously scripted one. The board of directors has at least five men on it at any given time, and elections for board members are held once a year. The entire incarcerated population of William Head votes, and in some years candidates face stiff competition for board seats.

The administrative structure of WHoS reverses the logic of prison programming seen in most other parts of the world. In most state prison systems in the United States, for example, incarcerated people cannot gather without the presence of an outside volunteer or prison staff person to, at least nominally, run the activity at hand. At WHoS, incarcerated men still end up incorporating people from the free world into their activities, but they have the power to invite the people they choose and to make plans together even when outsiders are not present.

The board chair holds a full-time position, paid by the prison administration, to run WHoS as his prison job. This formal recognition of the group's legitimacy and autonomy sets WHoS apart from any other prison theatre company I have encountered. Others, like the Drama Club at the

Louisiana State Penitentiary (described in the introduction and conclusion of this book, as well as Chapter 6), have the ability to meet on their own but not the support of a full-time prison job or the autonomy to write grants. Salaries for incarcerated people in Canada, like those in the United States, remain well below minimum wage. The board chair for WHoS receives $6.90 (Canadian) per day, minus a host of taxes and fees charged by the prison, which essentially cut these wages in half. Unlike people in most prisons, the men at William Head have to buy all of their own food from the prison commissary and cook it themselves in their houses. This means that the meager wages that they receive in their prison jobs are mostly spent on buying food from the prison itself. Despite these restrictions, the board chair for WHoS remains at a comparatively high pay scale among the jobs available to the incarcerated at William Head, and the money for it does not come out of the production budget for the theatre company.

Men who have been on the board credit this experience with teaching them business skills, budgeting, public relations, advertising, marketing, "how to deal with people," collaboration, delegation, and negotiation. Perhaps most significantly, the board members feel ownership over WHoS and its daily workings. Matthew Ross, the board chair from 2018 to 2019, writes, "The fact that it is 'ours' makes it more precious. Lots of history and freedom in this. We appreciate that we are part of something greater than ourselves. Shows we can obtain something higher than what we first expected."[44] The practical business management skills that board members at WHoS develop will serve them in many contexts in and out of prison, and the sense of achievement, pride, and inclusion in a meaningful historical legacy gives board members motivation to carry on the often daunting and unrelenting work of running the theatre company.

Managing WHoS' Money: Responsibility, Connectivity, and Placing Value on Artists' Work

Board members at WHoS feel the weight of their commitment to keep the company financially afloat. Andrew, a former board member who is no longer in prison, describes why WHoS functions differently than other organizations at William Head: "All the other things were just like social groups. . . . This [WHoS] was a business that was run by the inmates. . . . Ya it is still a self-run business . . . complete responsibility of it. If you screw it up really bad one way or another, there might not be one next year. So there was nothing close to it."[45] Incarcerated people often feel deeply disempowered by their inability to earn a living wage and contribute significantly (or at all) to their families' financial stability. Legal scholar Donald Braman has convincingly argued that this is one of the key ways in which incarceration strips people of their responsibility to their loved ones, communities, and the outside world.[46] By giving them fiscal ownership of the theatre company, WHoS makes its board members both responsible for and connected to one another, the theatre professionals they hire, and public audiences, which often include their family members.

In this sense, the theatre becomes an active form of public service for the company to engage with others on both sides of the walls. For Lincoln, who participated in WHoS before getting out of prison, the theatre company offered him his first experience of this kind:

You know, this was an opportunity for us to give to our community. . . . Never done that before. . . . My outside community—I had only ever taken from them. . . . So every now and then, you watch the rows [in the audience]. . . . We made people cry, we made people laugh, we made people stand and applaud. And it felt amazing.[47]

The board members and the rest of the company take seriously the matter of giving back to their audiences and the larger world. Since 2016, WHoS has been making charitable donations. Each year they choose a nonprofit that does work connected to the subject matter of the play. For example, when they produced *The Crossroads*, WHoS partnered with the Dandelion Society, which addresses issues of homelessness. WHoS gives 10 percent of its profits from each play to charity.

Managing the money for the theatre company also helps board members become reacquainted with what it feels like to budget and pay bills—a life skill that incarcerated people often lose when they have for years been cut off from the rhythms of paying rent, buying food, and budgeting for transportation costs. For those who entered prison as teenagers before they had their first jobs or apartments, money management may be an entirely new experience and a high stakes skill to acquire prior to their release.

WHoS sustains the quality of its creative endeavors by making a commitment to paying the professional theatre artists who work with them. The mechanics of how the funds are raised and how the artists get paid have changed over time, but the process always involves a highly regulated and rigorously defined set of partnerships among the men in the company, prison administration, and artists in the free world. In recent years, a local nonprofit theatre company called SNAFU has formed a sustainable symbiotic relationship with WHoS. Both the men at WHoS and the leadership at SNAFU write grants, which get funded by the Canadian government and arts agencies. The budgets for the WHoS productions are then assembled with resources from both sides of the walls, and professional theatre makers receive as close to a living wage for their labors as the funds permit. Even so, many of the long-term free-world collaborators at WHoS volunteer their time for about six months out of each year and receive pay only in connection with specific productions. Ultimately, these collaborators, like the men inside, are always giving far more of their time and talents than their pay would justify. However, the fact that they receive meaningful stipends for the production work makes it possible for them to continue giving so much of their time and energy each year. Otherwise, they would likely need to spend those long hours doing paid work somewhere else.

PPA Paying Artists to Work in Prisons and Beyond

Unlike WHoS, PPA has a small, salaried administrative team outside of the prisons. The artistic director, director of youth programs, and managing director receive full-time salaries with benefits, and at times they also have paid interns on staff. PPA's board of directors, who help with fundraising, includes local business people, two public defenders, a copyright lawyer, a university professor, and a former director of the Missouri Department of Corrections (MDOC).[48]

For the original production of *Hip Hop Hamlet*, PPA paid the Q Brothers and nationally renowned choreographer Redd Williams fees equivalent to what they would make in any other professional theatre engagement and covered their travel expenses to the prisons. Charlebois volunteered her labor at PPA for this production while on a paid sabbatical from her university, though PPA did reimburse her for some of her travel expenses. The MDOC does not have a mechanism that allows PPA to pay incarcerated collaborators, but at the time of the NECC production of *Hip Hop Hamlet*, some of the men in the cast were able to earn college credits from Fontbonne University—an arrangement that no longer exists for PPA productions but could be a useful model for partnerships between independent arts organizations and university programs in prisons.[49]

In 2018, PPA took the idea of professionalization in prison theatre even further by launching their New Play Initiative—a structured play development process bringing professional playwrights into prisons to work on new scripts. The incarcerated actors who work with the playwright throughout the process become the first cast to perform the show. The play then gets produced again shortly thereafter at a professional theatre in St. Louis, and the original cast from inside the prison are credited both in the program for the free-world production and in any future published version of the script.[50]

The New Plays Initiative has attracted nationally and internationally acclaimed writers as collaborators. Stacie Lents wrote the play *Run-On Sentence* with women at Vandalia, creating a drama about how prisons shape families—both biological and chosen ones. The incarcerated cast performed in January 2018, and the SATE Ensemble production in June of the same year received a nomination from the St. Louis Theatre Circle for Best New Play.[51] Playwright Pamela Sterling, who is known for her work in theatre for young audiences, collaborated with men at Missouri Eastern Correctional Center on a play called *No Plan B*, which will have its premiere in prison in 2020 and will be considered for a subsequent production at Metro Theatre Company.

The third production in this series will be an adaptation of Margaret Atwood's novel *Hag-Seed* with men at NECC. Limber wrote to Atwood through her publisher, explaining the work of PPA and expressing interest in producing *Hag-Seed*. Atwood emailed him and gave permission for PPA to create the first theatrical version of her novel.[52] *Hag-Seed* has several clear ties to PPA's work, as both an adaptation of *The Tempest* and a novel set in a prison—where the inhabitants stage a theatrical production of *The Tempest*. The PPA production of *Hag-Seed* at NECC is scheduled to be staged in January 2020, and the Shakespeare Festival of St. Louis will consider mounting a professional coproduction.[53] Documentary filmmaker Lisa Boyd has been following the collaborators on the New Plays Initiative, and her film *Prison Performing Arts: The Voice Within* previewed at the St. Louis Film Festival on July 21, 2019.

The New Plays Initiative at PPA structurally integrates the professional theatre world with prison arts programming. In several significant moments in US theatre history, incarcerated people in a theatre program and their free-world collaborators have managed to get the attention of professional theatre producers. The San Quentin Drama Workshop, named for the California prison in which it lived, produced work together from

1958 to 1965, "likely making it the first extended prison theatre program in the US launched by prisoners." Rick Cluchey, one of the lifers in the drama group, eventually left prison in 1966 and went on to become a close friend of Samuel Beckett's, a leading translator of his work, and the founder of Barbwire Theater. Cluchey had a successful career in professional theatre until his death in 2015.[54]

Another landmark transition from prison to professional theatre grew out of director Marvin Felix Camillo's work with an incarcerated theatre group who called themselves La Familia at Sing Sing Correctional Facility in New York. They developed the play *Short Eyes* by Miguel Piñero, a member of the imprisoned company. *Short Eyes* became the first play by a US Latino playwright to be produced on Broadway in 1974. All but three of the actors playing incarcerated men in the Broadway production had served time together. The play won two Obies and the Drama Critics Circle Award for Best American Play and launched Piñero's career as a writer. He became a founder of the famous Nuyorican Poets Café.[55] These extraordinary prison theatre companies in California and New York rose to notoriety and gave formerly incarcerated theatre makers real careers in the industry. They did so in ways that grew organically out of those troupe's experiences and connections.

PPA is attempting, for what might be the first time in US history, to build professionalization into the very structure of what it does with incarcerated theatre makers. This does not mean that any of the actors or writers who will one day gain their freedom after participating in PPA have assurances of careers in theatre, but PPA has managed to build months-long working residencies for theatre professionals to meaningfully collaborate with those inside the walls and then carry their work *with their names on it* into respected theatres and possibly also publishing houses. In doing so, PPA trains free-world theatre makers and audiences to recognize the talent of people inside the walls and to value their experiences. As Limber puts it:

> This kind of exposure [of the New Plays Initiative] widens the audience and the awareness of the work of PPA. By alerting the public to the high quality (as well as the importance) of developing the unheard voices of the men and women artists who are in prison, we boost our ability to gather audiences to attend in the prison and as well, financial support for what we do.[56]

Many grassroots prison arts programs do not believe that they have the funding to pay professionals to collaborate with them, but Limber argues that finding a way to make that financial structure work actually makes the organization more solvent in the end by drawing in donors.

PPA's commitment to paying theatre professionals and compensating incarcerated collaborators as they are able—with educational credits, professional recognition in the form of publication, and honoraria for those out of prison—offers a flexible, feasible, and ethical model for other prison arts organizations to follow. What may be possible in terms of compensation, especially for incarcerated people, varies widely from place to place, and the window of opportunity for such things can change drastically in a short amount of time. However, PPA and WHoS both treat currently and formerly imprisoned collaborators as people worthy of compensation and recognition, and this, in partnership with the development of skills, positions incarcerated theatre makers to take agency in their own growth as individuals and professionals.

Time Management, Collaboration, and Interpersonal Skills at WHoS

Like any other theatre company, WHoS has an annual production schedule and has to set its own pace for fundraising, planning, rehearsing, advertising, and performances. People in prison seldom have the opportunity to set a schedule that shapes the lives of others, and the development of this skill set among WHoS company members will prepare them well for many challenges in the outside world. Company members know that they cannot schedule visits with family and friends in the last several weeks leading up to performances because the troupe needs everyone in rehearsal six days a week,[57] and some have even added time commitments beyond what the professional directors have required: "The inmate stage manager went to other inmates' houses and quizzed them on their lines; he took it upon himself to organize extra rehearsals for the team during days off. It cannot be said enough, these guys worked harder than many who consider themselves professionals."[58]

In the development of *Fractured Fables*, this spirit of collaboration grew into the fascinating synergy that those of us in the audience observed on stage. According to Balkwill and Hansen, it began in the devising and puppet building process: "One person would start a puppet, another three might consult on how the thing looked, someone else might finish building it, and then yet another person would paint it."[59] The uses for the puppets, the number of them that were needed on stage, and the movements they would make grew collaboratively as well:

> Watching each other's discoveries in the construction lab and rehearsal hall, inspiration fed upon itself and fostered a connection between the puppets and puppeteers, between the inmate puppet builders and the inmate performers. There was a unified desire not to let each other down, to tell the best story ever told and to lift each other up to the heights of success. It was in its purest form a kind of artistic comradery.[60]

The company members' reflections on their experiences working with WHoS also bear out this spirit of connectivity and collective action. Actor Samuel says: "In WHoS and when we get out there [on stage], we're a team. . . . A lot of times we put our differences aside because we are not from the same backgrounds, or religion, or even institutions, and politics inside the institution . . . we get together and we produce a show for the public."[61] Collaborating across cultural differences, religious affiliations, and institutional divisions comes at a higher risk in prisons than in other kinds of spaces because those who live inside the walls cannot escape one another, often for years on end. Carceral institutions are specifically designed to keep people apart from one another and prevent them from interacting with residents of the free world. Prisons teach people not to trust one another and to keep to themselves. Theatre programming does the opposite as it builds ensembles and requires cast and crew to rely on one another. It cultivates healthy human interaction and provides a pathway toward this for some who had never had a way to practice collaboration or compassion publicly.

D.K., who began participating in 2013, credits WHoS with changing him "big time." He entered prison as a very young person and "grew up in here" without ever having the opportunity to live in the free world as an adult. He never had aspirations of being an actor but became one in WHoS. Because of this experience, he says he "wants to do good for the rest of his life." I.R., a new member of WHoS, describes growing up "in the hood" in a world of "violence, drugs, and partying." He joined the theatre company because he wants "positive things in [his] life." Sammy, another WHoS participant, found the group to be a kind of refuge from the other kinds of interactions he experienced in prison:

> For myself, establishing more of that patience and communicating with people and not getting aggressive—I think that was a lesson for

me . . . especially in a prison setting . . . it can get pretty fucking stupid over nothing, people start acting very immature. You can tell when a lot of guys are having difficulty working with people.[62]

The environment of the theatre company gave Sammy a model and a space for having different ways to respond to others, and when audiences arrive for the performances, they bring with them a new social dimension.

Several groups of elderly people from retirement homes came to a matinee when Blaze, the current chair of the WHoS board, was ushering. Blaze had recently been transferred to William Head from a medium security prison where no physical contact was permitted between incarcerated men and others. As the residents of the retirement home got off the vans that bring audience members to the performance space, they immediately reached for Blaze to help them from the vehicles and to their seats in the theatre. Blaze felt a shock at being touched and the way the elderly grabbed hold of him without hesitation. The audience members saw him as a help rather than a potential threat, and Blaze felt humbled by the immediacy of their trust and reliance on him. It delighted him to see that the visitors from the retirement home were even more excited and energetic leaving the theatre than they had been when they entered.

Spectators at these productions also report being moved by their interactions with incarcerated ushers before and after the play. After seeing a performance of WHoS' 2018 original play *Crossroads*, an audience member named Jeanne posted this comment on the WHoS website:

> What touched me . . . was the tenderness I saw in the inmates who welcomed and cared for the elderly and disabled people in the audience. My nephew, Gabe, has cerebral palsy and is in a wheelchair. The men guided him to the special place designed for him in the front row. One man offered him, and those of us with him, cookies and juice and another took the time to tell us his impressions of the show . . . a rave review. They included Gabe in their conversation and were attentive and respectful to him. I noticed that they did the same for the seniors as they came in one by one. Each person was treated like an honoured guest.[63]

Jeanne's experience mirrors my own, not only at WHoS but also at the many prisons I have visited around the world. People in prison consistently express profound gratitude and extraordinary courtesy to those who come inside the walls with open hearts. I am far more often treated rudely or deliberately intimidated in an airport, government office, or public street than I am inside a prison. I learn more about human dignity and kindness from the incarcerated people I meet than from any other group I encounter. Prisons have a striking way of making one recognize how people should and should not be treated.

Remember Me: Closing Night of *Hip Hop Hamlet* at NECC

Hip Hop Hamlet ends with a choral scene in which the actors no longer play the characters we have seen throughout the performance. They become a version of themselves—incarcerated actors, some of whom have removed elements of their costumes to make them seem more like everyday people. Speaking sections of the final scene in small groups, the performers address the audience:

> Hamlet asks questions; we ask them too.
> We hope our show asks them of you.
> Is revenge really worth it? Who can you trust?
> At the end of the day are we just cosmic dust?
> The play has madness, revenge, and grief,
> But friendship and love, even comic relief.
> There's more to this play than senseless violence.
> That's all for now—the rest is silence.[64]

In these lines the actor/writers question themselves and those of us who ventured inside a prison to watch them. We, as a great worldwide audience, have been pushed to think of people in prison as the ones who need to rethink their own actions—"Is revenge really worth it? Who can you trust?" Yet, all versions of *Hamlet* point to the rich and powerful (i.e., they who should have a corner on freedom compared to the rest of us) as the ones behaving most despicably. Shakespeare convinced centuries of readers and audiences that we can become invested in, and perhaps even love, people who do terrible things; their motives and emotions come from the same human impulses that propel each of us through life. At the end of *Hip Hop Hamlet*, performers and audience alike find themselves sitting in a prison, in a room we cannot leave until the guards open the doors. We cannot even go to the bathroom without permission and an escort. No one has the autonomy to make their own choices about when or where we will move inside this prison—"At the end of the day are we just cosmic dust?" When the players tell us, "There is more to this play than senseless violence," they remind us that there is more to them as people than whatever assumptions might have walked into the prison with us. The play ends with the entire cast saying, "Remember me. Remember me. Remember me. Remember me."[65] It feels like both a command and a promise. We should remember these people and the lessons they taught us, and we will be haunted by their memory, in the tradition of the ghost who first spoke the line.

One of the striking things about being in the audience on closing night of the NECC production was the presence of the then director of the Missouri Department of Corrections (MDOC) George Lombardi, who was seated on the opposite side of the audience from me and who was absolutely beaming with joy throughout the entire performance. (The online footage of the production confirms the accuracy of my memory.) The first to leap to his feet for a standing ovation at the end of the show, Lombardi smiled and clapped as though this were the most marvelous thing he had ever witnessed. He resumed his seat when the applause died down and listened attentively to the more than twenty minutes of discussion that followed. Lombardi was, for that time, just as locked into the room as the rest of us. Though he, of all people, had the ability to insist on his own release at any time, he stayed until the very end of the night—perhaps as a visiting dignitary or a person making sure he was seen, but certainly also as someone who appreciated the performance and did not want to miss a moment of it or the postshow discussion and reception.

A number of us in the audience, including myself, had no idea who Lombardi was at the time and turned our full attention to the conversation with the cast. Still stunned by how funny the production was from start to finish, I asked the first question: "Why did you make *Hamlet* a comedy?" J. Eric Satterfield, who played Claudius, responded that they never made a conscious decision to write a comedy: "I guess that's what the characters told us to write." Michael X. Campbell (Polonius) confirmed this, saying that since the men were doing the writing in small groups, they could not see where the script was going until they got into rehearsals. Wilcox reminded the audience that comedy and tragedy are very close to one another: "Hip hop is a form that celebrates irony. I believe that the humor highlights the tragedy. We laugh because we don't want to cry." Indeed, laughter and joy resurfaced multiple times as themes in the discussion. Mark Sevier (Laertes) smiled broadly when he told the audience, "This is the most fun I've had since I stopped having fun."

As the men described their labors to create the text and performance, it became exceedingly clear that this joy and fun had been hard won. Not only did most of them have to learn two new kinds of language—Shakespearian and hip hop—they had to do the immense work of crafting this production while still living in a prison, with all of the constraints, challenges, and sorrows that entails. As a result, their rewards would prove long-lasting. David Anderson (Narrator/Doorman) declared, "Everybody in the company will tell you, once you go through this and the confidence that you get and the skill set that you get are going to go with you through the rest of your life." Satterfield and David Nonemaker (Rosencrantz) felt so deeply affected by their experiences with PPA that they wrote a play of their own together, and Satterfield says he wants to spend the rest of his life writing for the theatre.

Wilcox wrapped up the conversation by thanking several prison officials in the room, ending with Lombardi, whom she revealed had driven all the way from Jefferson City—about ninety-five miles—to attend the performance. Lombardi, still smiling, addressed the actors, "You guys were absolutely amazing . . . and I really appreciate the way in which everyone explained the metamorphosis of yourself personally as you went through this transformative . . . process of learning about *Hamlet*." He expressed love for Wilcox and assured the assembled crowd that in spite of her impending retirement, PPA's work in the prisons would continue to receive MDOC's full support: "I want you to know that her legacy will live on because we're going to continue to do this forever and ever as far as I'm concerned because it's so obvious the impact it has on you personally and on the culture of our prisons." Much to my astonishment, he then exhorted the audience to donate money to PPA. I have never, before or after, heard a sitting head of a carceral system call for financial contributions to a prison arts program. Lombardi pled for our support earnestly, saying:

> I have never observed a program or an effort that has made such a profound impact on individuals and the group as well. . . . I think that what you also learned is that compassion—compassion for others is a critical, critical quality. It's what makes us human and humane, so keep doing this. We thank you for what you have done.

The audience leaped to their feet for the second standing ovation of the night.[66] The highest-ranking carceral official in the state had just said that theatre makes more of a difference than anything else happening in Missouri prisons.

Furthermore, Lombardi *thanked* the men in the cast. Compliments for incarcerated people and gratitude for their efforts remain in painfully short supply in most prisons. The remarkable nature of a person of such authority—publicly, on camera, and in front of prison staff—thanking the imprisoned cast was not lost on that closing night audience. People rise to be professionals in their fields not just because of their abilities and efforts but because others acknowledge and promote them. Lombardi understood that something significant had grown out of the men's many months of labor and used his leadership position to signal the value of those accomplishments. He saw benefits in this work not just for those in the production but also for the larger prison community and beyond.

What might happen if we all started thinking of experiences like these as preparation for professional life equal in its value and status to that received at elite graduate schools or apprenticeship programs? Having studied and taught at four different elite universities with top theatre programs, I would be hard-pressed to say that many of my peers or students received more thorough professional training than some of the veterans of WHoS and PPA. How might the world at large benefit from the talents, life experiences, and training of incarcerated people who have been meaningfully prepared for stability and advancement? Both WHoS and PPA offer not only models for how prison theatre programming cultivates professional skills but also invitations to the outside world to stop depriving ourselves of the abilities and talents of those who live in prisons.

The structural limitations that many prisons place on the programs they offer can severely diminish the scope of the impact that such work can have. For instance, many facilities refuse to allow family members of incarcerated actors to attend performances. Others allow no one from the outside world other than state-trained volunteers and prison staff to see the productions. Most prisons prevent those on the higher levels of security from viewing plays performed by those with fewer custody restrictions. Those in solitary confinement see nothing. If we treated the performing arts as a humanizing force—something intrinsically good for our well-being and the cultivation of empathy—then we would want even those with the worst behavior and the most profound social problems to have access to it.

If our prisons were designed to make people safer rather than to punish those who have done wrong, then we would want everyone who lives in such a place to grow while they were there—to become someone who has new skills and knows how to apply them in the service of a better society. We would want to be able to trust these people as our peers and colleagues and not have to live in fear of what they might do next out of desperation or a lack of concern for others. Theatre in prisons works in service of all of these goals, and it does so most effectively the more administrators open the gates and let outsiders interact with the incarcerated.

CHAPTER 3
THEATRE AS A STRATEGY
FOR SOCIAL CHANGE

When my collaborator Andy Martínez and I traveled to South Africa for the first time in 2014, the nation was celebrating twenty years since the fall of apartheid in 1994. Tee shirts and banners in the streets of Johannesburg proclaimed "twenty years of democracy." Yet, as we moved from place to place, we saw how legacies of colonialism, segregation, and brutal oppression remain apparent in South Africa today, as they do in my own country. And as in my country—in any country—the divides created by this history are nowhere more apparent than inside prisons. During apartheid and in the present, blacks and mixed-race people were and are incarcerated at disproportionate rates to their white counterparts, as has long been—and remains—the case in nations such as the United States and Brazil. As we learned, however, in South Africa, incarcerated people lived in segregated prisons with no outside programming until the late 1990s. This history, the nation's multicultural and multilingual performance traditions, and the urgency of the country's HIV/AIDS crisis together shape the theatre programming inside South Africa's prisons in unique ways.

Throughout my research in ten countries, I found no national culture of prison theatre more disposed toward direct and active social change than that of South Africa. Most of the kinds of change being sought by prison theatre programs have to do with community building and prosocial behavior among the participants. A far smaller number of prison theatre makers can claim that their theatre formulates a specific call to action for those who live and work inside the prison. This chapter examines how a group of prison theatre makers in South Africa used theatre to inspire action around social justice issues, specifically around HIV and AIDS. Near Durban, theatre professor Miranda Young-Jahangeer and her students from the University of KwaZulu-Natal devise performances with women inside Westville Female Prison, addressing injustices surrounding the treatment of women. They use theatrical performances to promote significant social changes in their own lives and those of other incarcerated women. The longevity and success of this program rely on the facilitators' abilities to listen to incarcerated people and share power and agency with them to as great an extent as the environment of the prison permits.

On the Agency of Imprisoned People and Africans

Unsurprisingly, people in prison have a hard time convincing those of us in the free world that they possess the intellect, ability, awareness, and problem-solving skills to better their own lives. We tend to assume that the sort of people who end up behind bars did not have the common sense or life skills to avoid their own incarceration, or alternately that they are not quite human in the Orwellian sense that "some animals are more equal than others." We assume, as journalist Sarah Koenig describes in her award-winning podcast *Serial*: "That we are not like them—the ones we arrest and punish, the ones with the stink. They're a slightly different species, with senses dulled and toughened. They don't feel pain or sorrow or joy or freedom or the loss of freedom the same way you or I would."[1] This distancing of ourselves from others enables the rampant human rights abuses that characterize most nations' prisons.

Philosopher Achille Mbembe describes a similarly devastating and dismissive attitude toward the people of Africa—one born of the same colonial logics that enable our present global culture of mass incarceration:

> First, the African human experience constantly appears in the discourse of our times as an experience that can only be understood through a *negative interpretation*. Africa is never seen as possessing things and attributes properly part of "human nature." Or when it is, its things and attributes are generally of lesser value, little importance, and poor quality. It is this elementariness and primitiveness that makes Africa the world par excellence of all that is incomplete, mutilated, and unfinished, its history reduced to a series of setbacks of nature in its quest for humankind.[2]

African prisons, then, might be said to hold the most exiled peoples of the world—those written out of the social contract of a continent already inscribed as a place of absence and loss. Mbembe posits as a fundamental tenet of his book *On the Postcolony* that "the African subject is like any other human being; he or she engages in *meaningful acts*" (emphasis in original).[3] The imprisoned women and men described in this chapter—and those held captive all over the world—also have meaningful lives, a certain amount of agency within the confines of the prison, and the ability to make significant contributions to culture, politics, families, communities, and nations. Young-Jahangeer sees theatre as a means to transform the prison into a place where those living inside the walls can "talk back to the institution."[4] The incarcerated theatre makers in this chapter face a particular set of challenges tied to the legacies of apartheid and prison culture in South Africa.

South Africa as a Carceral State

The newly democratic nation of South Africa has not managed to shake off the legacies of colonialism and apartheid that dominated so much of its history. Despite the best efforts of the African National Congress (ANC) and the Truth and Reconciliation Commission, equality remains elusive. Crime, gender-based violence, and poverty ravage the mostly black citizenry, and the country struggles to heal from its past and to articulate its current identity. Neal Lazarus, in an article entitled "The South African Ideology: The Myth of Exceptionalism, the Idea of Renaissance," writes:

> a sort of violence is perpetrated in the dissemination of the idea that we are all South Africans, that we are South Africans together. . . . Phrasing citizenship as a matter of identification, hence of affiliation, the language of the "New" South Africa glosses over the struggle to achieve it—a struggle that cannot be said to have been won, once and for all, merely because apartheid is no more.[5]

Sarah Nuttall similarly describes the "entanglement"—*not* the unification—of cultures of different groups of South Africans as they struggle to "come to terms with a legacy of violence in a society based on inequality."[6] Of the 161,054 men and women in South Africa's prisons in 2017, 80 percent are black, 12 percent are colored, and 1.6 percent are white; they serve as living representations of the ongoing societal divides in the postapartheid era. A study from 2013 found that black men in this nation are six times more likely than white men to be imprisoned.[7]

The divisions among South Africans can be plainly seen outside of prisons as well. During my travels to South Africa in 2014 and 2017, I was struck by the fact that everywhere I went in major cities (Johannesburg, Durban, Pretoria, and Cape Town), homes, shops, businesses, schools, and universities were surrounded by spiked fences, barbed wire, and impenetrable walls. No other country I have visited looked so much like a prison. In 2014, Andy and I stayed in an affluent part of Johannesburg called Rosebank, and despite the apparent wealth of the neighborhood's residents, every home and building looked like a prison. Everything sat behind ostentatious walls—great solid things with metal spikes and rows of concertina wire surrounding them. From a window in our hotel, we could see a well-to-do high school just across the street with a fancy swimming pool and a soccer field made of pristine Astroturf. When we walked up close to the school, all we could see were walls and barbed wire. The day care center across the street was similarly barricaded, as were all of the impressively large homes on the surrounding streets. In other wealthy neighborhoods where I have, by accident or design, found myself such as Beverly Hills, USA, or a ritzy residential section of Cairo, Egypt, I had seen high walls and ornate gates, but never this. In Johannesburg, it seems that the more successfully imprisoned you are in your home, school, or place of business, the better off you are. Where other rich places strove to confine discreetly, here the closed-in look, that elsewhere signified poverty, signified wealth. Wherever I went, South Africans constantly spoke about crime and warned me not to be out in the city at night, even when I was not alone and had Andy to brave the streets with me.[8] We took their advice seriously.

On two separate occasions in Johannesburg and Pretoria, we went to the theatre at night to see performances, and both times staff members at the theatre—kind strangers we met that night—insisted on driving us back to our hotel because they believed it was too dangerous for us to hail taxis on our own. These interactions exemplified the contradictions in how we encountered South African culture. We were constantly warned about crime, which was undoubtedly a pressing and dangerous reality, yet people also went well out of their way to make sure we were safe. I cannot imagine strangers in any major city in the United States offering to drive me home from a play because the streets were not safe. South Africans in these cities had spent decades, perhaps hundreds of years, walling themselves off from one another, yet they repeatedly opened their homes and vehicles to us in startlingly generous ways to make sure we were protected.

One of apartheid's cultural legacies may be the fact that a great many South Africans, of all racial and ethnic backgrounds, implicitly understand that prisons in their country were purposefully designed as mechanisms of segregation and racial oppression. Because it is the subject of our research, Andy and I spoke about prisons with most everyone we met in South Africa. Such conversations with casual acquaintances—people working in hotels, taxi drivers, or staff at theatres—did not react to mentions of prisons with the surprise, discomfort, or alarm that we often found in other countries. The South Africans I met seemed to harbor fewer negative assumptions about currently and formerly incarcerated people than citizens of other countries do. South Africans appeared to me to be reluctant to condemn their imprisoned compatriots as inherently and irrevocably criminal. After all, former president Nelson Mandela and other leaders of the ANC in the mid-1990s had served decades in prison before they ushered in a new era of democracy in South Africa. Despite this, rampant fear of what the *New York Times* has called "widespread violent crime" in the nation persists.[9] As Alexandra Sutherland notes, "Crime is South Africa's national obsession. Everyone is affected by it, and we live with one of the highest murder and sexual violence rates in the world."[10] The walls and prisons persist and are presumed by many to be urgently needed, despite their well-known legacies as structures of state terror and oppression.

Prison History in South Africa

In many parts of the world, including South Africa, prisons and the culture of mass incarceration have become so ubiquitous that we have trouble imagining a world without them.[11] However, prisons as we know them today were extremely rare on the African continent in precolonial times.[12] Detention or imprisonment was generally seen as an inappropriate consequence to crime because greater emphasis was placed on compensating the victim than on punishing the offender. British colonization and the slave trade laid the groundwork (and often the buildings, as forts and slave castles were converted into prisons) for the carceral systems that now dominate the landscape of criminal justice in many African countries.[13] (The same phenomenon can be observed in the United States in the conversion of slave plantations, like Parchman in Mississippi and Angola in Louisiana, into some of the largest, most notorious and enduring prisons in the South.) The logic of incarceration as many parts of the world know it today is not an irreversible product of human nature but a deeply ingrained and widely transmitted system of social oppression and stratification.

Prisons as permanent institutions took hold in southern Africa earlier than in the rest of the continent, and they formed "an integral part of a system of racial oppression, which toward the middle of the twentieth century, developed into the notorious political system known as 'apartheid.'"[14] Andy and I visited a former apartheid-era prison, now converted into a museum, in the Johannesburg neighborhood of Braamfontein. Built in 1892, Constitution Hill served as a prison for most of its history, with a brief interlude as a military outpost during the South African War (1899–1902). The prison endured for more than 100 years, housing both men and women—many of them guilty only of the crime of being black during apartheid. A great many political prisoners served time there, including Mahatma Gandhi, Nelson Mandela, Winnie Madikizela-Mandela, and Albertina Sisulu. In the mid-1990s after the fall of apartheid and Nelson Mandela's release from prison, the prison at Constitution Hill shut down.[15]

We saw the black men's section of the prison first. In the buildings that still stand, we saw room after cement room where men slept like sardines in a can. They had only blankets or thin pallets on which to sleep, and they were forced to sleep so close together that each man's head was wedged between two sets of other people's feet. An open toilet stood in the corner of each of these rooms, and the poorest and weakest men had to sleep nearest to the stench of the sewer. The museum has allowed the peeling paint, cold walls and floor to speak for themselves, adding little more than a few tasteful signs to help explain how the rooms were inhabited. Rough gray prison blankets with a few white stripes at each end have been made into skillfully constructed "blanket sculptures" to show where the bodies of the men would have lain at night. These stand-ins for actual people prove not only more artistic but also more moving than the mannequins that dwell in so many museum tableaus. The inhabitants of Constitution Hill actually made these sorts of blanket sculptures during their incarceration. They also engaged in papier-mâché and other forms of art making. The blanket sculptures on display at Constitution Hill's museum today were made by two formerly incarcerated men who returned to contribute to the museum.

Such evidence of participation by formerly incarcerated people in the curation of the museum appears throughout the many exhibits on Constitution Hill, as do opportunities for visitors to respond to what they are seeing. Message boards appear throughout the exhibits, posing specific questions to visitors and encouraging them to share their thoughts about things such as whether the people described in the exhibit were unjustly imprisoned or what Gandhi's most significant legacy to South Africa might be. The notion that visitors' active participation in the museum, indeed in South Africa's ongoing history, falls in line with the objectives of the Truth and Reconciliation Commission's efforts to capture the experiences of everyday people alongside the largest events in South African civil unrest. This impetus to include average citizens in the reformation of South Africa's national narratives about justice resurfaces in the theatre that I saw in its prisons.

Apartheid worked to maintain oppression and prevent the common people from organizing by segregating groups and individuals from one another. Constitution Hill had quite a few solitary confinement cells throughout its many buildings. In the white male section of the prison, the isolation cells had a small desk bolted to the wall and wooden floors. Nowhere in the prison did we see a bed. It seems that everyone slept on pallets or the gray wool blankets on the floor. The white men's isolation cells were stark and intimidating, even though they were about twice as large as those for black men and women. I could not help wondering what those slight differences would mean to a captive. How much comfort and human dignity does a wooden floor lend as opposed to a cold concrete one? What fragment of one's sanity and emotional stability might be better held in place by a few more feet of space in which to move?

I held myself together until we saw the black men's isolation cells. As I have felt in most of the prisons I have visited around the world, in some places pain seems to radiate out of the walls and floor with a cold intensity. The walls have seen so much suffering that they appear to have absorbed it. We walked inside the cells and closed the doors behind us to have a clear sense of what the people in this place endured. The back of each metal door was covered in writing etched in the paint. The small courtyard outside these cells is covered by a network of barbed wire laid out in a grid so that even when you step out into the sun, a cruel barrier looms between you and the sky.

In a separate area of the prison, women served their time away from men. The isolation cells for black women now contain museum exhibits. In front of each of the doorways to the cells, a large placard bears the photograph and a biographical sketch of one of the women who served time on this wing. Inside each cell a video monitor displays pieces of interviews done with the women featured on the placards, and beneath the video screens, artifacts of the women's lives are on display. One woman says in her video that she had the most beautiful wedding dress imaginable, purchased on the day of her arrest. She wore a prison uniform for a very long time, waiting for her incarceration to end so that she could show the wedding dress to her family. The bright yellow gown hangs in the cell beneath the video screen that plays her story. These contrasts between the vibrancy and tenacity of the people who endured incarceration under apartheid and the bleak reality of the prisons themselves manifested in the political and cultural upheaval that so radically changed South Africa.

The end of apartheid in the early 1990s brought with it significant reforms in the South African penal code, including a mandate for the desegregation of prisons.[16] However, the practical implementation of desegregation was left in the hands of high-ranking staff at each prison, who chose to separate incarcerate people based on race or ethnicity if the officials justified the practice as necessary to prevent conflict.[17] The use of incarceration as a means of state control actually increased, even as Nelson Mandela and others who had spent decades in prison held the highest offices in South African government. In the ten years immediately following the nation's first democratic elections in 1994, South Africa's prison population increased 60 percent.[18] In a parallel crisis in roughly the same time period, HIV/AIDS inside South African prisons spread dramatically, as "the number of deaths due to 'natural causes' rose abruptly from 186 in 1995 to 1,087 in 2000 with as many as 90 percent of those deaths believed to have been AIDS-related."[19] The prison reforms that accompanied the advent of democracy enabled volunteers to provide theatre programming in South African prisons for the first time,[20] and the theatre makers who began offering such programs in prisons partnered with incarcerated people in responding to the urgent and widespread nature of the HIV/AIDS epidemic.

South African Prison Theatre and HIV/AIDS

Well before it allowed prison programming, South Africa had a long and rich tradition of social protest theatre. Gibson Kente, known as the "father of township theatre," promoted a vibrant culture of performance among poor and black South Africans from the 1960s until his death of AIDS-related illness in 2004.[21] Athol Fugard—perhaps South Africa's most famous playwright—began working to desegregate the professional theatre in the late 1950s and has continued to use his plays to advocate for social justice ever since. Gcina Mhlophe turned her anti-apartheid activism into a series of one-woman plays in the 1980s and 1990s and gained international acclaim in doing so.[22] Though a great many memoirs of incarceration were penned during apartheid, no one could produce theatre in South African prisons until after the 1996 legislative reforms enabled programming to enter those spaces for the first time. As soon as theatre could be made inside the walls, incarcerated people urgently and consistently wished to dramatize the effects of the HIV/AIDS crisis on their lives.

Of all the prison theatres I have researched around the world, South Africa's stands out in consistently addressing the public health crisis of HIV/AIDS by seeking to cause cultural shifts inside prisons. In no other nation do prison theatre makers seem to address a particular theme in this way, except that of prison itself. Johannes Visser describes the work done in this vein by theatre practitioners from the University of Pretoria, who between 2006 and 2009 created approximately eight plays about HIV/AIDS that were performed for juveniles in detention.[23] Professor Alexandra Sutherland has run a drama program in a men's prison in South Africa since 2010 and describes this work as being driven by the group's interests, "primarily . . . based on issues—often dealing with life in prison, the stigma around HIV/AIDS, or the challenges of release back to family and community."[24] Christopher John, also known as Chris Hurst, who was at the time a colleague of Young-Jahangeer's at the University of KwaZulu-Natal, worked with men in the Medium B Correction Centre in 2003 to create a play entitled *Lisekhon' Ithemba* (*There is Still Hope*), "that addressed living with HIV/Aids [*sic*]" in prison.[25] Themba Interactive, a social service organization that provides information about HIV/AIDS by using theatre, worked in prisons from 2009 to 2014; their theatre company performed skits that provided public health information about the HIV/AIDS crisis and encouraged audience members to take their medications. Themba's program also used theatre to train incarcerated men and women to become peer facilitators who then held informational groups to shift the culture around how people in prison talk about and respond to HIV and AIDS.[26] This list of theatrical activist projects surrounding HIV/AIDS comes from a survey of the published literature on theatre in South African prisons, but I suspect many more such performances have taken place and not been recounted in print. The preponderance of theatre work on the topic of HIV/AIDS in South African prisons points not only to the magnitude of the epidemic but also to the urgent need for cultural as well as practical responses to it.

This makes sense given the fact that South Africa has the highest rates of HIV infection in the world, with an estimated 7.2 million people living with the disease in the nation. The nation suffered 110,000 deaths from AIDS-related illness in the year 2017 alone.[27] The approximately 10 million incarcerated people worldwide have higher rates of HIV infection and other communicable diseases than those of us who are not in prison.[28] Given the swift and widespread transmission of such diseases in prisons in countries with large and often overcrowded prison populations, such as the United States and Brazil, the most successful strategies of South African prison programs need to be replicated in other parts of the world.[29] The immediacy and persistence of the HIV/AIDS crisis in South African prisons also illuminate the ways in which struggles for public health and public safety are deeply and intimately intertwined.

The Prison Theatre Project at Westville Female Prison

The theatre work done by the faculty and students from the University of KwaZulu-Natal in the Westville Correctional Centre near Durban, South Africa, has been focused on using performance to address the needs and interests identified by the incarcerated populations there. In fact, the initial impetus to begin a theatre program at Westville came from an incarcerated man. Clement Ntuli, a former university student who was serving time at Westville, asked professors Chris Hurst and Beki Nkala from the University of Natal (which later in a process of desegregation merged in with the University of Durban Westville to create the University of KwaZulu-Natal) to help the men in the Medium B maximum-security section of the prison stage a play in 1999.[30] This collaboration led to the development of not just a successful production that toured outside the prison but also a series of theatre programs in different sections of the prison and several university courses in the university's Drama and Performance Studies curriculum for undergraduates and graduate students (or postgraduates, as the South Africans say).[31]

Westville Correctional Centre houses multiple separate prisons and includes housing for prison staff inside the gates of the large complex. Faculty and students at the University of KwaZulu-Natal have offered programming through their prison theatre projects in three of Westville's prisons: Medium B for men, Youth Centre for boys, and Female Prison. The programs in each of the Westville prisons have had different trajectories, and the work at Female Prison has endured the longest.

The founding facilitator of the program at Female Prison, Miranda Young-Jahangeer, first learned about the idea of doing theatre in prisons in 1999 when she read an article about Geese Theatre Company in England. In less than six months, "after a series of uncannily synchronicitous experiences," she had both joined the faculty at the University of KwaZulu-Natal and begun working with the women at Westville.[32] Throughout the twenty years that have followed, Young-Jahangeer and her students have maintained a steady presence in the prison and helped the women to create performances on a broad variety of topics, driven by their interests and desires. Their original plays have addressed many sensitive areas of concern for the women, including gender-based violence, lesbianism, South African and Zulu cultures, addiction, racism, classism, motherhood, power dynamics in prison, and, of course, HIV/AIDS.[33] The group has had enough stability, longevity, and sensitivity to one another's feelings and beliefs to be able to engage in meaningful debate and performance work around this wide range of difficult issues. The scope and depth of their theatre provide evidence of a profound level of trust and thoughtfulness—things that are often difficult to cultivate in the harsh and often adversarial environment of the prison.

Young-Jahangeer, in her six articles about the theatre at Westville, always attributes the success of the program to the women themselves and is careful to acknowledge her own privilege, whiteness, outsider status, and lack of fluency in the isiZulu language. She writes about the "four powerful women inside [who] had become my 'co-investigators' functioning as co-facilitators and partners in all aspects of the programmes."[34] This occurred in the very first year of the program, which means that Young-Jahangeer has seen certain women in the prison as being equals in this process from the beginning. In doing this, Young-Jahangeer is not putting herself down or sidelining her own contributions, but she gives credit where credit is due to the incarcerated women and university students who have worked as an ensemble to create the kind of theatre that they most want to share with each other and their audiences. Young-Jahangeer takes particular care in her article "LIVING with the Virus Inside: Women and HIV/AIDS in Prison" to foreground the experiences of a woman named Lilly, who was a member of the theatre troupe and who endured the myriad difficulties of being HIV positive while living in a prison.[35]

Young-Jahangeer has formed meaningful relationships not just with the incarcerated women but also with the staff at the prison. When Andy and I visited Durban in 2014, Young-Jahangeer took us to Westville and introduced us to Veli Khumalo, a staff person at the prison who at that point had been working with the theatre group for years. Khumalo's brother had held the same position at this prison, and when he passed away, she took his place. When I asked Khumalo if it had taken time to build a solid working relationship with Young-Jahangeer, she said that she took up right where her brother left off. He had gotten along with Young-Jahangeer and liked her work in the prison, and Khumalo saw no reason to feel differently.

The people who work in prisons every day have much power to enable or prevent programming for the incarcerated. Those of us who volunteer in prisons often find ourselves needing the help and good faith of staff members in order to accomplish even the simplest of tasks, such as getting through the front gate of the prison and making sure that the incarcerated participants are allowed to attend the programs. From what we saw of Young-Jahangeer and Khumalo's relationship, it was clear that they both had the same purposes—to provide quality programming and to give incarcerated women the agency and safety to use theatre to form a community and speak to their own situations. In spite of the many institutional forces that often pit volunteers and incarcerated people against prison staff and one another, the Prison Theatre Project at Westville Female Prison established a level of trust and commitment that has lasted two decades.

How the Prison Theatre Project at Westville Female Prison Addressed HIV/AIDS

The Prison Theatre Project at Westville Female Prison has focused on HIV/AIDS as a significant issue at the heart of many of their plays. Young-Jahangeer cites HIV/AIDS and violence against women as the two issues with which the women were most concerned in the early years of the group's existence.[36] Between 2000 and 2010, their plays addressed many aspects of the impact of the disease on their lives and communities, including

> issues around stigma; the need for women and communities to support each other around the disease; cultural interpretations of the disease (such as being bewitched by an enemy) as misinformation and the need for parents to speak openly with children about sex and HIV/AIDS. The issue of insensitive health care workers was raised twice (2000 and 2004).[37]

HIV and AIDS have had such a profound impact on these women that they have been able to generate a remarkable amount of theatrical material on the topic.

In one notable production from 2002, the women in the prison were responding to the terrible conditions at the prison clinic.[38] The AIDS epidemic was claiming many lives, and often the bodies of the deceased remained in beds at the clinic for days before being removed for burial. This meant that other women confined to the clinic would have to lie for days on end next to the dead bodies of their friends. The play that the women devised about this situation included a character of a particularly unkind nurse in the clinic. Young-Jahangeer did not realize until the performance of the play that the nurse in question not only was a real person but was being represented in such a way that she was recognizable to the entire prison audience. The nurse was in the audience of the performance along with 250 incarcerated women, and at some moment during the play, the nurse got up and fled the courtyard where the play was taking place. As the nurse ran, the women in the audience all raised their arms above their heads and shouted, "La la la la la!" mocking her in unison. (In a bizarre twist of fate, that same nurse ended up becoming incarcerated at Westville sometime later, and she joined the theatre program and became a much-beloved member of the troupe.)[39] This performance nearly caused a riot, but a humorous play put on by the boys from Westville Youth Centre immediately followed this one and dissipated the tension in the audience.

Soon after, the prison discontinued the practice of leaving the dead in the infirmary overnight, and Young-Jahangeer was reprimanded by the prison authorities.[40] The theatre program no longer has performances for such large audiences inside the prison, but the group endures and keeps devising new work. In many other places, such an incident would cause the discontinuation of the theatre program, but Young-Jahangeer believes that the political moment of postapartheid prison reforms saved their group. It would not have looked good for the prison administration to cancel the theatre troupe at a time when the recently elected ANC government was calling for programming for the incarcerated. Young-Jahangeer also feels that the serious relationship building that she and the women in the company had done with prison staff contributed to the administration's willingness to continue the program: "It was new to all of us–we were all inexperienced in how to handle both the situation and the consequences!"[41]

Young-Jahangeer and the women in the theatre group believe that the theatre "interventions at the prison were one of the primary ways in which consciousness around the disease was raised in the Centre."[42] Young-Jahangeer and her incarcerated coinvestigator Lilly list many cultural and practical changes related to HIV/AIDS inside the prison since the theatre group started in 2000. Lilly refers to a more open environment for dialogue about the disease and a much higher percentage of women willing to disclose their positive HIV status: "The drama did really emphasize a lot [around HIV]. We actually dramatized the things that were in us. We actually showed the people that what they were doing to each other was wrong. We were saying, 'Come on, guys! Wake up!' It was a wake-up call to them."[43] The prison authorities began hosting talks by experts on health and offering better nutrition and counseling to infected women.[44] Lilly was released from prison in 2018 and lost touch with the theatre program and Young-Jahangeer. Of the four original incarcerated core members of the theatre group, two have died from AIDS-related illness—possibly three if Lilly has passed without Young-Jahangeer's knowledge. The prison environment has seen lasting cultural shifts. Young-Jahangeer reports that overall women with HIV/AIDS at Westville are "living positively," taking their medications without fear of stigma. She says that deaths of AIDS-related illness nowadays are rare.[45] The theatre program did not cause all of these changes on its own, but its ongoing efforts have been part of a significant shift in how the full community of people inside the prison—staff and incarcerated women—are responding to HIV/AIDS.

A Plan of Action and Hope

The story of the Prison Theatre Project at Westville Female Prison outlines a successful partnership in creating theatre for social change. The women at Westville and Young-Jahangeer serve as models for how to use theatre as an intervention to change life inside the prison. We should not underestimate the ability of such partnerships between incarcerated people and outside volunteers to create real and lasting social change, even in the face of devastation. Nesha Haniff at the University of Michigan argues, "The act of teaching HIV prevention is inextricably linked to empowerment of the community and their ownership of the information."[46] Communities that have been historically silenced also need the collaborative and communication skills that theatre offers them, as they labor to change the dire circumstances of their lives. Like the theatre itself, this kind of grassroots work for social change is all about the embodied moment, and the experience of it can be fleeting and ephemeral. If people stop speaking publicly about the facts about HIV/AIDS, they may retreat into the myths and stigmas that have contributed to the epidemic. Then the disease will continue to spread, particularly inside prisons where infection rates are high and unsafe sex a common practice.

Empowering the incarcerated to become well-informed leaders in their own communities provides a lasting and potent strategy for fighting the war on this epidemic. Lilly frames her experiences in battling her disease at Westville as a kind of community action: "I spent eight months in bed not eating, vomiting. But here I am, and I am not going to take the credit for it all for myself. There is [*sic*] people around me. They came to see me, prayed with me, cried with me. Officials and inmates were there for me . . . and when I gave up, they said, 'No!'"[47] This collective will to not lose hope, even in the face of utter devastation, drives meaningful social change. Young-Jahangeer says that the "theatre builds social cohesion by telling not *my* story but *our* story."[48] South Africa's greatest human rights victories were won because of the extraordinary work of formerly incarcerated people like Nelson Mandela, and undoubtedly the Prison Theatre Project at Westville Female Prison paved the way for critically important interventions—what Jorge Huerta calls "necessary theatre"[49]—in this fight for the very lives of hundreds of thousands of South Africans.

CHAPTER 4
THEATRE AS A STRATEGY FOR HOPE

Most of the incarcerated people in this book began doing theatre *after* they became incarcerated, but Ngũgĩ wa Thiong'o went to prison *because* he wrote a play. Starting in the 1950s, British authorities used theatre as a means to acculturate the people of Kenya to colonial rule. This came about in reaction to the widespread popularity of "anti-imperialist" Kenyan theatre and dance.[1] The colonial government invested so heavily in the acculturating force of theatre that it even coerced those incarcerated solely for their political beliefs into writing plays about the virtues of confessing one's sins (and presumably one's misguided opposition to the current government).[2] The theatre of resistance survived this onslaught and continued to encourage Kenyans to preserve their own cultural traditions. In 1977, Ngũgĩ's play *Ngaahika Ndeenda* (translated as *I Will Marry When I Want*) sought to radically transform Kenyans' understandings of theatre. The play, written and produced in the Gikuyu language, starred workers and peasants from the village of Limuru and encouraged the audience of common people to see the performance and the culture it represented as belonging to them.[3] The authoritarian government of Kenya found *Ngaahika Ndeenda* so threatening that it closed the very popular production after six weeks and imprisoned Ngũgĩ without formal charges for more than a year.[4]

In his memoir about this year of incarceration, called *Wrestling with the Devil*, Ngũgĩ considers the idea of hope for those who have little reason to believe things will turn out well. His struggle for justice and freedom for all Kenyans resembles the way in which the prison theatre makers described later in this chapter have created and maintained hope by staging plays. Because Ngũgĩ had never been tried or sentenced, he did not know how long he might live in confinement or when, if ever, he might be released. A man serving time with Ngũgĩ gave him advice about how to think about his future:

Wasonga Sijeyo once called me aside and told me never to build any certainty of release on false hopes: "It is good to have faith, to keep on hoping. For what is life, but hope? Never prevent a man from hoping, for if you do, you are denying him reasons for living. To hope for a better tomorrow, to dream of a new world, that is what is human. But don't be so certain of the hour and the day as to let it break you if the hoped-for freedom does not come at the expected hour and day."[5]

When he had set his sights on a particular opportunity or time for his release, Wasonga felt himself pierced by the "tenterhooks of hope," only to be devastated on three successive occasions when he did not attain his freedom as expected. Over time he grew "reserved and cautious" about the way in which he looked toward his own future.[6] This wisdom about the amorphous and unspecific nature of hope, gained through experience, helped to guide Wasonga throughout the remainder of his incarceration.

Ngũgĩ himself stayed focused on hope for the collective—for the people of Kenya in a broader sense. He sought not only to give himself "reasons for living," as Wasonga described but also to help his people to share hope's "dream of a new world." The play that landed Ngũgĩ in prison advocated for the liberation of the oppressed, and his focus while inside the walls took the form of another revolutionary cultural act; he wrote the first novel ever penned in the Gikuyu language—*Caitaani Mutharabaini* (*Devil on the Cross*)—and did so by writing in secret on toilet paper.[7] Upon his release, he brought this novel, a manifestation of his struggle and his hope, out of the prison and into the hands of a publisher so that it could be shared and disseminated to others. His imprisonment came about because his work in the theatre had profoundly motivated so many people toward hope and resistance, and his time inside the walls, with which the Kenyan colonial government meant to silence him, moved Ngũgĩ to call out to his people in a different literary mode.

Martin Luther King, Jr., who also did some extraordinary writing while incarcerated, argued that we should understand hope as a force shared by a community, rather than as a kind of optimism about one person's desires. As such, hope cannot be an easy or passive state of being. It necessitates much collective labor and strife in service of large-scale concepts such as justice, freedom, and peace. Religious studies scholar Vincent Lloyd writes, "King's goal is to show that when hope does not result in struggle, it is misunderstood."[8]

Prison theatre can serve an activating force for such a struggle, giving richness and meaning to the difficult work of finding and maintaining hope inside the walls. Feminist theatre scholar Jill Dolan explains, "For me, performance and politics have always been intertwined. At the theater, I first learned to articulate and sometimes to see realized my own hopes for an otherwise unimaginable future."[9] This sense that the theatre helps us to conjure up collectively what we could not imagine on our own holds particular meaning for folks in prison, who must work hard to envision a future beyond the grim and monotonous reality of life in confinement. To paraphrase both Mahatma Gandhi and Augusto Boal, we must rehearse the kind of revolution we would like to see in the world.

For those in prison, particularly those with long sentences, living again in freedom would be a revolutionary act. In her book *Women Doing Life*, Lora Lempert describes the necessity for lifers to stay focused on a better future:

> Hope is central for women who are sentenced to life without parole. It enables them to envision better, different futures than their present circumstances allow and so is central in the struggle against the erosion of generalized despair.[10]

To that end, when incarcerated people come together in the creative enterprise of theatre making, they can help one another to envision a hopeful future that could benefit them and those they love.

Somebody's Daughter: The Hope to be a Part of Something

On July 16, 2015, I visited the Dame Phyllis Frost Centre, the only maximum-security women's prison in the state of Victoria, Australia. Maud Clark and Kharen Harper—the Artistic Directors of Somebody's Daughter Theatre Company—had invited me there to spend the day in rehearsal for the original musical called *I'll Be on My Way* that they were creating with the women. Of all the theatre companies I have ever known, Somebody's Daughter has the best name, reminding everyone who encounters them that every woman in prison is someone's child—a person connected to the outside world who has loved and has been loved, or who should have been.

The company hires professional artists and theatre makers—many of them in full-time positions—to work with adult women in prison and after their release and also with boys and girls in youth facilities and in rural communities. The day of my visit, Harper and I spent the day in rehearsal from 10 a.m. to 4 p.m., along with actor Amy Jones, visual artist Kate

Osborne, musical director Justin Holland, and about a dozen women. This level of professionalism enables prison theatre troupes with paid artists to produce higher quality, better rehearsed and produced work than other programs whose process is conscribed by volunteer labor, limited time inside the prison, and lack of access to musical instruments, sets, lighting, props, costumes, and other materials. Somebody's Daughter is largely funded by grants from the Australia Council, which provides support for arts programming, but Harper and Clark have been deeply concerned about the fiscal sustainability of their work as Australia's government has become more conservative and less supportive of public arts funding. So far, that has not stopped the Daughters from devising plays.

On the day that I spent with them, the Daughters were working on *I'll Be on My Way*—a musical about homelessness. Though the overall feel of the play was quite joyous, the script dealt with a host of difficult issues that read like a list of the nightmares that women in prison have endured: domestic violence, addiction, failed foster care placements, juvenile detention, and incarceration. As the characters experienced each of these things, their story arcs tended to resolve with the cast banding together to support one another. The crises they faced abated but did not disappear. Katie Langford, one of the actors who was incarcerated at the time of the production, asserts that "the play is about hope, dreams and how to overcome adversity. It was also a wish list to policy makers of what we needed individually to move out of homelessness, incarceration and addiction."[11] In this sense, the prison could not contain these women. They wrote for an audience larger than themselves and asked others with more power to take notice and make changes. The women learned to cope and continue, but no deus ex machina came to rescue them. The characters found strength in one another as a band of drifters and misfits who often got lost but found their way again with the help of other women.

The women in the troupe came from many different cultures, and musical director Justin Holland collaborated with them to compose songs that would highlight as many of their life experiences as possible. Katie Langford trained at the Guildford School of Acting, worked as a professional actor and radio presenter, and ran her own theatre company in England prior to her incarceration in Australia. When I met her, she was one month shy of her release and deportation to her homeland. She had just enough time to perform in *I'll Be on My Way*. Her character Agatha frames the show, chatting to the audience and the other characters as the play began, introducing the world of the play and the characters. Agatha sells things from her little cart as she tries to earn enough money to fly home to England. In the meantime, she, like most of the other characters, is homeless but not despairing. She lives a hard life but hopes for a better future. Her song, "When I Get Home," sounded like something from a Broadway musical and described her longing to get back to the East End. Katie says it "was written thinking about all the things I love and couldn't access whilst in prison: tea, marmite, being naked when I wished! [sic], Michael Caine my cat, the places and streets of home." She calls it both "a love song to home" and a "gift to the girls serving with me—I wanted to write something that would take them somewhere else—a magical, bonkers place that was far away from the beige and barren prison."[12] Knowing that she would soon leave her friends behind in prison, Katie left the other Daughters with a new kind of dream—a clear picture of what her life would be like in freedom.

At the end of the play when Agatha finally has earned enough money to get herself home, she leaves with both joy and sorrow. She has attained her dearest hope but must say goodbye to the friends who helped her to survive for years: "Dear Friends . . . the time has come to move on. . . . I will take you all in my heart. My sisters, you have given me soo much [sic] . . . moments that will I always cherish. Be kind to yourselves and remember—no matter what people think or say—<u>You matter</u>."[13] The character Agatha's journey mirrored the actor Katie's life as she prepared for her release from prison, which came shortly after the play closed. Katie left many good friends behind her in a place where she never wanted to be, and now she lives in London in freedom, carrying the other Daughters in her heart.

Another woman who had recently been released had written a rap song before her departure; one of her friends still in the theatre company performed it in the play. (When I said I lived in Michigan, the woman singing this song had a hard time believing that I had never met the rapper Eminem.) The character Ajax who performs this rap has recently been released from prison and is visiting her parole officer. She had gotten high before going to the parole office and spent the entire play trying to figure out how to pass a drug test so that she would not be sent back to prison. Her song comes near the end of the play, when she makes the hard choice to try to get clean. She and another character ask the parole officer to send them to a rehab program. The song's chorus hammered out the tedium of being counted over and over again each day by prison officials, the beat lending a rhythm to the repetitive ritual. Even though she has not escaped her addiction, the song emphasizes that Ajax has made progress and wants to fight for a better life:

What a journey to recovery
These walls heartbeat on my way to discovery
I've been beat up I've been pushed down
Too many times I've been stripped of my identity
But I'm still alive I've learnt from my enemies
So thank you guys you helped me find my sanity
Thank you thank you thank you!
I landed on my own two feet
Found a better heartbeat
In the end I know I'll defeat
Cause I'm sick of pressing rewind and putting it on repeat[14]

We see Ajax and her friend ask to be sent to treatment, but then they exit the stage. The audience never knows how the parole officer responds to their request and the fact that they must surely have failed their drug tests that day. We live in hope with them but do not know what the world actually has in store for these women.

Another woman led the cast in an Albanian folk song in her native language, accompanied by a belly dance, which required much rehearsal on the day I visited. Though she was imprisoned in a country on the other side of the world from her homeland, this woman recreated a piece of her family and culture as she trained her castmates to sing and dance. She brought immense joy to the task and instructed all of us with both care and precision. It mattered to her that we translated this piece of her heritage as best we could.

In the staging of the play, the circle of women uses this song and dance to rescue a woman from an abusive relationship and spirit her away to safety. First, the women chase off a threatening lover and then encircle the battered woman with their love. Aisha, the character played by the Albanian woman, tells a folk tale about a little girl who lived with a sly fox who was mean to her. As the girl grows up and gets stronger, her fairy godmother helps her magically escape through the woods. The girl at last arrives at her grandmother's house where she recovers in safety. Aisha explains that the fox in her own life had been her mother—"a very cruel woman." In the end, the fox no longer has power over the girl, but Aisha explains that "it took until she was twenty-one years old."[15] The kind of hope these characters describe does not come easy. Every victory is hard won and usually the result of years of struggle, but each of them walks away with her head held high, looking toward a future where she might finally have a bit of peace.

One song seemed deeply personal to all of the women. At the time of my visit, officials had recently banned smoking inside all prisons in the state of Victoria. Many carceral systems throughout the world have adopted this policy, citing smoking as a public health threat. A prison employee in the United States told me that such bans also reduce the illicit drug trade inside facilities. Once cigarettes are no longer sold in the prison, those who trade in illicit substances behind the walls can make just as much money selling black market tobacco as they could peddling harder drugs and do so without incurring the risk of time added to their sentences. When I related this to someone I know who lives in a US prison, he called this assertion "very dubious" and said that in Michigan a person caught with tobacco would be taken to court and charged with smuggling—the same consequence for trading in heroin. Whether or not it actually reduces illicit drug use in prisons, smoking bans have appeared in prisons in many of the nations I visited, including England, Scotland, Canada, New Zealand, Australia, and many parts of the United States.

Many of the Daughters I met were avid smokers and felt the loss of their cigarettes keenly. At the news of the tobacco ban, incarcerated men in Deer Park (at the facility nearest to where the Daughters were) had rioted, knocking down doors and walls, causing much structural damage to the prison. The women made no formal protest of their own but had what they described to me as "a rough week" on preemptive lockdown while the men rioted—the smells of things burning in the men's facility drifting into the women's facility, replacing the familiar scent of cigarette smoke. After their week in their cells, the Daughters reunited and wrote a comedic song about "chop chop"—the prison slang for cigarettes—to express their displeasure and longing to smoke once more. It began with one of the women leading a protest, shouting, "What do we want?" The chorus answered, "Chop chop!" "When do we want it?" "Now!" They then sang a litany of things they would rather endure if only they could have their cigarettes back:

You can lock us up
Throw away the key
Take away our dignity
Dress us in a blue track suit
Deny any access to forbidden fruit
. . .
You can put us on regimes
Throw us in the hole

Trump up new charges
Even cancel parole

. . .

We can't cope anymore
And we need you to hurry
A rolly a gasper
Even menthol will do
Just a little hit of nicotine
To help us get through . . .[16]

The song ends with the women begging, "please please please please with a cherry on top!" and an interruption by a voice-over instructing all of the women to return to their units for count. Just as in real life, their pleas remain unrecognized by the authorities. Neither the men's uprising nor the women's performance caused any change in prison policy, though both the actions of both groups expressed voluble resistance to this new restriction on their freedom. However, the Daughters also found a way to comfort one another and their incarcerated audiences through humor and perhaps a bit of catharsis. They could not alter their reality, but they could collectively remember, complain, laugh, and hope for a future when they might have more choice about the texture of their everyday lives.

I spent the better part of the afternoon that day with a woman named Jemma whose scene partner could not come to the rehearsal for some reason. Kharen Harper asked me to help Jemma with her lines, so we took a copy of the script they had been developing and sat in a corner to work on it. The dialogue was fairly simple, but Jemma struggled to remember the smallest phrases. The facilitators later explained to me that the facility had put Jemma on medications that were affecting her memory at the time and that in other productions Jemma had played the lead and remembered many lines. That day Jemma could not have been more delighted to have my full attention for a little while. We made no progress with getting her lines memorized, though we spent the better part of an hour in focused study of the script. Jemma labored intently and wanted badly to contribute something to the play. Holland called us over to the piano to work on Jemma's song. I approached with much trepidation because I so wanted Jemma to succeed and feared she would not do any better with the music than she had with the dialogue.

Much to my relief, the Daughters had found an ideal way to let Jemma's talents shine. She had been cast as one of the two clowns in the show, and the song she and her partner would perform had only two words in it: *stop* and *go*. A vocational training program at the Dame Phyllis Frost Centre sends some women to construction sites where a lane of traffic has been blocked off. Two women wearing orange vests stand at each end of the obstructed road with signs saying *Stop* and *Go* to direct passing cars. Holland had written a song for the clowns to sing with their traffic signs. He played a cheery tune on the piano, and Jemma would chirp, "Go!" I sang, "Stop!" These were our only lines throughout the song. That much we could remember. As Holland changed the music, our voices and bodies would follow. He slowed down, and we acted bored and sleepy as we sang our lines. The piano would shift suddenly and snap us back to attention. The tune picked up an angry minor chord, and Jemma poked me with her stop sign. In synch with the music, she and I teased, flirted, played, danced, and eventually used our traffic signs as light sabers in a mock fight, each of us singing our one word repeatedly in the mood of our current actions. Jemma made a marvelous clown, and that number proved a favorite of the Daughters. Jemma, who might not remember the lines for even the briefest of scenes, shined in her song. She had found a way to fulfill her hope of contributing something wonderful to the play.

Later, when I saw a film of the full production, my heart swelled in seeing how well Jemma did throughout. Clearly her memory issues had been resolved—perhaps her medications had been adjusted—and she said her lines and clowned quite brilliantly. Near the end of the play after a large scene with the entire cast has broken up, her character says, "Us clowns always get left out of the party."[17] Then her fellow clowns reveal that the three of them have a rodeo gig and need to hit the road. They exit in a flurry of excitement with the hope that they will soon bring joy to new audiences. Seeing Jemma run offstage with the women who so clearly embraced her made my heart leap as I remembered her struggles in rehearsal. With the patience and love of her castmates and her own perseverance, Jemma had done precisely what she hoped to do; she gave something beautiful to the group and was celebrated for it.

Each scene and every piece of music gave the women an opportunity to contribute a part of herself, her present reality, past, and/or imagined future. In a place where the institution consistently irons out a person's individuality, opportunities to express one's feelings and culture, publicly and with celebration, are rare and precious. To paraphrase Joan Didion, the Daughters sang their stories in order to live.

Romeo and Juliet at Teatro na Prisão: Hope for a Happy Ending

Just as Somebody's Daughter created hope in desperate situations, a group of women I met in a prison in Brazil used the theatre to insist that they would survive in spite of all that they suffered. On July 9, 2013, my colleague Andy Martínez, several of my University of Michigan students, and I made our first trip to a Brazilian prison with Professor Natália Fiche and her students from the Universidade Federal do Estado do Rio de Janeiro (UniRio). Fiche and the Teatro na Prisão program at the federal university have been doing theatre work in prisons since 1997, and I had come to Brazil to begin building an exchange program in which Fiche and I would bring our students to each other's countries and prisons to share best practices.

When we arrived at the Penetenciária Talavera Bruce (a women's prison), Fiche and five of her students led us to a huge metal gate where a guard slid open a small panel just large enough for him to look us over. Then he opened up a door in the gate and admitted us two at a time, searching the large bags of costumes that the UniRio students carried with them. Andy, my student Hector Flores Komatsu, and I were near the back of the group, and as those in front of us were being admitted through the door, the guard decided that Andy and Flores would not be allowed to enter because they were wearing shorts—albeit long ones. Someone dug through the costumes and found two pairs of stretch pants that they could wear. Both pairs of pants were bright pink, but the fellows were very good sports about wearing them for our visit to the prison. The guards confiscated the offending shorts and held them at the front gate until the end of our visit. It seemed a deliberate act of humiliation—a test to see how badly we wanted to spend an afternoon with the women inside.

Fiche told us that they had never before given her a problem about people wearing shorts. Apparently, prisons all over the world have this in common; the dress code seems to shift often and arbitrarily so that visitors and volunteers cannot possibly keep up with the rules. We face this all the time in the United States. During the last several years of my father's incarceration prior to his release in 2014, the dress code for female visitors in the prison where he lived in Texas became progressively more regulated than it had been in the preceding two decades. When the prison staff decided that a woman's clothes were too tight or low cut, had too much writing on them, or were deemed unfit for any other reason, they forced women to wear blue hospital gowns over their clothes. Visitors to prisons, particularly wives and girlfriends coming to see their partners, tend to want to look their best and have often been meticulous in dressing themselves for the precious few hours they can spend with the people they love. My mother and I witnessed at least two women forced to wear the hospital gowns burst into tears when the men they loved arrived in the visiting room; the women's shame and grief became palpable to all visiting families around them. If Andy or Flores were ashamed of their makeshift outfits the day they wore the pink sweatpants, they did not show it. They laughed good-naturedly about the incident and moved right along with their day. In this case, the shaming force that prisons often inflict upon their inhabitants and visitors did not spoil our trip.

Once we got inside the prison gate, a guard took our passports, asked us to sign the visitor's log book, and had us walk through a metal detector. We then followed another guard across a courtyard and into a cement building. The room in which Teatro na Prisão was meeting at Talavera Bruce is concrete on all surfaces, like the rest of the building, and has a small raised stage at one end. The dozen or so incarcerated women in the group welcomed the UniRio students, Fiche, and even us visitors with smiles and hugs. Those of us who had done work in US prisons were surprised to see that even with a guard in the room, male volunteers and incarcerated women were allowed to hug without repercussions. All of the guards we saw beyond the front gate were women, and at least one of them stayed in the back of the room the whole time we were there to watch the workshop. We gathered from the UniRio students that this is not usually the case. Because we were from another country, the workshop was also visited by the warden. Fiche had previously received approval over email to video record that day's workshop, and she had set up a tripod with a camera when we entered. The warden came in shortly thereafter to tell Fiche that she was denied permission to film after all.

Teatro na Prisão uses both improvisatory games based on Theatre of the Oppressed and traditional theatrical scripts as starting points for its work. The group tries to hold a performance in each prison twice a year at the end of each semester. At the time of our visit, Fiche was working to try to gain permission from the authorities to allow the women to perform twice each semester: once for their families and once for the other women in the prison. They were in rehearsals for an original devised performance based on *Romeo and Juliet*.

The UniRio students and incarcerated women set up chairs to make an audience of us visitors, and they put a small partition upstage right. This served as an area for costume changes and also became Juliet's balcony when she would poke her head over the top of the partition to talk to Romeo. The women had a great time with the costumes, which were diverse and rather impressive—well worth the women's enthusiasm. They even had makeshift swords made out of papier-mâché for the fight scenes.

While the women were trying on costumes and the debate over filming the workshop was happening, we had some time to talk to the workshop participants before they began their rehearsal. One woman told me about her five children, two of whom had died. Of the remaining three, two lived with her mother. In my limited Portuguese, I did not understand what she was telling me about the whereabouts of the third child, but it seemed important to this woman that we know that she had a life and family beyond the walls of the prison. She had people who loved her and hopes for a future reunited with them.

This workshop was using the story of *Romeo and Juliet* but not Shakespeare's text—even in Portuguese translation. The UniRio facilitators had given the women a basic outline of the scenes, and the women improvised using Shakespeare's characters and plot—or at least as much of it as they liked. This particular adaptation of *Romeo and Juliet* began on the streets of Verona where the Montagues and Capulets were sizing each other up for a fight. This opening scene was very funny because one actor in particular (I believe she was a Capulet) was doing such a good job of goading her opponents with gestures and facial expressions. As in Shakespeare's original, Prince Escalus (a government official in Verona) appeared and stopped the fight with a speech about keeping the peace. The rival families dispersed with another round of intimidating looks and hand motions.

Then the whole cast attended the masquerade ball at the Capulet residence. Everyone appeared in sequined mardi gras masks and danced to *funk carioca* music—a kind of Brazilian hip hop that comes from the *favelas*—as though they were at a modern-day nightclub. The cast was obviously having a great time and seemed surprised and excited by this choice of music. The UniRio students had brought a small boom box and played a number of selections of background music at different points in the play. Apparently in prior rehearsals, they had played more classical dance music, and the women in the workshop found it boring and refused to do much dancing. With *funk carioca* as their inspiration, the dance party became a whole lot of fun for the cast and audience alike.

Romeo and Juliet fell in love at the dance, and when Romeo left the party, he was so overjoyed that his happiness was positively contagious. He ran to his friends to sing Juliet's praises and then collapsed in a lovelorn heap downstage center to contemplate the many virtues of his love. Juliet's head popped up over the partition in the back of the stage, and she began a soliloquy about Romeo's virtues. He quickly leaped to his feet and ran to stand beneath her balcony. They had an enthusiastic exchange and ran off shortly thereafter to be wed by the friar. The two women playing Romeo and Juliet were allowed to share what appeared to be a pretty decent kiss, albeit with Juliet's wedding veil between them—a level of physical contact that I would not expect to be allowed in prison theatre in the United States.

At this point in the story, we encountered a most excellent bit of comedy along with a casting change. In order to give more women the opportunity to have significant roles, a new actor took over for Juliet just after the marriage scene. A UniRio student named Paulo de Melo had been telling me about the double casting before we arrived at the prison. He referred to the first actor as "the long-haired Juliet" and the second as "the short-haired Juliet." The long-haired Juliet played the character as demure and a bit shy, while the short-haired Juliet was far more outgoing and demonstrative in her love of Romeo. The first time we saw the short-haired Juliet, she was helping Romeo to sneak into her bedroom so that they could consummate their wedding night. She darted out from behind the upstage right partition, grabbed Romeo by the arm, and dragged him into her bedroom. A number of actors were hidden behind the partition, and they enacted Romeo and Juliet's love making by throwing articles of clothing into the air along with whoops and shouts. We, the audience, loved it.

Romeo emerged from the wedding night all aglow with his love for Juliet and stumbled into the street fight that killed both Tybalt (Juliet's cousin) and Mercutio (Romeo's dear friend). Then Juliet distraught by this news took a sleeping potion to fake her death. Romeo found her, believed her to be dead, and then—in the first major break from the Shakespearian plot—proceeded to get falling down drunk. (The women unanimously disliked Shakespeare's ending to the tragedy and decided to change it.) Romeo passed out, and Juliet first worried that Romeo was dead, then became very irritated at Romeo for having got drunk. She shook him awake and forced him to his feet where he stumbled around still drunk and trying to explain himself, yet overjoyed by Juliet's unexpected recovery. The families reconciled. Another *funk carioca* dance party ensued. Curtain call.

The UniRio facilitators later explained to me that they had been introducing the play to the women in sequential order, starting from the beginning, and when they reached the point when the lovers commit suicide, the women revolted. They had no attachment to the sanctity of Shakespeare and thought he had been terribly wrong to kill off Romeo and Juliet in the bloom of their youth and love. These women live in a prison every day, and they insisted on—they *needed*—a happy ending. How could they, after months of rehearsal and investment in these characters, let them become little more than collateral damage in a turf war that might never end? These actors would play people who lived, survivors of the unceasing violence that surrounded them all of their lives and divided neighbors from one another. Most prisons in the world have seen more than their share of suicides,[18] and this company of incarcerated actors had no desire to act out something they knew all too well and had likely witnessed firsthand. The Teatro na Prisão adaptation of *Romeo and Juliet* became a roadmap to hope for women who wake up in prison every morning and decide once more not to kill themselves.

After the applause died down, the women and UniRio facilitators cleared away our chairs and formed a circle. Not only did they include all of us in their circle but they deliberately spaced themselves between us so that each visitor held hands on both sides with an incarcerated woman. The music began again, and one of the UniRio students jumped into the circle and started dancing. We all cheered. He pulled one of the incarcerated women into the middle with him and then exited to rejoin the circle so that the woman could have the spotlight to herself. We danced this way for quite a while, each person in the middle bringing in a new person before rejoining the group. Then we held hands again, and Fiche talked to the women about how important their weekly attendance at the workshop is. She made sure that each of them understood that the community they had formed relied on their presence in order to continue. Then we broke the circle. Out of what felt like nowhere, a table appeared with food and drinks that the UniRio students had brought with them to the prison, and we were all encouraged to eat and drink as we mingled and talked about the performance. When the refreshments were gone, we all hugged and thanked one another before we left—the women heading off into a different area of the prison as we made our way back to the front gate to reclaim Flores and Andy's confiscated shorts.

In the years since I watched Romeo and Juliet live to see another day, their joy and hopefulness have stayed with me. Unexpected happy endings in prison shine like beacons of resistance. When one cannot secure one's own freedom from incarceration or an oppressive government, then perhaps imagining a world in which Romeo and Juliet can overcome their previously inevitable tragedies gives performers and audiences alike a sense of hope. Perhaps the kinds of devastation that we predict for women, the poor, the uneducated, the oppressed, and the imprisoned are neither logical nor inescapable. If in this one instance, incarcerated women have more authority than Shakespeare to decide the ending of the play, what else might be possible? The women imprisoned at Talavera Bruce refused to die, and instead they danced to *funk carioca* toward the futures they would like to have.

Someone Worth Knowing: Hope for the Rest of Us

Some intangible light shone out of the women I met in these prisons in Australia and Brazil. Their performances served not just to buoy them through another day but also to draw audience members like me into their hope. Like Jill Dolan, they reminded all of us present that we can and should dream of a better life for ourselves and everyone else, especially when we are in the theatre. I wanted—still want—to know if a better life awaits them, if they could be my neighbors and bring their gifts to the wider world. They have something to offer that makes the world more beautiful, richer, more interesting. A man named Curtis Dawkins wrote an exquisite collection of short stories called *The Graybar Hotel* while serving life in a Michigan prison. One of his characters describes another incarcerated man and captures precisely what drew me in as I watched the women in both of these theatre companies: "He had a kind of knowledge no one really wants to come by honestly because it involves unimaginable loss. He had literally been to hell and back, and part of him knew it. Someone like that— someone who had layers burned away to reveal something essential—is worth knowing."[19] It devastates me over and over again when I realize how few people outside prisons get to know the extraordinary people I have met inside the walls. The theatre, like Dawkins's stories, makes this clearer and, on some level, all the more painful.

My students give me hope because they go into prisons, build meaningful relationships, and carry the beauty of the people they meet out into the world again. Stina Perkins became my research assistant in her first semester at the University of Michigan and stayed involved in PCAP throughout her four years of study. In that time, she facilitated creative writing and theatre workshops in Women's Huron Valley Correctional Facility and joined a team of students and formerly incarcerated people to launch PCAP's podcast *While We Were Away*, which gives people who have come home from prison a platform to describe the challenges and joys of life after incarceration.[20] As the capstone presentation for her Engelhardt Social Justice Fellowship in the summer of 2018, Stina gave a talk called "On Seeing Fireflies" that described her years of work with currently and formerly incarcerated people:

> I've learned more about hope—and about vulnerability and creativity and expression—from the people inside than I have in any other corner of this world. And that's because these men and women, who have been "blinded," so to speak, by the despair and pain in Pandora's box, more than most of us, understand what it is to see—and they've shared this with me, through their stories and their feedback and smiles. Learning about hope in this way is important, not because it changes material conditions directly and immediately, but because hope gives us the energy to dedicate our lives to the tireless search for change—in all the ways we think we can, but also in all the ways we don't yet know we can.[21]

The Daughters and the women of Teatro na Prisão channeled that energy to do what "we don't yet know we can." It moved through the room as a palpable force in the way Vincent Lloyd says that hope makes us ready to get up and do something: "Hope is neither cheerfulness nor vague inspiration, but rather grave resilience that makes possible clear perception and right action."[22] Like Martin Luther King, Jr., whom Lloyd describes, these groups of incarcerated women steeled themselves with the kind of slow-burning resolve that makes the survival of year after year of captivity possible. They did so with joy and celebration in the face of incredibly painful realities, and they gave their hope to audiences as a gift. I hope we are wise enough to take and use it.

CONCLUSION
GLORIOUS BEINGS LIVE HERE

At the end of the play, when [the incarcerated cast] is sitting in a line
and the audience is all looking at you . . . you're all glowing. You're all
shining from what you've just done, and your beauty is so evident.
And everybody loves you, and everybody sees your humanity. . . . To
me a value of putting on a play in prison and inviting people from the
outside who may not have been in a prison before is to break their
preconception of . . . who's in here and to see that glorious beings
live here.

—Johnny Stallings, Open Hearts Open Minds

The triumphs of prison theatre makers should not overshadow the tortures
of incarceration. As Ngũgĩ wa Thiong'o wrote from personal experience,
"A narration of prison life is nothing more than an account of oppressive
measures in varying degrees of intensity and the individual or collective
response to them."[1] Prison theatre should make us see this more clearly.
The often invisible mechanisms of state control stand in stark relief against
the talent, intellect, humor, skill, and vivaciousness of those who play upon
makeshift stages in visiting rooms and chow halls. In this sense, performances
created inside the walls defy the logic of oppressive regimes, as described
by Uruguayan philosopher Eduardo Galeano: "People are trained to accept
this order as *natural*, therefore eternal. . . . The law of the jungle, which is
the law of the system, is sanctified, so that the defeated peoples will accept
their condition as destiny."[2] All of us who live in countries that have prisons,
particularly those with extraordinarily large penal systems, have been told
that we have no meaningful alternative to incarceration—that this is what
justice looks like and that it can only look this way. Theatre programs in
prisons call this logic into question by showing us that people inside the
walls can work together in peace, create something beautiful, accomplish
difficult tasks, and give back to others. Why then can they not be welcomed
back to the free world and supported as people with something to contribute
to our communities? After their hour upon the stage, we take these people
away from the public again, strip them naked, search their body cavities for
contraband, and lock them away, sometimes for life. These humiliations are

ultimately the prison's response to their achievements. Our governments do this in the names of their citizenry—in our names. They say it serves our best interests and our safety. They say a lot of things, and for lack of a better response, we usually believe them.

We put such trust in the powers that be that we forget what we already know. In her excellent book *Unruly Women: The Politics of Confinement and Resistance*, Karlene Faith reminds us of something we should already know: "whenever a group of people with weapons is given the authority to lock up and control a stigmatized group, abuses are inevitable."[3] Those who do not work in prisons—and even many who do—lose sight of the fact that we are, in fact, the people with weapons and authority because we have not insisted that no one should do this in our names. We instead create justifications that separate people into groups of those who deserve the state-sanctioned violence of imprisonment and others who do not. Faith asserts that such distinctions cannot reasonably be made, "We are all innocent and we are all guilty; there are no purely 'good' or 'bad' people."[4] The veracity of Faith's claim is obvious when we apply it to ourselves, but we tend to lose sight of it when we talk about Others—the ones for whom prisons were made.

The Redemption Narrative and How Prison Theatre Can Disrupt It

Much of how we perpetuate this enduring fiction lies in the rote redemption story we tell ourselves and ask the incarcerated to reinforce: A person commits a crime, which defines them for the rest of their lives. Everything they think, say, and do from that point forward must in some way be an act of contrition for what they have done wrong; otherwise they are irredeemable. In the idealized version of this story, the person repents, reforms, and earns release from prison. An incarcerated character in Rachel Kushner's novel *The Mars Room* describes what it feels like to be made a living representation of a crime: "All the talk of regret. They make you form your life around one thing, the thing you did, and now you have to grow yourself from what cannot be undone: they want you to make something from nothing. They make you hate them and yourself. They make it seem that they are the world, and you've betrayed it, them, but the world is so much bigger."[5] Here Kushner cuts to the heart of why this redemption narrative does not function. Human beings cannot grow or improve when they are tethered permanently and irrevocably to the past, when things that cannot be changed become the sum total of a person's existence and their potential to be anything else in the future.

Adding complexity to the redemption narrative troubles us greatly because we must then see a person instead of a crime. Responding to a person proves far more vexing and complicated than addressing the worst thing that someone has ever done. Playwright Eve Ensler spent eight years leading a creative writing workshop at Bedford Hills Correctional Facility, a women's prison in New York State. She describes the way in which this work disrupted her world view:

> The scariest part of prison was falling in love with the women, the inmates in my group. They were smart and funny and beautiful and deeply kind and remorseful and in so much pain, and these same women had killed people, taken actual lives. This complexity, this ambiguity, was almost unbearable. It made me want to flee the prison. Everything was suddenly in question.[6]

In Ensler's description, and indeed in their own writings, the women in this workshop did grapple deeply with the crimes and actions that had sent them to prison, but what troubled Ensler and frayed the edges of the familiar redemption narrative were the nuances and complexities of these women's lives, behaviors, and feelings.

In this same essay, Ensler tells the story of a woman in the writing group who was a child molester. Ensler and many of the other women in the workshop "despised" this woman for what she had done. Then one day this woman described the circumstances of her life. From the age of five, she had been molested and raped by her mother and stepfather, then sold to paying customers. Her mother died when she was fourteen, and at fifteen this woman had been forced to marry her stepfather, whom she then helped to molest other children, one of whom died at their hands. The woman spent her first five years in prison not understanding why she was there. She had never known that molestation was wrong because she believed it happened to everyone. When she could finally grasp what she had done, she began harming herself regularly.[7] Clearly, something needed to interrupt the cycle of harm in this woman's life, but was prison the most appropriate intervention? How can the traumas of captivity, violence, and institutionalization be our best response to the life of a person who arrived at this point as a direct result of years of torture?

The sharing of this story in the writing group changed Ensler and deepened her commitment to working with incarcerated women. After years of work together, Ensler shaped what the women in this workshop wrote into a play called *What I Want My Words to Do to You*, which was performed by professional actors both inside the prison and in free-world venues. The process of making the play was filmed for a documentary of the same title and broadcast in the United States on public television.[8] The play and film became vehicles for extending the disruption of the redemption narrative to wider audiences. In a broad sense, prison theatre does this revelatory work for audiences on both sides of the walls, bringing us closer to a complex understanding of what incarceration does to individuals and societies.

The Imbecile You Will Not Find in Prison

Prison theatre asks us to reckon with the damaging logic and, more importantly, the actual people who have been deliberately hidden from us. In theatre, we often talk about the reversal of expectation as a comic device, and the very act of making art in a place designed to flatten out individuality serves this purpose. Of course, not all prison theatre leans toward comedy, but it does tend to be laden with surprises—some of which emerge in the play and others in how we understand the prison and its inhabitants because of the theatre. One of the abiding revelations in prison theatre has to do with what Rachel Kushner describes as the imbecile for whom the prison was constructed. In *The Mars Room*, Kushner's incarcerated protagonist describes what the prison expects of her and the women around her:

> Everything in prison is addressed to . . . the imbecile. I've never met her. Plenty I have met in prison cannot read, and some cannot tell time, but that doesn't mean they are not shrewd and superior individuals who can outsmart any egghead. People in prison are clever as hell. The imbecile the rules and signs are meant to address is nowhere to be found.[9]

The process of entering most prisons teaches volunteers, audience members, and certainly incarcerated people that everyone who walks through the doors will be treated as the imbecile. You are likely to be touched brusquely without your permission, told where to stand and sit, mistrusted, and instructed not to make even the most basic decisions for yourself. You will be told to follow a great many rules, which will never be explained to you satisfactorily, if at all. Some of these things are done for your safety and others for the sheer exercise of power. You cannot discern which is which. Part of the prison's power is to convince you that you are the imbecile who cannot navigate this space adequately on your own. Then, if you are lucky enough to get to see a play performed in such a space, you will realize quickly and irrevocably that the people you have been told are the imbeciles (perhaps even yourself)—for whom all these rules were made—can do remarkable things. They offer you gifts of joy and artistry and community. You receive these and perhaps share them with others, and then the space designed for the imbecile crowds you out or keeps you in. You do not get to choose whether you remain or leave because, of course, you are not trusted with this decision. But, whether you walk out of the gates or stay, you do so knowing that the people inside are not the imbeciles for whom the system was designed.

If indeed the prison is designed for the imbecile who cannot be found, then what can the theatre do to address this pressing injustice? Augusto Boal's work with the Theatre of the Oppressed undergirds much of the prison theatre I have seen. He believed that in order to create social change, we must be able to imagine what a different and more just world would look like. He and those he trained taught people throughout the world to use theatre to rehearse for a better future.[10] At a simple level, prison theatre casts incarcerated people in roles outside their present circumstances. It provides a literal representation of those in prison as capable of inhabiting other environments and identities. To this same end, Galeano argued, "*We are what we do, especially what we do to change what we are*: our identity resides in action and struggle. Therefore, the revelation of what we are implies the denunciation of those who stop us from being what we can become" (emphasis in original).[11] The theatre then functions both as an assertion of identity, made and claimed by the incarcerated and as an inherent act of defiance against the logic of the prison and all of us who let it stand. If we listen well, we can remake ourselves and our nations, aligning our values to honor the human dignity of all people, as the incarcerated so plainly urge us to do.

The Strange Gifts of Prison Theatre

Besides challenging all those with whom it engages, prison theatre also imparts a variety of strange and, at times, wonderful gifts. Phyllis Kornfeld, a visual artist who has been making art with imprisoned people since 1983, says that she begins her work with the goal of "access[ing] that part of you which has never been incarcerated."[12] In a sense, prison arts work does this for all of us—the process of creative engagement helps us to imagine how we would be if no one lived in captivity.

In everyday practice, many prison authorities describe the practice of prison theatre as cultivating virtues in incarcerated people. Jennifer Sachse, warden at Missouri Eastern Correctional Center, reflects on what she has seen the Prison Performing Arts (PPA) program accomplish in the prison she runs: "Most will say that the end product, a play or performance, is the measure of success for PPA. I have found that the process by which the end result is achieved, is the actual prize. Patience, tolerance, cooperation, communication, sympathy, and empathy are all crucial pieces to the play's success."[13] George Lombardi, who served both as Missouri's director of prisons and its director of corrections, concurs. He also had a long-standing relationship with PPA and now sits on its board of directors and has observed that PPA plays a significant role in

> the transformation of offenders from insecure, sometimes angry and troublesome individuals to compassionate and altruistic personalities. This is profound. It is my observation after forty-one years in this corrections business that if there is a quality missing in many offenders it is lack of compassion for others—either because they never had it to begin with or it has been suppressed because of childhood trauma. . . . Anything that can inculcate compassion in their being is a good thing and anathema to future criminal behavior I believe. PPA is a great catalyst for that occurring.[14]

Theatre programs in prisons provide opportunities for incarcerated people to develop intellectually, emotionally, and creatively. They tend to provide enough structure to make people feel safe in trying new things, opening up to others, and listening to viewpoints they might never have heard otherwise. At the same time, they cultivate specific skill sets that help participants feel confident about their own abilities and capacity for growth. All of this lays the foundations for the cultivation of the virtues that Sachse and Lombardi describe.

Theatre also provides an opportunity for incarcerated people to feel that they have something to give to others. In the July/August 2018 issue of the *Angolite* prison news magazine, incarcerated reporter Rudy

Martinez published a story about the Angola Drama Club visiting men in the residential hospital wards at the Louisiana State Penitentiary. The actors, attired in outlandish drag with oversized fake bosoms and rear ends, terrible wigs, and flowered dresses, brought a baby doll into the hospital wing. An incarcerated actor named Will Smith, playing a female character called Manish, would hand the doll to a man in a hospital bed and explain that she was a single mother caring for this child. As the patient held the baby, Manish would ask, "Do you want to be his daddy?" Other comedic bits included a drunken doctor character called Dr. Jack Daniels and a pair of outrageous nurses who claimed to raise heart rates by shaking their huge false bosoms over the patients' faces. According to Martinez, the men in the hospital ward took great joy in the laughter provoked by the Drama Club members and felt grateful for the personal interaction. An incarcerated man named Reginald Mason remarked, "All this is about love. I like seeing these fellow inmates come here to cheer up the patients with their comedy."[15] Because of Angola's isolated location in the middle of a Louisiana swamp an hour outside of Baton Rouge, many families have trouble getting to the prison to visit their loved ones. This made the Drama Club's warmth and cheer all the more valuable to hospital patients who might not have anyone else to comfort them in their illness.

At times the gifts of prison theatre surprise even those who volunteer to participate. While serving time in Cotton Correctional Facility in Michigan, Patrick Bates saw a post in his housing unit for people to sign up for workshops being offered by the program that I run at the University of Michigan. He had known men who had done creative writing with the Prison Creative Arts Project (PCAP) and thought that was what he would be doing. He had put his name on the wrong list but stayed in the group even after learning he had signed up to do theatre:

> I fell in love with the fact that I could find an outlet for my showmanship. This is a place where we can't find too much happiness. I looked for ways to better myself in every way. I was always looking for ways to be productive. Some would look at me signing up for my first workshop as an accident. I see it as fate and the universe working in my favor at a time where I didn't see much favor in my life.[16]

The prison authorities called him Bates, but he asked us to call him Pat. In the four years that followed, Pat took two different PCAP theatre workshops every week and upon his release from prison in January 2019 became one of the most dedicated participants in our free-world programming. He took PCAP's facilitator training within weeks of regaining his freedom and immediately became a co-facilitator of our community arts workshop at a public housing complex in Ann Arbor. Pat also audited the Theatre & Incarceration course that I co-teach with Cozine Welch (a formerly incarcerated poet) and advised my students about how to navigate difficulties they encountered when facilitating theatre workshops in prisons, youth facilities, and groups of formerly incarcerated people.

Pat's engagement with PCAP theatre programming during and after his imprisonment translated into a community of support during his first year of release and connections that have led to some paid work and possible opportunities for further employment at the university. Pat also gives much to us as a community on our campus and beyond. The students in our Theatre & Incarceration course felt that Pat had a significant impact on them personally and on their learning. A graduating senior, Julia Barron said:

> Meeting Pat was . . . life-changing because he humanized the struggle of what society calls a once incarcerated individual, a returning citizen. I quickly realized this term "returning citizen" added to Pat's anxiety because it forced him to realize that he had been locked away from his family, friends, loved ones, cultural heritage, society, and even the ever so quick development of technology.[17]

Julia took it upon herself to help Pat learn to use his smart phone and access our course readings from the class website. They soon became good friends, almost like siblings raised in separate Latinx families in Michigan. As the semester progressed, Julia struggled to cope with the harsh realities faced by the boys in her theatre workshop in a particularly bleak youth detention center. Pat, who had lived in similar facilities when he was a child, helped Julia to better understand how to navigate such an environment and what she could do to support the boys in her workshop. Pat did not have security clearance to attend the celebration Julia and her co-facilitators hosted for the boys at the end of the semester. When I later described how joyful it had been and the many kindnesses that the boys had offered to me, my students, and one another, Pat wept openly at the beauty of what they had achieved. Julia says, "Meeting Pat has been one of the best things to happen to my life because not only do I get to love an incredible human being, but I have the honor of helping Pat realize that second chances are for every human being."[18]

Many other students reported that Pat had a similarly profound effect on their lives. Shannon Harper (a first-year student) grew up in Detroit, as did Pat, and felt it difficult to find community at the university until she joined PCAP. Instead of offering a theatre workshop in a prison, she chose to work alongside Pat as a co-facilitator of the community workshop that meets in a public housing complex in Ann Arbor: "I don't think I was ready to meet amazing people and then leave and maybe not be able to see them again or know what is happening to them." In Pat and her workshop team, Shannon found a network of support that buoyed her through a difficult semester: "Pat taught me to always see the bright side of things and to check on the people you care about. He always asked people how they were doing and assured them that he was there if they needed him."[19] Quinn Blackledge, a student in his final semester and another co-facilitator of the community workshop, felt similarly supported by Pat in their collaborations. He was "struck by Pat's innate leadership" and the "undeniably beautiful energy" he brought into the class and workshop. Quinn claims Pat was "absolutely central to my education of theatre, prison and life."[20]

Liv Naimi, a third-year student, greatly valued Pat's presence in our classroom: "Pat's insight into our reading and his willingness to share his personal story with us allowed me to learn more about myself, mass incarceration's impact on individuals and families, the people in my [prison] workshop, and how crucial art can be. It was also something that I did not think I deserved usually." Liv, who uses they/them pronouns, had concerns that Pat gave so much of himself that it may have cost him dearly. They felt cognizant of "how much more work he had to put in to be in that space than I did." While the students in our class grappled with the daily realities faced by the incarcerated people in their workshops, Pat faced challenges with transportation, employment, and rebuilding relationships that are common to many people in their first year out of prison. He shared much of this and his prison experiences with us in class in response to readings and discussions. Liv felt grateful for his openness but also concerned: "I was often worried that Pat felt he needed to disclose trauma or hard things in order to gain respect in class . . . I hoped he didn't feel tokenized, but I was often aware that in a space where you have to remind everyone that you've been in prison all the time nonstop, maybe he did."[21] Pat's openness and generosity drew us all in and made the students feel protective of him. His vulnerability and concern for others stood in stark contrast to the fears that our university expressed in a new policy that same semester, requiring all employees and students to disclose any new felony charges brought against them.[22]

The students soon drew Pat into their campus activism surrounding the university's restrictive policies on students and employees with criminal records. He addressed the Central Student Government and attended two meetings of the university's Board of Regents to help the members of these governing bodies understand the ways people with criminal records have something to contribute to our campus. Pat credits the PCAP theatre workshops he did while incarcerated with teaching him the public speaking skills that he now uses in his advocacy work around criminal records and prison issues. His consistent presence on the University of Michigan campus helped him to get hired by a new collaborative research team called the Carceral State Project, which is a group of professors, students, and community collaborators working on issues related to confinement and detention. In prison he, like all the incarcerated, was interpellated into the role of *the imbecile*, though he was not and could never be that person; now he addressed elite university professors and students about the very real deficiencies in their knowledge of the lives of others.

Pat had never envisioned himself as a person who could do all of these things. In fact, he told me repeatedly in that first semester after his release that he had never before known that he could have the opportunity to be something else. He believed from childhood that he belonged in prison, that he deserved nothing better. His early stints in youth detention facilities had taught him this, and the older men in prison raised him when his family could not. All the role models he had lived with him inside the walls. Some of them taught him the violence that drove much of his early life in prison, and years later some of those same men taught him peacemaking skills, encouraged him to get involved in PCAP programs, and took pride in Pat's development as a force for kindness and generosity inside the prison. Many of those long-serving men remain in prison, and some will never come home. They, too, deserve programming, but in many prisons they would not be eligible to receive it.

For Those Who Remain: The Case for Including All Incarcerated People in Programming

We often tend to measure the success of prison programming in terms of how it prepares people for life after incarceration and neglect to advocate for access to programming for those who may never rejoin the free world.

In many prison systems, particularly in the United States, people with long, indeterminate, life or death sentences remain ineligible to participate in most kinds of programming. Others, like the Obama era Second Chance Pell Grant program, which provides federal financial aid for college education to incarcerated students, prioritize those who will be released in five years or less.[23] The rationale for this kind of restriction often has to do with limited resources and a desire to privilege those nearest to rejoining the free world. While this makes a certain kind of sense, it also misses the bigger picture; the culture and communities we create inside prisons have significant impacts on the outside world.

Lifers understand this reality better than anyone else. Mary Heinen McPherson was serving a natural life sentence at the time that she cofounded PCAP in 1990. She asserts that long-serving imprisoned people shape the prison environment by "hold[ing] key work details/ positions inside penitentiaries. They earned those assignments by classification through hard work and responsible, competent, diligent behavior. Lifers . . . support prison administrators' efforts at maintaining peace and security . . . [and] help maintain the stability of the institution."[24] Mary believes that an investment in those serving long sentences enables everyone inside the prison to live more safely. Martín Vargas, another PCAP participant who served forty-five years of a life sentence, agrees and emphasizes the impact lifers have on younger people coming into prison:

> There are few, if any, programs for learning developmental skills, and if theatre is what it takes to help someone come out of his or her hell-shell, there should be one in every prison. Young felons learn from lifers, who have been there the longest. It would be better for everyone, if what those young minds learned was how to take criticism well, and not that they have to prove themselves to everyone watching.[25]

Longer-serving incarcerated people often speak of the lifers who served as surrogate parents to them in prison and in turn invest in the next generation of incarcerated youth. They can choose to teach violence and crime or to draw young people into a different way of life inside the walls.

Lifers tend to set the tone of an institution, and some prison administrators realize that an investment in long-serving people serves the well-being of everyone inside the walls. George Lombardi, former Missouri director of corrections, thinks that all incarcerated people should have access to meaningful programming:

> Anything that can keep life sentenced folks engaged with the world in any way is of benefit to them, to the culture of the prison and to the safety of staff and fellow offenders. They have great influence on the population of their prison environment and so it is wise to keep them engaged in productive activities and thus impact the overall morale accordingly.[26]

Lombardi even includes people with death sentences in the category of those who should receive programming:

> Missouri still has the death penalty. In the early 90's, we eliminated Death Row and put all the 100 plus inmates at the time sentenced to death in the general population of one of our Max prisons—so from then on they had complete access as any other inmate to everything in the prison. . . . So having them engaged with [theatre programming] is a no brainer for me. It simply makes sense.[27]

Why should it be a radical thought that those we have condemned to die still have something to contribute to living communities inside prisons— especially when they themselves are forced to constitute such a community even as they wait for death? Many other US states and countries in other parts of the world segregate those awaiting execution from the rest of the prison population and deny them any access to programming other than religious counseling. If the state of Missouri—a Southern state formerly in the Confederacy—can peacefully integrate those with death sentences into programming, what prevents other prison systems from granting this level of human dignity to those the state will execute?

Theatre programs encourage longtermers, lifers, and those with death sentences to develop strategies for emotional well-being and growth that help them to support a better environment inside the prison. As a founding member of PCAP's first workshop, the Sisters Within Theater Troupe, Mary learned skills that carried her through the decades of her imprisonment:

> From the earliest improv, I acted out what I needed to problem solve in my personal life inside. Theater and the Sisters gave me safe space

and a sense of security where I could act out my problem and see it from other eyes and actions and work through responses. I can't tell you how important this became in real life. Living with hundreds and hundreds of women was beyond challenging, and acting helped me solve crises and deal with acute, severe, debilitating trauma. The theater games and the element of play saved my sanity. Those times were precious and necessary for my survival.[28]

Mary's life had a significant and measurable impact on those around her in prison. During her twenty-seven years of incarceration, she filed and won thirteen class action lawsuits as the named lead plaintiff suing the Michigan Department of Corrections on behalf of the women serving time in the state. These lawsuits established precedents for more equitable and humane treatment of women in prison throughout the United States.[29]

After a commutation from Governor John Engler freed her in 2002, Mary continued her advocacy work for currently and formerly incarcerated people. She won a Soros Justice Fellowship in 2011. In the 2015–16 school year, she co-taught my PCAP courses with me at the University of Michigan. Since 2016, she has worked full-time as PCAP's Program Coordinator, training and supporting the more than eighty volunteers per week that we send into Michigan's carceral facilities. In this position, she mentors university students alongside currently and formerly incarcerated youth and adults and speaks at national conferences about prison issues. Her life stands as a visible testament to the extraordinary value of those we have imprisoned. She undoubtedly has shaped the lives of thousands of others for the better and continues her advocacy today.

How would the world be different if Mary had not had the networks of support that she needed, including the Sisters Within, to survive prison and continue her work? How many others with similar potential have we already lost because of the violence of incarceration? Would theatre programming have made a difference in any of their lives? Theatre clearly helped but did not save Mary, and she would be the first to say that what we need most is to get people out of prisons, not make their lives more comfortable while they are there. In the meantime, Mary continues to do the challenging work of reaching back into the systems that harmed her to try to help those who endure inside the walls. In her words, "Theater breathes life into the dungeons and cages of confinement."[30]

Theatre Doesn't Save Anyone in Prison, but It Helps Some People Get out of Bed

Given that theatre does not actually free people from prison, the question of what this work can do remains. Galeano wrote poignantly about the untold numbers of "artists and writers [who] have never had the opportunity to recognize themselves as such" because of the harsh conditions of their lives.[31] He also had a tempered view about the power of the arts to change structural oppression: "To claim that literature on its own is going to change reality would be an act of madness or arrogance. It seems to me no less foolish to deny that it can aid in making this change."[32] My friend, Professor Viviane Narvaes, expressed a similar sentiment in a talk she gave at the Universidade de São Paulo on May 19, 2019: "Theatre in prison doesn't save anyone, but it helps some people get out of bed in the morning."[33] Having a positive reason to face another day in prison makes a meaningful difference. Narvaes should know. She has been making theatre with incarcerated men and women in Brazil since 2009.[34] In addition to the kind of work she does with the Teatro na Prisão program inside prisons, as described in Chapter 4, Narvaes has also directed a play with a mixed company of current and former students from the Universidade Federal do Estado do Rio de Janeiro (UniRio), one of whom—Edson Sodré—lives in what Brazilians call an "open prison."

While serving a sentence of 108 years in a prison in Rio de Janeiro, Edson Sodré joined a theatre workshop offered by Teatro na Prisão. He had no interest in the theatre but had heard that another man in the same prison had managed to escape from a tunnel underneath the stage. Sodré participated in the workshop but also crawled under the stage to see if he could make his way to freedom. He found a human skull inside the tunnel and turned back to both the prison and the theatre. He fell in love with theatre, started writing plays, and has remained a part of Teatro na Prisão continuously since that fateful first encounter in 1997.[35]

By 2018, Sodré had done more work with Teatro na Prisão than any other incarcerated person, served twenty-eight years of his sentence, and recently transitioned into an open prison with authorization to study at UniRio. This meant that he could leave the prison at 7 a.m. each weekday as long as he returned by midnight every night. On weekends he would have to stay in prison. He enrolled in classes for his bachelor's degree in theatre and began studying alongside some of the students who had been facilitating the theatre workshops he had taken in prison. Sodré had thought that he had earned three years of good time (time off for good behavior) toward parole for completing high school courses and working as a janitor in prison. Since parole in Brazil is generally granted after a person has served thirty years, he believed that he would be released from prison very soon. Then a judge clarified that his three years of good time would only be counted as part of time served for the 108-year sentence but that they would not be included in the calculations that could earn him parole. In essence, he learned that when he thought he was due for release, he would actually have to serve at least another two years prior to being eligible for parole.[36]

Around this same time in June 2018, Narvaes directed Sodré and two other UniRio students in a reading of a Portuguese translation of a ten-minute play by Tennessee Williams called *Escape* (translated as *Fuga*). In the play, three members of a chain gang sit in the bunk house of a prison in the Southern United States. The men play cards as they discuss an escape that another man named Billy is making that night. Their commentary on Billy's actions and their own circumstances is imbued with references to the plight of black men in prison. They characterize blackness as an ill-fated mark that they can read in their cards as well as on Billy's and their own skin. They listen to the baying of the hounds that chase Billy and speculate about where he might be and whether he will make it to the passing train that could carry him away from his pursuers. They hear gunshots but do not know whether Billy has been hit until they see his body returned to the prison. The play ends as they watch this through the window of the prison bunk house:

STEVE

He's free, dat's how I look at it. Billy's free.

BIG

Yeah. He's free.[37]

Billy spent what precious little time he had out of prison—surely less than a couple of hours at most—hiding and running for his life, yet as his compatriots so poignantly observe, he made it to freedom. He did not die in prison, as the other characters might, as so many members of chain gangs in the United States have been worked or beaten to death.

This reading of the play took place while my PCAP students and I were in Rio as part of our annual prison theatre exchange program.[38] As a result, the audience for *Fuga* that night was comprised of a nearly even mix of Brazilian and US theatre people. We had much to say to one another about the commonalities in our prison systems and the fact that what Williams wrote in the late 1930s or early 1940s still had deep and troubling resonances in both nations.[39] During our discussion, Sodré reflected on the irony that his attempted escape from prison resulted in him becoming a student at UniRio, reading a play called *Escape*. He said that in actuality he had escaped *to the stage* rather than under it.

Mostre-me a saída

Because the reading had been such a success and because Sodré was suffering so greatly from the knowledge that his time in prison would last years longer than he had realized, Narvaes and the cast decided to adapt the short text into a larger play with three layers of storytelling:

1. The text by Tennessee Williams
2. The carceral state of Brazil in its complexity
3. Our own stories of prisons (whether they be experiences of being incarcerated or experiences of giving classes in prison)[40]

The task of adapting *Escape* and putting on the new play actually provided a greater measure of freedom for Sodré; he was able to get special dispensation from a judge to allow him to leave the prison for weekend rehearsals, since they were now an extension of his college education.

When I returned to Rio a year later in June 2019 with a new group of PCAP students, we saw a forty-minute production of the adaptation of *Escape*, entitled *Mostre-me a saída* (*Show Me the Way Out*). The play opened with the actors standing behind plastic curtains as projections of actual Brazilian news footage illuminated the stage. We saw images and heard sounds of military occupations of *favelas*, police shootings, the assassinations of ordinary citizens and civil rights leaders like Rio city councilwoman Marielle Franco, and much more. The sheer volume and scope of state-sponsored violence that Brazilians are currently experiencing overwhelmed the stage.

Sodré approached the front of the stage and began to tell a story from his own experience of incarceration. Throughout the play he performed alongside Luan de Almeida (a recent graduate of UniRio) and current student Peterson Oliveira. Together these men played both the characters in the Williams text and also versions of themselves as writer/actors of the adaptation. In his opening monologue, Sodré described what he called the Banana Rebellion. One day while Sodré lived in a closed prison, a confusion arose when prison administrators asked for more bananas than were available that day. The incarcerated man assigned to bring food to the officials went to look for the bananas, which had all been eaten. The functionary in charge said that the fact that the bananas ran out was the problem of the incarcerated clerk, who had no power to bring more into the prison. A discussion began, which ended with two shots fired into the leg of the incarcerated clerk. The other men in the prison rose up in protest and were mowed down by beatings and hundreds of gunshots. Then came what Sodré called the *hora da cobrança*—the hour of reckoning:

> The prisoners are taken to the patio and stacked on top of each other under a flag of a skull with a dagger through it. This image recalls the slave ships. Some individuals are removed and ritually tortured to make examples of them. It's a pedagogical moment when prisoners learn that human rights are thrown out, beaten, and exploded.

The weeks that followed in the prison played out like a zombie film with dozens of men wandering around with their arms and legs in casts and their heads bandaged. "But the story of the bananas was never told! They said it was a mass escape attempt!"[41] At the end of this scene, the three actors march like a police battalion and chant together: "*Tropa de Elite qual é sua missão? Entrar na favela e deixar corpo no chão!*"[42] ("Elite troops, what is your mission? Enter the *favelas* and leave bodies on the ground.") The actors then reassemble in a different configuration and begin a new scene as the characters in Williams's *Escape*.

Sodré as a character named Texas recites stage directions to alert the audience that we have entered into a new world. The other two actors immediately drop their Williamsonian personas and interrupt with a "footnote to the scene" to acknowledge their "problem of representation." When they began reading the Williams text, they had not immediately understood the racial undertones of the script and assumed that the one named Texas would be white, simply because of his name. With further study, they discovered that all three characters in the prison were black, and this created a dilemma for them because Sodré is white. Sodré felt that the play was written for him because he lives in prison. He lives in the most "fucked up" situation of the group of actors yet acknowledges that he does have some white privilege in the prison. Peterson asked him, "Isn't it because you're white that you are in the open prison and performing here [at the university]?" Peterson and Luan said that the structural problem of racism in Brazilian society continues with no way out (*não tem saída aqui*), that it follows them as black students in the university.

For the first two-thirds of the play, the actors continued in this manner—attempting to start the performance of *Escape* but getting sidetracked by the chaos of their own lives and the need to explain the deplorable conditions of incarceration in Brazil. By the time we at last saw these three beleaguered and abused figures play out the Williams text, the audience understood that the characters from the past had much in common not just with the actors on the stage but also with all oppressed people in Brazil today. The last interruption in their portrayal of *Escape* came right after the first shot at Billy is fired offstage. Luan stepped out of the character of Big Boy to say, "In the 1930s, Williams was denouncing the shooting of one prisoner. In 2019 the Brazilian army used 203 shots to kill a family and a worker who tried to help them. All of this is unacceptable."[43] This reference to a real tragedy, which occurred less than a month prior to this performance, immediately precedes the devastating conclusion of both *Escape* and *Mostre-me a saída*.

After the Williams characters say that Billy died free, a blackout fell across the stage, and I thought the play had ended. Instead of a quick return of the actors for a curtain call, we heard a lot of rustling in the darkness on stage. When the lights came up again, the three actors were wearing plastic body bags, arranged in a striking tableau with one man lying across a small table and the other two standing at odd angles. It was as if the imprisoned men were already dead or as if the dead had stood up to show that they were finally free. I could not stop crying because of the force of the loss of the people I have known who died in prison and those who I know today who are likely never to see freedom again while they live. I had never seen such a striking image to convey either the living death of incarceration or the absence and invisibility of all those who lost their lives inside the walls.

We—the audience, cast, and crew—stayed in the theatre a long time that night, discussing what we had witnessed and how it made us feel. In the end, Sodré returned to prison, as he does every night.

The Work of Little Ants

Two days after we watched *Mostre-me a saída*, my father suddenly fell very ill. He coded on an operating table during emergency surgery and died for four minutes before medical personnel could resuscitate him. My sister called me in Brazil to tell me to come home. The first available flight did not leave for a full twenty-four hours, and I spent this day and night in terror, not knowing as I finally boarded a flight to the United States whether my father would still be alive when I landed. In the midst of my panic and sorrow, my prayers for him to survive, I kept reliving the last moments of *Mostre-me a saída*—Luan's voice ringing in my ears: "*Ele tá livre.*" At least *he's free.*

My father lived another five and a half months in hospitals before complications from this episode took him from us. If he had still been in prison when his health failed, he would undoubtedly have died before a doctor (or his family) ever saw him. Like the characters in *Escape*, the incarcerated in Texas are still chained together in a row whenever they are taken out of prison. The few times that my father received medical care during the twenty years of his incarceration, he spent two days traveling each way, back and forth to the hospital, while handcuffed, shackled, and chained to the man next to him.

Mostre-me a saída haunts me, as do so many of the other plays I have seen performed by incarcerated people. As Johnny Stallings reminds us, so many glorious beings live behind prison walls, hidden from the rest of the world. Prison theatre gives us brief glimpses of what these people have endured and what they have to offer to humanity. Many of the prison theatre makers I met outside the walls described ways in which they felt overwhelmed by this work or inadequate in the face of so many injustices. Narvaes, ever the Marxist, finds hope in continuing to labor:

> I, too, feel very sad and anguished when I stop to think of the level of sickness in the world, of the injustices and inhumanity in which we are mired. . . . I think our work is like that of little ants—heavy and constant—and that we are contributing to a change in the long term. Very probably we will not see a world without prisons, but the utopia moves me. . . . We are doing our small part with all the limits of the theatre and the academic work as well.[44]

The men, women, and children behind the walls persevere, and like the little ants, so do we.

PART II
CRITICAL PERSPECTIVES

CHAPTER 5
DANCING IN THE WINGS
DOES PRISON THEATRE OFFER A RADICAL
CONTAINMENT OR A PEDAGOGY OF UTOPIA?

Selina Busby

In this chapter, I will consider how a specific prison theatre project functions on a continuum of radical intervention and radical containment, asking if it is a piece of theatre with the intentionality of creating the space for social transformation or if it merely creates a more docile prison population. In doing this, I am borrowing Ric Knowles's notion described in his text *Reading the Material Theatre*.[1] I shall focus on a project that I tutored each year during 2008–12 with students from the Royal Central School of Speech and Drama, working in partnership with Second Shot Productions as well as the staff and residents of privately run category B prisons in England. I will consider the degrees to which the transgressive or the transformative potential of the Children's Play Project in prisons functions this continuum, and I am using Knowles's description of radical containment being the control of transgressive elements in society in the interests of the reproduction of the dominant order.

The Project

This project has taken place in three different local category B prisons in the United Kingdom. Category B prisons incarcerate adult male prisoners (over twenty-one) who are a risk to the public. According to the Ministry of Justice National Offender Management Service (NOMS), category B prisons are for "prisoners for whom the very highest conditions of security are not necessary but for whom escape must be made very difficult."[2] A "local prison" houses those who have been recently sentenced within the area in which the prison is based, and this may include men who are on remand before trial.

I am going to focus on one of the prisons in which we ran the project during 2010–14. This prison was built by Her Majesty's Prison Service in 1994. Since 2003, it has been maintained and operated by a private company with a contract to manage the prison still in operation during the writing of this chapter in 2019. This makes it one of fourteen UK prisons currently run privately. It has a capacity to house 1,145 male residents. The prison's mission statement stated that it aimed to

> positively change the lives of prisoners by providing a secure and decent environment, in which staff can provide a range of interventions and services designed to reduce re-offending and thereby allowing a safe reintegration back into the community.[3]

The Children's Play Project was part of the mission to run "interventions and services to reduce re-offending." The project involved five BA Applied Theatre and Drama Education students at the end of their second year of studies working on a drama residency in the prison. They worked with between eighteen and twenty-five of the residents, who were all under twenty-five years old. These residents were all new to this facility and were all fathers with children living outside the prison. The men volunteered to work on a theatre project, over a two-week period, in which they devised and performed a piece of children's theatre. At the end of the residency, the children, partners, and extended families of the participants were invited into the prison to see the performance, followed by an extended visit.

Under the support of the governor (or warden in US parlance), who was supportive of arts initiatives, and in partnership with a small arts organization called Second Shot Productions, an Arts and Media Department was set up within the walls of the prison. As noted by Marie Hutton, in an unpublished evaluation of the Children's Play Project, it was the first and only prison in England and Wales to appoint a creative director.[4] In October 2011, Second Shot Productions, operating as a social enterprise from within the prison, offered local businesses and charities its professional services, such as film making, graphic and web design, and music production. During 2012, eight serving and two former HMP prisoners were running the production company. Second Shot Productions worked all year around, offering a number of drama and media projects and producing a number of plays with subjects that included restorative justice, substance abuse, gang culture, and bullying in prison. Hutton's report notes that "a number of Second Shot's production endeavors have won Koestler

Awards and, for the first time in a custodial setting, six prisoners working with them, were awarded the Silver Arts Award."[5]

These initiatives and the Children's Play Project were sanctioned as part of the prison's efforts to reduce reoffending rates for its ex-offenders and an attempt to create better opportunities for its inmates to re-enter the community successfully.

Desistence and the Family

In the United Kingdom, according to the Ministry of Justice, "around half of all crime is committed by people who have already been through the criminal justice system."[6] In 2012, the Prison Reform Trust's report *Out for Good* noted that 47 percent of adults released from prison were reconvicted within one year of release, and this statistic rose to 57 percent for those serving sentences under twelve months.[7] The cost to the British taxpayer of reoffending is estimated to be £9.5 to £13 billion per year.[8] Lowering the cost of reoffending is therefore a high priority for the government, and the reintegration of offenders into society, or their resettlement, has been identified as a linchpin for reducing offending. Reducing reoffending, or the encouragement of desistance, has become the aim of many prison initiatives involving the arts and sports since 2002 when the Office of the Deputy Prime Minister published a report that claimed:

> There is a considerable risk that a prison sentence might actually make the factors associated with reoffending worse. For example, **a third** lose their house while in prison, **two-thirds** lose their job, over a fifth face increased financial problems and over **two-fifths** lose contact with their family.[9]

This report was followed in 2004 by publication of the NOMS *Reducing Reoffending: National Action Plan*. This plan outlined the seven pathways for reducing reoffending: accommodation; education, training, and employment; mental and physical health; drug and alcohol rehabilitation; finance, benefit, and debt; attitude, thinking, and behavior; and children and families.

The Prison Reform Trust's report *Out for Good* states that "there were approximately 200,000 children in England and Wales who had a parent in prison at some point in 2009."[10] This report provides a detailed consideration of the ways in which retaining contact with families during imprisonment helps prisoners to "maintain" familial relationships and how this, in turn, has "powerful" implications for resettlement outcomes upon release.[11] In 2012, the *Pathways from Crime* report implies that unemployment is a driver of offending, while meaningful employment is a driver of desistence."[12] And so the family, and maintaining family contact, has for some time been seen as a key factor in desistence.

The prison discussed in this chapter ran a range of initiatives that attempted to utilize the seven pathways in the rehabilitation of its inmates, specifically with regard to the "children and families" pathway. Her Majesty's Inspector of Prisons described the provisions for family contact at this prison as "generous," "innovative," and "creative."[13] The Children's Play Project was sanctioned by the governor as part of the "Families First" program. This program aimed to keep prisoners' contact with their families at a maximum as a means to aiding their reintegration into society upon release and as an aid to their "desistence" from crime.

According to criminologist Shadd Maruna, desistence is "the process of abstaining from crime among those who previously had engaged in a sustained pattern of offending."[14] Measuring desistence is difficult, and Maruna outlines part of the problem by asking questions about the permanent nature of the change that implies desistence when he observes that the word itself suggests the halting of criminal behavior as an event or a decision to stop. In his 2008 text *Making Good*, Maruna compares desistence to the process of stopping smoking. He argues that people decide to stop, but that it often takes several attempts and slippages: "deciding to desist and actually desisting are two very different things."[15] The only way to truly consider if a person has desisted from a life of crime is to look back retrospectively from the end of their lives.

In the pursuit of these aims, the prison management were prepared to take a risk and allow five students into the prison to work with the men in order to devise and perform a piece of children's theatre. After the performance, the residents of the prison and their families were permitted a relaxed visit. As a means of promoting healthy family relationships, the usual formal visiting rules were relaxed and the men could talk to, and play games with, their children and partners in a more open and freer environment than they would usually be allowed. The men themselves were motivated to take part in the project because of the access it gave them to their families in this relaxed visit, and this proved to be a powerful incentive.

Lynda Clarke's research on fathers in prison, compiled in 2005, reveals that many men serving custodial sentences believe that it is not possible to be a father while in prison. This stems from the lack of time spent with their children, the lack of privacy when visits do occur, the lack of familiarity with their children's lives, and the inability to financially support their families.[16]

Hutton's interviews with the participants on the Children's Play Project echoed these findings, with the fathers expressing frustration at not being able to be real "fathers." One interviewee stated:

> you can't even be a dad in prison can ya? You can't have a relationship with nobody while you're in jail. . . . Just visits and that and going down and not being able to move off your chair you can't be a dad, all I can do is speak to her on phone or send her a card . . . so it's not really good being a dad in jail.[17]

Taking part in this project was an opportunity for the fathers to engage with their families in an extended visit. Hutton observes that "the overwhelming feeling was that by having been sent to prison, they had let their children down and failed them as a father."[18] She believes that, in a way, the project allowed them to reaffirm their identities as fathers.

For the prison authorities, the project was a means of addressing their "Families First" program in an attempt to address reoffending rates, and for the participants themselves, the project represented an opportunity to demonstrate their ability to do something for their families. It also allowed them to see their relatives in a more relaxed setting than would usually be permitted. However, there is a tension here between the stakeholders in the project, and I would suggest that this is one often at play in prison theatre projects.

Theatre in Prison—Radical Containment or Pedagogy of Hope?

The foreword to *Doing the Arts Justice* starts with the sentence, "Within the Criminal Justice agenda the arts have a history of being used as a tool to work with offenders to reduce crime and re-offending."[19] In this report, Jenny Hughes asserts that the arts are "associated with positive criminal justice outcomes and can play a part in changing the individual"; she goes on to say that there are weaknesses in the evidence for this impact, both technically and conceptually.[20] Since 2005, numerous reports and evaluations have sought to find evidence of the impact of the arts being used within the criminal justice system. This includes those that assert the arts as being useful in aiding the development of transferable soft skills,[21] in the development of self-esteem and self-confidence,[22] and in contributing to desistance.[23]

This is not the place for a detailed consideration of the potential efficacy of theatre as a tool for transformation or change per se, and there is a good deal of literature on this topic.[24] Maruna, when talking about desistence, claims that the emphasis should not be on the change but rather on the "maintenance of crime-free behaviours in the face of obstacles and frustrations."[25] In other words, both desistence and change are ongoing processes. Citing DiClemente, he argues that "achieving long term personality change can take between seven and ten years."[26] It is therefore unlikely that a two-week drama residency like the Children's Play Project will encourage its participants to reform. More in line with Michael Balfour's search for a "théatre of little changes,"[27] I am optimistic or hopeful that this project might offer the possibility for some reflection that may eventually lead to the consideration of change.

In 2015, I outlined a theory for pedagogy of utopia in which I draw on both bell hooks's and Henry Giroux's definitions of pedagogies of hope.[28] Drawing on this earlier work I am claiming in this chapter that the Children's Play Project might offer a potential "discourse of critique" and is based on a "mobilizing foundation," but that it also goes further and opens up what Paul Ricœur describes as "the field of the possible."[29] The field of the possible is a place where it is possible to re-examine what "is" in order to see what "might be," or what Ricœur calls the "not yet." I suggest that the "not yet" in this instance might be strengthened relationships between the inmates and their children.

This allows me to think of the practice as a "radical intervention," but I am troubled with this project's goals of contributing to desistence. I wonder if this element means that it is offering a form of "radical containment."

It could be suggested that this model demonstrates a form of radical containment aimed at controlling the "transgressive elements in society"—the offenders—in the interest of the "dominant order"—the prison staff and wider society. I am caught somewhere on Knowles's continuum of radical hope and radical containment. This is not a new concern; in 2004, Baz Kershaw asked, "How do the practices of drama and theatre best engage with systems of formalised power to create a space of radical freedom?"[30] In our project, it was obvious that one of the main motivations for taking part was for the men to spend quality time with their children on the visit afterward. The project exploited this desire of the men to see their families in a relaxed setting. The participants were being bribed with the promise of seeing family members; this kept the inmates docile, contained, and self-regulating. Early on in the 2011 version of the project, one of the men participating stated, "I'll do anything for that visit."

In a specific example of how this self-regulation was enacted during the project, I will now describe a set of events that occurred during the 2011 version of the Children's Play Project.

Radical Containment—or Just Plain Violence?

In 2011, as in other years, the participants worked hard during the devising and rehearsal process. They regulated their behavior throughout the intensive process to avoid the threat of being "sacked" and removed from the project. More than this, they also regulated the behavior of their peers. This troubles me, as it is far from Kershaw's outline of a practice of radical freedom that can reach "beyond existing systems of formalised power" and create "currently unimaginable forms of association and action,"[31] and it is actually closer to the territory of radical containment. In fact, it moved the project closer to something reminiscent of Foucauldian panopticons, authoritarian hierarchies, self-regulation, and coercion.

As with every other year, the 2011 Children's Play Project concluded with the relaxed family visit. During this visit, the participants were able to move freely around the performance and audience areas, mingling with each other and their guests. The prison usually provides a buffet tea with sandwiches, cakes, and ice-lollies for the inmates and their families. The afternoon takes on the feel of a family day at a museum or National Trust property, and there is face painting, ball games, ice-cream, and lots of family interaction—all most unusual in the confines of a prison setting. Prison officers are clearly in attendance, but the inmates are under less intense surveillance than is usually evident during visit days. In 2011, the inmates were acutely and accurately aware that this time is potentially dangerous for the security team within the prison. Compared to standard visits, the family visit after the play provides a greater opportunity to smuggle drugs or other contraband into the prison.

As the day of the performance grew nearer, it became evident that they were collectively keen to make sure the day ran smoothly. The annual speech made by Second Shot Productions' director made it clear that any illicit activity would result in the project, and therefore the visit, being canceled. One of the prisoners stated at the end of her speech that there "would be trouble" if anyone attempted to use the project to smuggle illegal drugs into the prison. The inmates all made it clear that they were in agreement, keen to let the director know that they were "all singing from the same hymn sheet." At this point, it was apparent that they were making an agreement to regulate their own behavior and to "police" the performance day themselves. Hutton notes in her evaluation that this was a clear warning to others, and it was evident that these participants did not take a romantic view of their fellow inmates' reasons for taking part in the project. In fact, they believed that some of their fellow performers specifically enrolled in the project as a means to bring banned substances into the prison.

In the postshow interviews, Hutton discovered that there had indeed been a plan to smuggle drugs into the prison during the relaxed visit. One of the participants told her that, rather than report it, he took matters into his own hands. This resulted in one of our cast entering the cell of the intended recipient of the drugs and "giving him a thump" as a warning that he would be subject to a more serious assault if he went through with the plan to use the performance as cover for drug smuggling, thereby jeopardizing the product for everyone else.

The perpetrator of the assault claimed that he deeply regretted his actions, but Hutton notes that he was still adamant that "it was the only way it could have been solved."[32] He also acknowledged that he had hoped at the time of the incident that his actions would act as a deterrent to any others with similar intentions.

This incident is one of many troubling issues regarding how theatre might be perceived as a form of controlling transgressive elements within the prison and creating a docile prison population. As an applied theatre researcher and practitioner, I am uncomfortable with the idea that theatre is being used to encourage inmates to police themselves and to do so violently. I am troubled that this project, which started out with the aims of radical freedom that might transcend repression, oppression, exploitation, and injustice, merely reinforced these qualities.

Pedagogy of Utopia

Ricœur's theory on imagining a utopia is defined in his text *Lectures on Ideology and Utopia*. He suggests that the social imagination allows us to imagine utopian variations on reality. He outlines the way in which creating moments of distanciation from reality allows people to stand outside of their current circumstances and critically appraise the ideological conditions surrounding them.[33] My suggestion is that making theatre creates moments of distanciation that allow participants to appraise their current situations and open up the field of the possible, thus enabling them to imagine alternative ways of living. In the Children's Play Project, the fathers create a play amid a great deal of laughter, and they also talk about their current circumstances and what they anticipate for the future. In these moments, they critique what *is* and plan for what *might be*. Both Ricœur and I consider this the moment where "utopia" may be glimpsed. Ricœur argues that

> the result of reading a utopia is that it puts into question what precisely exists; it makes the actual world seem strange. Usually we are tempted to say that we cannot live in a different way from the way we presently do.[34]

Pedagogy of utopia therefore allows for participants to see the current situation clearly and, at the same time, start questioning it. This may invite them to imagine a new version of reality, or at the very least begin to see that a different way to live is possible. Utopia, therefore, may be triggered by prison inmates as they work on a drama project, creating a piece of children's theatre for their families. While acknowledging the damage a prison sentence does to the parent-child relationship, participating in this project allows incarcerated fathers to tangibly demonstrate that they are serious about parenting by creating something for their children.

As the fathers worked on the project, they were focused on their children. During the two-week rehearsal process, as a group we made invites that featured the characters of the play, and each father sent them in the post to their guests. The men shared stories about the play with their children and partners on the telephone. In workshops, they relived these conversations with the students. They claimed that the play and its progress had become the focus for communication with their families. The children wanted to know what character their dad would play and what costume he would be wearing. The pirate dance sequence, in particular, became a source of amusement with partners being amazed that the men were learning to dance.

Hutton notes in her report that

> what was clear was that for these fathers taking part in the play project was quite literally a labour of love and a way to express their love for their children in a manner that is rare in the prison environment.[35]

The developmental and rehearsal process was not always smooth. The men struggled with their lines and maintaining their focus, and the pirate dance was often a cause of frustration as well as amusement. They found the dance moves and timing difficult. As the day of the performance drew closer, they worked especially hard at getting this bit right. They would arrive at rehearsals in the mornings talking about how they had practiced the "dance number" in their cells and on the wing the previous evening because they wanted to get it right for the children. This became a constant refrain throughout the rehearsal process, and they often told us that they "kept with it because it was for the kids." The inmate who played the chief pirate, "Captain Mack," specifically wanted the role because his six-year-old son was obsessed with pirates. He told his son that he was a pirate but kept it a secret that he was the captain of the pirate band. After the show, he described the moment when his son recognized that his dad was the lead pirate—he told us how his "face just lit up when he realized." In the interviews, this participant said that this was an opportunity to show his family that he was "doing something positive" for them while in prison.

His son's reaction made the hard work worthwhile. These moments, interviews, and anecdotes start to reveal the hope in this work. These were men who were conceiving a vision of their futures and attempting to make changes. I am not making the claim that this short intervention was a catalyst for life change that led to desistence. In the moment, these men were committed to the idea that change was possible and that they could be better fathers to their children. Anderson et al. observe that "arts projects might awaken belief in the participants capacity for or opportunities to change their lives for the better."[36] Maybe this is what was happening with our participants, as it's possible that the project might have awakened a belief that change was possible and that they were in the "field of the possible," and that makes the work utopic for me. I also suggest that working on the project may have raised their expectations and constructively challenged their self-identities, as after the performance they saw themselves as capable people. What kept them focused and rehearsing in both the rehearsal room and the wings at night was the fact they were doing it all for their children. I think these men were exploring the possibility of being there for their children in a way that they previously had not.

Hutton's report focuses on one participant who had served many prison sentences during the previous five years. At the time of the production, his daughter was two, but due to his time in prison, he had only lived with her for twelve weeks of her life. He said in his postshow interview: "I haven't really been a dad, I can't even really class myself as being a dad." He went on to say that the play project was "only a little thing but it feels like I've given something back."

As part of the play process, he started to build a relationship with his daughter and could begin to see a role for himself in her life if he could change his behavior and avoid further prison sentences. Or he could glimpse an imaginative variation of his future. Ricœur states that the intention of the utopia is to change—"to shatter the present order."[37] For me, imaginative variations of the present are at the core of this practice—not *my* imaginative variations, but those of the fathers.

So the work takes another step on the continuum toward representing pedagogy of utopia or at least hope. The participants are grounded by the present opportunity to work toward giving their children something positive and to spend time with them. For a short amount of time, some of that "grounded present" led to positive consequences.

In the postshow interviews, there was some evidence that the play had contributed to positive consequences for some of the participants, with tangible outcomes. Some confessed to not making the changes they had wanted, and one had been released only to reoffend and to be back within the walls of the prison and awaiting trial. Others, however, were looking for other courses and projects to take part in, and one had requested a transfer to a training prison. Two were continuing their work with Second Shot Productions and learning media skills. These few were trying to make long-term changes to their lives.

Does this negate the violent incident? I am not sure. Both participants involved in the violent altercation completed the project. Both had family members in the audience for the relaxed visit, no drugs were smuggled into the prison, and all the men on the stage that day had a glimpse of success. The applause and standing ovations from family and the prison officers were evidence of that. One told Hutton that "surviving" the project allowed him to see "that I can do something with my life and not be a failure," and maybe this moment of success is enough. These "small changes" in self-perception or family relationships are sufficient for me to see the value in this work. But at what cost? And does the end justify the means? I am still troubled and conflicted about that.

CHAPTER 6
"THE ACTORS HAVE ALL THE POWER"
ANGOLA'S *LIFE OF JESUS CHRIST*

Stephanie Gaskill

On a sunny summer afternoon, a middle-aged black man knelt alone in the dirt of a rodeo arena with his hands lifted toward the Louisiana sky. Beating his chest, the man tearfully begged forgiveness for his role in his friend's arrest and execution. Hundreds of people sitting on aluminum bleachers set aside their cokes and hot dogs and leaned forward, giving the man their full attention. This was one of the most dramatic moments in *The Life of Jesus Christ*, a full-length passion play featuring actors serving some of the longest prison sentences in the world. The man in the arena, Levelle Tolliver, who played Judas Iscariot, is one of almost 5,000 Louisianans facing life without any possibility of parole. His fellow cast members hailed from the state's two maximum-security facilities: the Louisiana Correctional Institute for Women (LCIW) and the Louisiana State Penitentiary, better known as Angola. Infamous for its violent history, Angola has become equally renowned for "moral rehabilitation," former warden Burl Cain's particular brand of faith-based reform. Framing himself as a Christian evangelist and progressive reformer, Warden Cain drew religious conservatives and liberals alike to the prison for twenty years (1995–2015).

Because of Cain's fame, *The Life of Jesus Christ* attracted more public attention than most prison theatre productions. Though most of its members were incarcerated, the audience included outside visitors, and publicity surrounding the play suggested it was their presence that mattered most. Cain framed *The Life of Jesus Christ* as an opportunity for the public to see that moral rehabilitation can transform "lawbreakers" into "law-abiding citizens." Like other prison productions, this passion play can imply that recognition of incarcerated people's humanity is contingent on their admission of past wrongs and adherence to prevailing norms and values.[1] Outside observers are in a privileged position to evaluate actors' contrition and transformation. Yet actors in *The Life of Jesus Christ* also framed themselves as evangelists to an audience of sinners and reinterpreted the biblical story as part of a broader social critique of the racial prejudice and systemic inequalities endemic in the criminal justice system. And, ultimately, the play forged a sense of solidarity among incarcerated people for purposes beyond appealing to public benevolence.

Background and Context

Written by Scottish playwright Peter Hutley, *The Life of Jesus Christ* came to Angola via Cathy Fontenot, then an assistant warden at Angola. Fontenot had seen the performance in Scotland at the estate of Sir Jack Stewart-Clark, whose grounds reminded her of Angola's green fields. She believed the prison would be a perfect venue to mount a similar production. The warden called on Gary Tyler, the longtime president of Angola's Drama Club, to direct the play, with the help of Suzanne Lofthus, the head of the Scottish production company that staged the performance at Stewart-Clark's castle. The warden at LCIW allowed incarcerated women to play female characters in the production. Sets and costumes were all created on-site at either Angola or LCIW. Men constructed helmets and shields out of repurposed football gear and garbage cans in Angola's hobby shop; women sewed costumes in LCIW's garment factory. Actors prepared for their roles by researching biblical history and watching Jesus films, including *Jesus of Nazareth* and *The Passion of the Christ*.[2]

Initially, *The Life of Jesus Christ* was to be a promenade play; audiences would follow actors throughout the prison grounds as they reenacted scenes in different locations around Angola. But the administration decided that a stationary performance at Angola's multipurpose arena would be more convenient. The Louisiana Prison Chapel Foundation sold tickets for the Inmate Welfare Fund to pay for programming. The play was mounted three times: May 2012, March 2013, and November 2013. In addition to the several thousand visitors who saw it in-person, the play received broader attention through national media coverage and a feature documentary, *Cast the First Stone*.[3]

The Life of Jesus Christ was reminiscent of both a baseball game and a church service. There were moments of intense action interspersed among long lulls. The smell of hot dogs and nachos wafted over the arena as audience members ferried back and forth between the concession stand and the bleachers. People snapped action shots with their smart phones and cheered and shouted in response to the action in the arena. Yet audiences also reacted as though they were listening to good Sunday preaching. Women waved their hands in the air in praise. Men shouted "Amen!" when Jesus recited a familiar verse. At times, it seemed that the only reminder they were not in church was the constant beeping and buzzing of guards' walkie-talkies. In short, *The Life of Jesus Christ* was both reverent and raucous.

The Life of Jesus Christ as a Showcase for Moral Rehabilitation

But not too raucous. *The Life of Jesus Christ* was supposed to be an opportunity for the public to see that incarcerated people were no longer unruly. Outside visitors sitting in the middle section of the bleachers were flanked by two sections of incarcerated people. Those facing stage left were trustys, who had earned special privileges by avoiding disciplinary write-ups. Those facing stage right had not yet achieved this status. There was also a small contingent of women from LCIW who usually sat in a clearly demarcated section among the non-incarcerated audience. In addition to the men and women acting in the play, the incarcerated people in the stands were being watched and evaluated by other spectators. Cain meant for their conduct to reflect well upon his program of moral rehabilitation. During the intermission of one performance in November 2013, he gestured toward the two sections of incarcerated people and proudly declared, "This is moral rehabilitation. Sitting here respectful, quiet, watching *The Life of Christ*." He suggested that watching a specifically Christian play is in itself moral rehabilitation and that "respectful" demeanor during such a performance was evidence of moral rehabilitation.

A White couple I met during intermission of the first performance in March 2013 suggested that Christianity and control were foremost in their minds as well. Traveling from Baton Rouge to see the play, Bill and Linda were sitting with about twenty other senior citizens from their Baptist church. They proudly informed me about the New Orleans Baptist Theological Seminary's satellite campus inside Angola and credited Warden Cain for the peace inside the prison. They appreciated that Cain had succeeded in both "giving prisoners spiritual upbringing" and keeping them "under control." Their attendance at the play was a Christian duty and support for sound penal policy.

The very presence of women in the play was also presented as evidence of self-control achieved through moral rehabilitation. Officials feared that men might take advantage of the opportunity to engage in sexual relationships with women, regardless of the consequences. Longtime Angola Drama Club member Bobby Wallace, who played the role of Jesus, recalls explaining to his fellow male castmates that such behavior would not only lead to punishment but also jeopardize the future of the play. *The Life of Jesus Christ* was supposed to prove that incarcerated men and women could perform together without succumbing to sexual temptation.

Acting out Rehabilitation

But *The Life of Jesus Christ* was not just evidence of reform: it was the method as well. Practitioners and scholars of theatre programs in prison often characterize dramatic performance as a form of individual rehabilitation. Incarcerated actors identify with their characters, helping them to think, feel, and act differently.[4] In his remarks to the cast before the first performance, Cain echoed this sentiment, insisting that incarcerated actors must have changed if they were depicting a biblical story.[5] They could not depict Christ and be un-Christ-like. Moreover, Cain suggested that their performances would have a "profound effect" on actors' lives offstage, making them "better people" who can better influence others inside and outside the prison.

Women in particular affirmed Cain's point. Sandra Starr, an African American woman who is serving a life sentence for murder at LCIW, plays Mary Magdalene, a woman caught in adultery and brought before Jesus for judgment. For Starr, learning about Mary in preparation for the play was "like looking in a mirror, seeing my own self." She describes how a long history of abuse ultimately led her to shoot and kill her boyfriend. She imagines Mary also felt starved of love, seeking affection in a manner for which she is condemned by society until finally found real love from Jesus. By playing Mary, Starr hoped she, "could find that connection and make that change, in her, but for me."[6] Starr was reliving her own experiences as she embodied Mary's life, expecting she would find the same love and self-worth Mary found in Jesus. In turn, she hoped that her change will be communicated to audiences.

Incarcerated Actors as Empowered Evangelists

Starr's framing of her performance suggested that the power of interpretation lies with the public audience, appealing to mainstream understandings of reform and redemption. However, incarcerated actors also assert understandings of the play and its purpose beyond a showcase for their own rehabilitation. "The play is just the stories in the Bible," Levelle Tolliver says. "But the actors have all the power."[7] Without actors embodying the biblical characters, expressing their feelings through their spoken words and actions, the "stories in the Bible" would not have the same emotional impact on audiences.

Many of the actors in the play are Christians themselves and see the performance as an opportunity to evangelize. Rontrell Wise, who plays the archangel Gabriel, prayed God would use him to spread the gospel to everyone, including his family and friends.[8] Cindy Anderson, serving a life sentence at LCIW, had both grand and humble expectations, expressing certainty that "the whole world" would learn about the play and hope that her father would be "saved" as a result of the performance.[9] Bobby Wallace, a graduate of Angola's Bible College, said he took on the role of Jesus in part because he is a Christian hoping to confront unbelieving onlookers with a choice to acknowledge or dismiss Christ's sacrifice.[10]

Indeed, some of those involved with the play suggest the gospel message is especially meaningful when portrayed by incarcerated people. Analyzing the play for LCIW's *Walk Talk*, Gail Willars wrote that "Jesus consistently reveal[s] himself to those of us deemed lost or unredeemable," making "outcasts and the criminals [into] messengers of God." Willars maintained that it is those who are rejected by society who understand his story the best, to the point that Jesus does not reveal himself "to the rest of the world."[11]

This interpretation is dramatized in the feeding of the five thousand. Shortly before intermission, Jesus feeds a large crowd, miraculously multiplying five loaves and two fish to feed the people gathered to hear his teachings. (Stage hands pass the bread through a small hole in the ground to actors who block the audience's view.) With their baskets full of bread, Jesus's disciples and followers run into the metal bleachers, murmuring, "The bread of life," as they distribute chunks of bread to both incarcerated people and visitors.

Audiences respond enthusiastically to this scene. I once saw a guard from Angola, a middle-aged African American woman, hold her bread in the air and exclaim, "Thank you, Jesus!" Similarly, Frances Morrison, a self-identified Baptist who brought her grandchildren to the play, told me this was her favorite part. "My grandkids were recipients of the bread," she said, "and it made it so special to them. It brought the miracle to life."[12] Many in the audience react as if the actors facilitated an actual miracle. "Free people" are no longer morally superior to people in prison. Rather, incarcerated people are purveyors of Christ's miraculous power; the audience depends on them to receive a divine blessing from God.

Rehabilitation as a Social Message

Despite this evangelistic bent, the play's cast includes people from a variety of non-Christian religious traditions, each with their own interpretations of the performance material. Gary Tyler encouraged his actors to set aside their disparate motivations and focus on their common purpose in depicting the life of Christ. Serey Kong, who plays the Virgin Mary, is a Buddhist. Though she is disillusioned by Christians' failure to practice what they preach, Kong thinks, "Jesus' message is the bomb as far as not judging people."[13] Levelle Tolliver, who plays Judas, is a devout Muslim, as is Elton Thomas, who plays the Disciple Thomas. Both Tolliver and Thomas emphasized Muslims' reverence for Jesus, as well as the universality of his message of peace and forgiveness.[14]

It is this broader theme of redemption that helped Tyler overcome many Drama Club members' initial reluctance to participate in a production that was introduced by prison officials. He convinced his actors that the play would promote unity within the prison population and demonstrate to a public audience how they have changed. He saw it as his responsibility to help each of his actors "become a better person." Though he does not consider himself a Christian, he believes that Jesus was a model of "greatness" that people can follow to make themselves "better men."[15]

Tyler also believes that the play's message is about "forgiveness and redemption." But his emphasis here is not on what incarcerated people do to merit forgiveness. "When you find it in your heart to forgive someone," he says, "you can remember sometime in your life when you did something that you wanted to be forgiven for."[16] Here forgiveness and redemption are contingent upon audience members' recognition of their own failures, not those of people in prison. Incarcerated people are not proving that they are worthy of forgiveness because they are striving to be like people in the audience. Rather, people in the audience are compelled to offer forgiveness because they and their loved ones are already like people who are in prison: in need of forgiveness. Ultimately, Tyler maintains that the main purpose of the Drama Club "is to enlarge life in general by putting it on stage."[17] In *The Life of Jesus Christ*, he is "enlarging" audiences' sense of what rehabilitation means rather than simply affirming their standards.

Angola's Drama Club: *The Life of Jesus Christ* in Context

In many ways, Tyler is a strange choice to direct a play about Jesus, and Angola's Drama Club seems an unusual vehicle for promoting moral rehabilitation. Again, while he considers himself to be spiritual, Tyler bluntly states that he is not a religious person and his organization is more well-known for "secular" plays.[18] However, since its inception in 1975, the Drama Club has frequently focused on themes of forgiveness and redemption. In 1989, Drama Club members Michael Walden and Early Laverne performed Walden's play, "Ultimate Mercy," which portrayed frustrations with the pardon board, namely its failure to recognize and reward individuals' efforts toward rehabilitation.[19] In 1993, Percy Tate starred in a one-act play entitled, "Concerned Parent and Child Abuser," in which a man relives and regrets the rage that led him to beat his daughter and end up in prison. Kim Cobb of the *Houston Chronicle* described the organization's repertoire best: "These are clear morality tales with heavy lessons in personal responsibility and the destructiveness of anger."[20]

Beginning in the early 1990s, when Tyler became president of the organization, the Drama Club also began cooperating with religious groups inside and outside Angola. Once, actors dramatized the martyrdom of Stephen and Paul's encounter with Christ on the road to Damascus. In 1990, the Drama Club put on a play to accompany a sermon entitled "The Black Prodigal Father," delivered by Pastor Pate of Church Point Ministries, an African American church in Baton Rouge. "Not only is the drama emphasized," Tyler said of the religious-themed play, "but the social message is of paramount importance."[21] Thus the Drama Club has a history of combining religious content and social commentary.

"Cast the First Stone"

Perhaps the clearest representation of this combination is the scene depicting Jesus's ministry is his initial interaction with Mary Magdalene (Sandra Starr). Audiences first encounter her when Jesus is teaching a crowd of people. Mary/Starr stands on the outskirts of the group in a long, flowing, bright pink dress with bold jewelry that makes her stand out from the others in their muted-color, unornamented tunics and robes. She flirts brazenly with a soldier, suggestively stroking his chest, whispering in his ear, and batting her eyes at him. Suddenly, a group of men seize her and roughly bind her hands together, throwing her down before Jesus, accusing her of adultery, and demanding that Jesus decide her fate. The crowd of men and women around him shout and jeer, picking up rocks to stone her as she weeps. Jesus sits down and begins writing in the sand, finally retorting, "If any one of you is without sin, then let them be the first to throw a stone at her." Though one man picks up a stone, the others hold him back. One by one, all her accusers slowly file away. Jesus turns to the woman, concluding that as no one has remained to mete out punishment against her, he will not do so either.

Though brief, this scene inspired the title of the documentary about the play (*Cast the First Stone*) and proved to be a crowd favorite. Audiences burst into applause and cheer as Jesus embraced the woman and told her to "go and sin no more." Georgia, an elderly black woman I interviewed during intermission at a March 2013 performance, singled this out as her favorite scene. "They had to think about how they had sinned too and couldn't go through with the plan," she said. Many members of the audience echoed her sympathy for Mary Magdalene. During the 2012 production, a female guard sitting behind me loudly voiced her disapproval when one of the Pharisees suggested that Mary should be stoned to death. Similarly, there was wild applause and cries of "Hallelujah!" when Jesus shamed the crowd and dismissed Mary without condemning her. For the audience, the power of this scene lies in the fact that Jesus not only forgives Mary but also reminds the crowds of their own sins, implicitly rebuking them for their hypocrisy.

Gail Willars, the reporter from LCIW, suggested this scene should lessen the public's appetite for vengeance, insisting society should follow the example of Jesus rather than the crowd.[22] Similarly, Suzanne Lofthus, who flew in from Scotland to help direct the play, said that after discussions with incarcerated people involved in the production, she hoped that audience members might reflect on how this scene applied to their own relationship with people in prison.[23] Jesus's reaction to Mary Magdalene and the crowds eager to stone her reminded everyone that "Jesus' teaching says I'm exactly the same as that person down there."[24] Maintaining that all are sinners in the eyes of God, Lofthus implied that audience members should consider whether they are any less deserving of punishment.

The Shepherds and the Crowds: Political Context and Communal Redemption

While her story challenges audiences to recognize their own faults, Mary Magdalene still represents traditional understandings of individualized sin and redemption. But *The Life of Jesus Christ* also presents scenes that assert the importance of communal liberation. One of the most memorable scenes of the play occurs when an angel announces the birth of Jesus to a group of shepherds. The shepherds are warming themselves around a small fire near the audience, when one begins a bitter monologue about shepherds' wretched circumstances. Another catalogs the oppressors to which he and his people have been subject: Assyrians, Greeks, and finally, Romans. They agree that they need a messiah to "kill all these Romans" and united their people again. The actors crescendo through this conclusion, shouting in unison and pumping their staffs in the air. But almost immediately, the angel appears to proclaim the birth of Jesus, and all the shepherds fall on their faces in reverence.

Here, the incarcerated actors playing shepherds in Angola's *The Life of Jesus Christ* enact their own contemporary social conditions as well as those of the characters in the story. Reflecting the disproportionate incarceration of African Americans, the group of shepherds usually consisted entirely of black men and women. The actors' description of their oppressors in their roles as Judean shepherds resonates with the discrimination and inequalities they have faced as both African Americans and incarcerated people. But what is most striking is the way that actors embody the shepherds in this scene. They fall down to their knees with their heads bowed in deference and submission when the angel appears. Yet for a significant portion of the scene, their bodily postures convey open defiance and intense anger. For a moment, these actors are able to physically express the frustration and rage of racial discrimination and incarceration.

Moreover, in later performances, the shepherds indirectly implicated the audience in their suffering. Whenever a shepherd referred to "the Romans," he would deliberately point toward those of us sitting in the "free people" section. When the shepherds called for a leader to "kill all these Romans," they gestured with their arms and bodies toward us as well. Though the shepherds' anger was quelled by the appearance of the angel, this simple shift in body language conflated audience members with Romans, identifying both groups as oppressors who were worthy of potentially violent retaliation from the people they marginalized.

Here, the focus shifts from individual redemption to communal liberation. In neither case is the people's anger and sense of injustice condemned. There are few visible or audible reactions at these points in the performance, but some do indicate that they take to heart the implied accusation of the shepherds. Anne Bucey, who attends an Episcopal church in Baton Rouge, reflected upon the fact that people incarcerated at Angola are "mostly black and poor" and are likely in prison "because they lack the cultural and financial capital that other people in our country have."[25] Similarly, Cindy Dunlop, who flew from England to attend the performance, maintained that after seeing the play, she was more and more convinced "that if the attention given to locking these men up had been given to directing their lives at an early stage, they could have been productive members of society."[26] Some audience members, at least, read the play through a lens of institutional racism and systemic societal neglect.

"It Wasn't About the Outside World"

Nevertheless, for actors, even communicating this radical social message to an audience was not the primary purpose of *The Life of Jesus Christ*. Bobby Wallace recalls that after he played Jesus for the first time, God asked him why he thought the play had been a success. Initially, Wallace replied the performance was an opportunity to "show the world a different perspective on people who are incarcerated whom they deem to be worthless." But God had something else in mind. God reminded Wallace of all the people he had met and impressed over his decades of athletic and educational pursuits in prison. They all wanted to come see their friend play Jesus. "When you got out there," God told him, "nobody called you Bobby. They called you Jesus." Wallace's performance was an opportunity for them to witness one of their own transcend his incarceration, not only displaying his talents but embodying a position of reverence. "So, it wasn't about the outside world," God told Wallace. "It was about what was happening inside."[27]

Indeed, Wallace's preparation for the performance affected the prison population in ways the audience never witnessed. In 2011, shortly before the play was supposed to open, the Mississippi River, which surrounds Angola on three sides, began to flood. All incarcerated people were required to build walls of sand bags to prevent the prison from being inundated. Because he had grown out his hair and beard for his role, Bobby was clearly recognizable as the man who was going to play Jesus. Several men mocked him, jeering, "Look, they've got Jesus in the field; they don't care nothing about Jesus." Wallace grew frustrated and was tempted to quit working. But he continued because, playing the role of Christ, he felt he had to hold himself to a higher standard. "I did not want to cause people to stumble," he remembers.[28] He even chose to stay in the fields when one of the guards gave him an opportunity to leave. "I'm with my people," he replied, and turned away. The other men in the fields rushed toward him, incredulous that he would choose to continue working in the sweltering heat. "Y'all are my people," Bobby reiterated. "You letting that Jesus role get to you," they told him. He insisted that though he wanted to leave, he felt compelled to suffer with them instead, as Jesus would have done.[29] Here, Wallace's portrayal of Jesus cemented his connections within the prison community rather than serving as a bridge to the outside world. The play was meaningful because it forged a sense of solidarity inside of Angola as much as it impacted people beyond the gates.

Conclusion

"Now you may go to your homes. But remember what you have seen and what you have heard. And may God be with you." In these final lines of *The Life of Jesus Christ*, Luke, the gospel writer and narrator of the play, released audience members but enjoined them to *remember*. Yet no one could control how people would remember, what they would take away from the play. After the final performance in November 2013, I walked behind an older African American man who walked with a group of younger children. Wearing a faded blue baseball cap whose adjustable strap read, "I ♥ Jesus," the man waved to a line of men in denim uniforms returning to their camps under armed guard after seeing the performance. Then he warned the children: "Don't ever do anything that would bring you here." One of the boys remarked that most people in Angola were serving life. Considering the seriousness of such sentences, the man shook his head meditatively as he exited the stadium to the parking lot.

Yet the play motivated some to do more than lament Louisiana's long sentences. During the 2016 regular session of the state legislature, Bobby Wallace reprised his role as Jesus during a Senate committee hearing on a bill that would have extended parole eligibility to lifers. After his release on parole in 2013, he remembered those he left behind. He presented his own transformation during *The Life of Jesus Christ* as proof of the possibility of rehabilitation. "I really humbled myself, and I gave my heart over to Jesus," he told senators. But his transformation through his performance as Jesus also imbued him with moral authority to advocate for reform. "I'm feeling like I'm back in this role again," he said, "because you're Pilate." Like Pilate, they had to choose whether they would grant mercy to men like himself.

Pilate initially made the right decision by releasing Jesus, but he eventually succumbed to popular demands, washing his hands of responsibility for Jesus's fate and allowing him to be crucified. "Don't wash your hands," Wallace warned the senators. "Give mercy. Do what's right in your hearts."

The Life of Jesus Christ attempted to present people in prison conforming to prevailing religious values and social norms, but also privileged incarcerated people's perspectives on the life of Jesus, interrogated deeply ingrained racial prejudices, and confronted audiences with racial injustice inherent in the criminal justice system. Individuals interpret incarcerated actors' performances as proof of Cain's administrative control, but also as evidence of structural inequalities inherent in American prisons and society more broadly. And ultimately, the play proved to be a transformative experience that fostered a sense of solidarity among incarcerated people and motivated actors to advocate for their own upon their release.

CHAPTER 7
CITIZENS THEATRE, SCOTLAND, FACILITATES CHANGES IN LIFE DIRECTIONS THROUGH CREATIVE ARTS MEDIUMS

Neil Packham and Elly Goodman

We—Neil Packham and Elly Goodman from the internationally renowned Citizens Theatre, Scotland—have over twenty-eight years' experience working in community arts, including theatre projects with people facing the challenges of addictions, recovery, homelessness, mental health, people seeking asylum, refugees as well as those serving sentences in prison. This chapter provides an insight into the Citizens Theatre's creative residency in Her Majesty's Prison Barlinnie, Glasgow, which is Scotland's oldest, largest, and most notorious prison.

This is a personal account of our experience from meeting the prisoners for the first time, exploring the journey of the rehearsal process and investigating the power of performance. We look at the practical challenges involved during the making of a piece of theatre within a prison and the effect it has on the individual and the wider establishment. This chapter will focus on how our artistic intervention has generated positive change and personal development within the incarcerated community. It will also explore the continuing relationship they have with the Citizens Theatre upon their subsequent release.

Why Theatre in Prison?

Theatre can be created almost anywhere, and why should prison be an exception? Aren't prisons supposed to be about punishments in an environment surrounded by constraints? We believe that the rudiments and disciplines of theatre making unlock creativity and celebrate the potential of positive change.

When we start a new performance project, there is always sense of venturing into the unknown; meeting any new group for the first time, you wonder how many people will be attracted to a theatre project in the first place. Did the information get passed around all the halls? How many people have seen it? Will they commit to the duration of the project? Or will other factors, such as release or transfer, get in the way? Will the allure of a work party, such as the carpenters, kitchens, or hairdressers, which is known to have a better prison wage incentive, entice them away? What will the working space be like? Which prison staff will be supporting us? What will the dynamic of the group be like?

At the beginning, I was unsure if I could see it through. After session one, I knew that I could enjoy it. Lots of support, encouragement from tutors, was very good. I had never been on stage before, so now I have another life experience.

When working in prison, you have to learn to navigate everything such as adhering to important security procedures, agreeing on dedicated staff, and procuring an appropriate space in which to work. Technical equipment, props, and costumes must be checked and verified. We remember observing the security gate staff's bemused expressions as three large, stuffed sheep and a toy goat passed through the X-ray machine at reception. The absurdity of this moment encouraged conversations that wouldn't normally happen and assisted our visibility within the establishment.

Building the Group

Over the years of our residency, the promotion of our work has been a major consideration. We have had to think of inventive and appealing ways to communicate with 1,500 men over the six halls of the prison. It is crucial in this busy and fluctuating environment that even at times when we are not there physically, that our presence is known within Barlinnie's walls.

In our quest to promote the Citizens Theatre projects, we have created posters, programs, brochures; recorded albums; filmed productions; held interviews with *Barbed Wireless* (the prison radio station); and visited individuals in their prison cells. However, our most successful promotional tool was a replica train ticket detailing information for the *Platform 2:10* performance project. Each train ticket was then slipped under cell doors. This yielded the most positive results; it aroused curiosity, given that a train ticket is neither seen nor required within a prison. This advertising campaign attracted a large cast of men who were interested in taking part.

Platform 2:10—A Large-Scale Production

In 2010, we were invited to be part of a nationwide project *Inspiring Change,* funded by Creative Scotland (Scotland's national arts funder). It was a partnership between New College Lanarkshire and eight national Scottish arts organizations.

Platform 2:10, the Citizens Theatre's most ambitious prison project to date, led sixty-five prisoners over a five-month period to produce this original play. The men worked alongside industry professionals in set design, playwriting, set construction, acting, song writing, producing live music, rigging and operating lighting, sound engineering, and stage management. They also recorded an album of the music, *Songs from the Heart.* This groundbreaking project was an opportunity to explore and interrogate the potential of coordinated, high-quality arts intervention. It had three main aims; to stimulate prisoners' engagement with the Learning Centre, to improve literacy skills, and to demonstrate the potential of the arts to support in the process of rehabilitation.

A participant interviewed in a focus group as part of an academic case study described the opening scene of *Platform 2:10*:

ALEC

> I think it was a good idea. I don't know initially where they got the idea for the project, you know? A prisoner stands alone on a platform waiting for a train.

INTERVIEWER

> And he has a decision to make.

ALEC

> Aye. You know because we get libbed [released]. You know, we've all got a date for getting out. . . . Well, we're going to have to make that decision. Because we've all got family and friends.

INTERVIEWER

> That specific decision.

ALEC

> Oh, aye, every single one of us will have to make that decision of whether we go to the licensed grocer or whether to get the bus straight home. Every single one of us is going to make that choice. Because every single one of us has been locked up for some time.

It appears clear that even this single vulnerable moment prompted an opportunity for greater reflection about a prisoner's decision-making. It also offered the potential to reflect on his offending behavior and the impact imprisonment had on his family. Approximately forty men a day are released from Barlinnie, so arriving at this crossroads is a regular occurrence.

During the early stages of the rehearsal process, in a noisy and distracted room, with a group yet to bond and clearly struggling to grasp what we were aiming to achieve. A young member of the cast started singing the first lines of Pink Floyd's "Wish You Were Here." The prison officer playing a station guard said the first line, and the two of them continued with the opening scene. There was complete silence in the room, total attention turned to the actors until the moment they completed the dialogue. Everyone stood up and applauded, while the actors humbly sat back down. From that moment on this cast member's belief in the project grew. This was an important moment because this young man had clearly made a commitment to the production having made the effort by learning the first two pages of dialogue the night before in his cell, coupled with the fact that a prison officer had put himself forward to take part as a fellow cast member.

Not According to Plan

Everyday can provide an unpredictable challenge, and on one occasion there had been an incident where Ryan, a cast member and talented rap artist, had to be removed from the room by force. There had been an altercation with a fellow prisoner, which was escalating. Prison officers within the room assessed the potential danger and called for backup. Though we logically understood why Ryan was extricated from the rehearsal room, it was disturbing to witness and a massive loss to us and, more importantly, to him. The next day it was clear that he was not going to be allowed to return to the project. This was a significant opportunity for a young man, who had contributed so much to the production to date and been given an opportunity to demonstrate his unique talent and possibly, for once in his life, to complete a positive journey. After much negotiation, we were able to film his rap so that his contribution could at least be seen and heard in the production. We did not lose a great moment in the show, but more importantly, he did not feel his efforts were wasted or that he had completely failed yet again. Despite all the negativity that exists around this young man's life, he undoubtedly possesses an incredible talent, which sadly appears to thrive more successfully in a prison community than on the outside. Due to his multiple and long-term offending behavior, the prison is his stage and the inmates his audience.

Our advice to anyone undertaking an arts project in a prison is get to know as many members of the prison team as possible, both management and the officers. They must feel valued and have an investment in the project. The power of this can never be underestimated. The majority of the prison officers understood and were supportive of the men, impressed by their ambition. Others struggled to acknowledge the profound impact it had on the men involved and perhaps (understandably) felt that it challenged their security routine. Despite the endless bureaucracy and anxiety, the production was a success. There were many emotional and rewarding moments: family members witnessing their partners and sons achieve something positive, the surprise of the standing ovation they received from their fellow prisoners, the tears of disbelief and relief from the cast that they had achieved the impossible.

A result of *Inspiring Change* was the continuation of the Arts and Criminal Justice Fund from Creative Scotland. It had been recognized through the analysis of the project that what was called for was the establishment of a consistent three-year service of drama provision within the Learning Centre. Along with the positive personal impact on prisoners, it proved itself as an alternative method to drawing people who would not normally attend into education.

Three-Year Creative Residency

The application for our three-year creative residency was successful, and we began the next chapter of our work in Barlinnie Prison. It was important that our residency complemented the existing learning provision. The program's guiding principle as with *Inspiring Change* would be that it would use drama workshops to engage and support prisoners in a creative approach to learning. Many prisoners have negative experiences of formal education. We wanted the project to provide new outlooks and alternative approaches to acquiring skills, while requiring a level of personal reflection.

The residency was divided into specific projects throughout each year. This included acting courses, creative writing and spoken-word performance projects, playwriting courses, a design and scenic painting project, and three theatre productions devised and performed by the men. Each component enabled participants to explore their creativity through a range of techniques including improvisations, script work, writing, song writing, music, and performance skills. Literacy and vocabulary were expanded; story structures developed; scripts and songs penned. The men took creative risks, and as they progressed through the duration of the project, they grew in confidence, enabling them to take the brave step of performing in front of friends, family, and their fellow prisoners from across the establishment.

We have collaborated with a number of highly respected industry professionals who make up a vital component of the team, in particular, Rikki Traynor, a digital sound artist who makes the possibility of sound design accessible and encourages the men to explore its potential. Rikki works closely with the group to create a soundscape that supports each performance piece. This is a useful device for people who are interested in this medium and offers an alternative to our sessions. Another crucial member of our team is Wendy Miller, who is a creative writing tutor, working for the Learning Centre within the prison. She has partnered with our team for a number of years, provided a crucial link, and is an important contact between the prison establishment, the Learning Centre, and the Citizens Theatre.

The Barlinnie Arts Festival

During the first year of our residency, we became aware of the extent of creative activity taking place in the prison and not just with us. We weighed the possibility of an arts festival within the establishment and discussed it with other artists and senior prison management. It was decided that the creative work within the prison would be drawn together to create the first Barlinnie Arts Festival. In November 2013, an entire week was dedicated to this, with a packed program of live music, film, visual art, standup comedy, poetry, and theatre. This was the ultimate endorsement from the governor/ warden and his recognition of the potential power of the arts in the criminal justice system. The governor/warden hosted a dinner for the Scottish Prison Arts Network delegates and Scottish Prison Service senior staff on the final day of the festival. We were aware that this had been a particularly stressful period for the prison staff. There was an audible intake of breath when the governor/warden in his closing speech announced, "After the success of this week-long festival, next year it should be two weeks long!" His pro-arts enthusiasm challenged some of his security staff, yet for us, it was a welcome and progressive outlook, one on which we would continue to capitalize while he remained Governor/Warden.

Keith's Story

The following year the performance project *Back of the Bus* marked an important milestone in our history of working in Barlinnie. We were devising and rehearsing in the recreation room of the wing known as A Hall. This is inhabited in the evenings by prisoners and houses six full-sized snooker tables and two table tennis tables. Prison officers observe the prisoners' activities from a raised platform. With space at a premium in the establishment, we had to make this work for our needs, even though it was not really fit for theatre rehearsal purposes.

On day one, we were met with new faces along with a couple of familiar ones from past projects. This can work in our favor or against us, as new recruits watch one another's behavior and take stock of the attitude in the group. The familiar faces reassure the group that the experience will be a good one, and they extol the virtues of the previous process. However, there is a slight danger of cliques forming as people feel comfortable and part of a clan based on the experiences that they shared together. This catapults previous participants instantly into a higher status position in the room, as they are comfortable with our style and know what to expect. This is not always useful when you are trying to create a new dynamic and want to resist spending too much time reminiscing on the success of the last project. A full evaluation happens at the end of each project in order to encourage the group to reflect on their experiences and explore the possibilities of how they might continue to engage with the arts while in prison and post release.

Our process always starts with activities that encourage the group to work as a team. This can be through short, playful physical theatre exercises that elicit a sense of competition while nurturing the importance of team work. We use a number of techniques that work this way, motivating the group to become enthusiastic about the way we use language so that they can create their own material, learn to edit, and work toward the art of making theatre. Dialogue is so much easier to memorize when it is scripted using your own words. We encourage the men to develop text and scenes that are influenced by their own experiences. However, we endeavor to expand their view of themselves and not be defined by their crimes.

At the time of developing this production, we had worked with a man called Keith, on a number of theatre and spoken-word performance projects. Keith was in his early twenties and, even at this young age, had been in prison multiple times. At the time, he was incarcerated with his younger brother and both had a natural aptitude for writing and performance. They would regularly encourage one another in their creative work and both thrived off the group, capitalizing on the playful nature of the workshop and rarely missing a session. Keith and his brother were confident, witty, and sharp, which quickly earned them credibility within the group. Keith was a very good storyteller and had painted a picture of his misspent youth, describing the deprived and rough suburb of Glasgow where he had grown up and the characters with whom he hung about.

Keith invited us to look through the window into his world. His story began to take shape and he gave it the title *Front Seat Fools, Back Seat Cools*. This was a significant point. We realized, despite our vastly differing backgrounds, that we had all come across the same equivalent characters in our former years. As Keith shared his story, we realized as a group that we could all relate to the themes of his world. This in turn gave us the vehicle to add our own stories that worked under the creative narrative of bus journeys and where they took us, physically and emotionally. Keith's story inspired the play *Back of the Bus*, which included everyone's creative contributions. Songs were written by group members, which were created at one of the snooker tables. Momentum gathered, and the group gained confidence in the material as it developed into a play. During the rehearsal process, the group had morphed and changed, with some men coming to the end of their sentences and subsequently being liberated. This included Keith, who had left his creative mark on the process yet was not there to see its completion. We reconnected with him at the Scottish Prison Arts Network event after he was released, where he spoke in public about the effects the arts had on his life.

John's Story

At the time, there were key individuals in the cast, who we did not know were going to play a further significant role in our working life at the Citizens Theatre. During the Barlinnie three-year creative residency, John had taken part in ten out of our eleven theatre projects. He had been liberated and reconvicted with great regularity having been in and out of prison for the past fifteen years. His crimes had been connected to issues with anger, sectarian and racial violence. John had attended the necessary relationship and anger management courses in prison; nothing seemed to be working for him. The prison system was familiar territory; it appeared, similar to Keith's story, not a deterrent. He hadn't found the incentive to break the cycle of offending behavior.

On first meeting, John was not someone who you might think would be attracted to the arts. He was a man of few words, although he appeared interested, he had a quiet air about him and was not easy to read. It was hard to believe that several Citizens Theatre projects later, he would be willing to play a female role within a show. There was nothing remotely feminine about John. However, embracing the notion of putting a wig on and taking part in the playfulness of the role was a crucial element to his journey of change. There were glimmers of the changes he was implementing in his life. His thinking was developing in an open and more positive direction.

This has been captured in a poem he wrote about the core issues linked to his violent behavior. Being able to make sense of his world through poetry and creative writing enabled him to express his feelings and finally address the problems and the hopelessness of his situation.

"Burden of the Sash" was included as a foreword in Martin Travers's play about sectarianism entitled *Scarfed for Life* published by Methuen Drama in 2013:

> Back for a religious breach
>
> I can't preach
>
> Flag waving, bigotry chants
>
> Sash wearing I wasn't caring,
>
> I'm on a bigotry journey
>
> I'm guilty and ashamed
>
> People still shiver

At the mention of my name

I can't get out, I'm in pain

I'm trapped in a life I don't want

I can't escape 'cause I'm too deep in the game

A night in the cells, bars as my only guide

Finger prints, photos, the charge Barcode,

On a shuttle bus to the court

I wish I could abort

This place is like a fort,

Sentenced for my crime

As time goes by tick, ticking away, I've had enough today.

Buckfast[1] has sent me to Alcatraz

The journey to Bar-Hell

I'm achieving in jail

Now I can get space to myself

That's my journey that I regret

There's no excuse for sectarian abuse[2]

To have his poem acknowledged in print was a pivotal moment in John's recovery. This had contributed to his journey out of the cycle of repeat offending. He had realized that he was being taken seriously, and he was being listened to for the first time. John was released and has not returned to prison to date. He informs us that this is the longest period that he has remained back in the community without reoffending. He attributes his positive change to his involvement with the Citizens Theatre, stating that from his perspective:

It was the only thing that worked. I first got involved with the Citizens Theatre when I was in Barlinnie Prison. The sessions were very relaxed, fun and encouraging. As the weeks went on, mine and the rest of the group's confidence began to grow. After we had written and performed our own play, we were all so proud of ourselves. I believe that confidence building and pride in good works are beneficial to rehabilitation. Since leaving prison I have been attending the Citizens Theatre groups. I also took my family to see the Christmas show, and I have started to attend regular performances. For someone who has just left prison and with poor prospects, the Citizens is a lifeline without which I know I would be back in prison. I know of others who share the same view. If these projects can help just one person change their life for the better, then I believe it's a success. More people deserve a chance to change their cycle of despair.

He has since been involved with a number of theatre projects including performing on the main stage at the Citizens Theatre, at a community theatre festival in Bristol, England, and a sell-out performance at the Edinburgh Fringe festival. He also completed a yearlong college course studying creative industries.

In his personal life, he is in a stable relationship and has a stepson, whom he had invited to see him perform in a Christmas show (his first Christmas on the outside in nine years) where he played a snowman. After the play, his stepson was seen wearing John's snowman carrot nose, as they journeyed home to enjoy their Christmas together—a poignant image of the path that led him to positive change.

John returned to Barlinnie Prison a year later with other former prisoners, only this time they were guests. They were invited to attend the Citizens Theatre *Tales from the Wagon* production and watch the next generation of men perform in the prison. John said it was an incredibly emotional experience to visit as a guest and to leave by the front gate. It was another landmark moment for him that signified his change.

Postproduction

It is important to acknowledge that when the production week is over and the evaluation session has taken place, the Citizens team leaves the prison and does not resume until some months after. The men must develop coping mechanisms for the separation and emptiness that follow a performance, especially because some of the productions take place just before Christmas, an understandably difficult time of year to be separated from people you love. This is why year-round arts provision is necessary in a prison environment for consistency, continuity, and progress.

Even though we have worked in many prisons and criminal justice settings, each performance offers something unique and special to its performers and audiences. Choosing to participate and commit to a positive activity during their prison sentence should not be underestimated. Having these important moments acknowledged by family and friends, we believe, is key to promoting emotional well-being and contributes to rebuilding relationships on the outside.

When the men are reflecting in their "peters" (Scottish name for prison cells), we hope that they have recognized that being part of this positive experience enabled them to recognize their worth. Once we acknowledge this, it introduces the notion of change. It is hard to part company after such an intensive process together, and as theatre makers, we try to maintain the group's morale. Their achievements are also recognized with a certificate. Although this is not an official academic endorsement, this important gesture acknowledges their positive engagement and dedication to the project.

Then the moment is over. The prison guards escort the men back to their respective halls and cells. We leave the establishment through the front gate and resume our own lives on the outside.

Carrying the Story Forward

Our creative residency had yielded a number of significant relationships with former prisoners who have since reconnected with the Citizens Theatre. One man had spoken about developing a theatre company called Streetcones on the outside, solely made up of former prisoners. He had been very determined and had contacted senior managers at the Scottish Prison Service looking for endorsements and support for his plans upon his release. Its aims were to use their lived experiences and explore the theatre process to help others from making bad decisions and potentially entering the prison system. Since his release, he and other former prisoners have taken many important steps as a group and have made progress in their quest to help others.

Thank you so very much. Made me feel human again.

One of the most positive experiences of my life. The exhilaration and enjoyment from performing for the first time were exceptional. Brilliant working as part of a team with a common goal. Citizens Theatre team were inspirational.

The Importance of Play

The men who have been in our plays speak of the power of play and the importance of removing the prison uniform, even for a short while, to change into a costume. The opportunity to reimagine yourself and be someone else while performing should not be underestimated. Every performance that we have undertaken has yielded the same responses.

> I never thought I'd have the confidence to do something like this—Bu the team made me feel good about myself. Thank you for helping me achieve one of the best and most positive challenges of my adult life.

It transports us back to the child we once were with the dressing up box, inventing characters through the world of play. The theatre gives permission to revisit and reconnect with play as adults. Some men have described this as "pressing the pause button on the reality of being locked up." It is vital that the arts are fully recognized for the part they have to play within a prison setting, for the tools they provide to those who seek to take charge of and rebuild their lives.

It is important that we see people as people, not numbers or prison uniforms, and as these projects and performances have shown, they are capable of truly astonishing audiences and performers alike. These plays inspire journeys in personal development, helping participants to make themselves better placed to step forward into self-determined life paths filled with positivity, hope, and the possibilities of change.

CHAPTER 8
BAD GIRLS, MONSTERS, AND
CHICKS IN CHAINS
CLEAN BREAK THEATRE COMPANY'S
DISRUPTION OF REPRESENTATIONS OF
WOMEN, CRIME, AND INCARCERATION

Caoimhe McAvinchey

The iconography and vocabulary that frames women who offend is as partial as it is prevailing. Marcus Harvey's *Myra* (1995), a painting of Myra Hindley—convicted, with Ian Brady, of murdering children in the UK in the 1960s—is a scaled-up reproduction of the police mugshot circulated widely in the media, made with children's handprints. It was temporarily removed from display after being vandalized at the Royal Academy's *Sensation* exhibition (London, 1997) having elicited public outrage because of its subject, mode of construction, and framing as art.[1] The film *Monster* (2003), about Aileen Wuornos, convicted for the murder of seven men and sentenced to death in the United States in 2002, reflects in its title a singular, highly emotive representation of women who commit violent crimes. These words and images have a potency that seep across generations and cultural borders, iterating, time and again, that women who offend are doubly transgressive: violating both legal frameworks and expectations of appropriate gendered behavior.[2] *Bad Girls: The Musical* (2006) is a stage show set in the fictional women's prison HMP Larkhall, and based on the eponymous popular British television drama.[3] The show's poster features a glitter ball and chain, clamped to the ankle of a woman's toned, naked leg teetering on a red, metallic, high-heeled shoe. The edge of the poster interrupts the rise of the woman's leg just above her knee. The shadow of prison bars frames this central image and two press quotations boldly declare, "A hell of a lot of fun" (*Daily Telegraph*) and "These girls aren't just bad, they're wicked" (*Mail on Sunday*). This marketing material plays up to existing cultural references of incarcerated women as "babes behind bars," "jail birds," and "chicks in chains" and prisons as playgrounds for homoerotic fantasies: ideas and images circulated through films in the Women in Prison exploitation genre such as *Big Doll House* (1971), *The Big Bird House* (1972), and *Caged Heat* (1974).[4]

The Feminist Spectator in Action: Feminist Criticism for the Stage and Screen is Jill Dolan's call to action for those who make, consume, and critique cultural work to attend to the choices we make in our practices, "to see what and who is stunningly, repeatedly evident and what and who is devastatingly, obviously invisible in the art and popular culture we regularly consume for edification and entertainment."[5] The circulation of culturally constructed images of women in prison, particularly on television and film, might suggest that they are not invisible subjects. However, monstrous and sexualized constructions offer two-dimensional tropes rather than any insight into the societal structural disadvantage and intersectional violence of oppression that shape the lived experience of many criminalized women. The stigma, abhorrence, and sexualized valence that surround women, crime, and punishment are, to use Sara Ahmed's phrase, "sticky":[6] it transfers and adheres to all criminalized women despite the evidence that violent acts are anomalous and the majority of women in prison are sentenced for nonviolent crimes, presenting a greater risk to themselves than to the public.[7] Corston's statement that many are "more 'troubled' than 'troublesome'"[8] is supported by government enquiries and research detailing the specific, gendered disadvantage that shapes their lives—racism, poverty, abuse, mental ill health, addiction, and limited educational or employment experience.[9] Within the growing global economy of punishment, increasingly managed by private companies administering the state business of justice, more than 10 million people are detained across the world. Within this, women historically make up less than 10 percent of the prison population. Until the 1970s, research focused on the majority ensuring that the default criminological subject was male.[10] Despite significant advances in feminist criminology and penal reform campaigns to highlight inequities endured by many women who offend and the major social, economic, and health implications of incarceration, the needs of women continue to be marginalized in politics and in practice.[11]

In this chapter, I consider how Clean Break disconfirms the limited and limiting cultural representations of criminalized women, too often reduced to "bad girls," "monsters," and "chicks in chains." Clean Break is a women-only theatre company, established by Jenny Hicks and Jacqueline Holborough in 1979, while at HMP Askham Grange. Holborough reflects on the imperative that galvanized their endeavor, "The system says go away and forget these people we've forced you to live with to the exclusion of all others. We said no. We want to explore this stuff. We want to own it. And we did."[12] Over the last four decades, the company has developed from a collective of women with experience of prison into a theatre company, commissioning and producing professional theatre makers to stage the stories of women, crime, and social justice. Alongside this, it has pioneered a unique education program, offering free training and support for women with experience of incarceration in its women-only center. While the artistic and education programs informed each other, there was a clear distinction and tension between them. In 2018, Clean Break entered a new phase of work, placing its Members—their voices and stories—center stage. In this chapter, I attend to work produced between 1990 and 2016, prior to this shift in the company's organizational practices.

I examine four productions to consider how, both in form and in content, Clean Break's practices are, in Dolan's words, "an activist project of culture-making":[13] *Sweatbox* (Chloë Moss, 2015), *Wicked* (Bryony Lavery, 1990), *Pests* (Vivienne Franzmann, 2014), and *Joanne* (Deborah Bruce, Theresa Ikoko, Laura Lomas, Chino Odimba, and Ursula Rani Sarma, 2016). Jill Dolan's, Nicole Rafter's, and Miranda Fricker's work supports a consideration of how Clean Break's theatre practice with and about women who have experience of the criminal justice system extends the representational vocabulary available beyond a limited repertoire of sexualized or monstrous tropes; attends to the lived experience of those who are too often invisible, on and off the cultural main stage; and contributes to understanding about the societal structural disadvantage that informs the lives of many women who offend. I argue that while all of Clean Break's work directly engages with the lived reality of criminalized women, the ways in which it does this are necessarily varied, using theatre to reconfigure the representational landscape to see beyond fact, figures, and statistics to the particularity of the individual lives blurred by them.

Staged Realities

Clean Break has made a significant contribution to contemporary British theatre through producing new writing, which always places the stories of women and criminal justice system center stage. *24%* (Paulette Randall, 1991), *Mules* (Winsome Pinnock, 1996), *Yard Gal* (Rebecca Prichard, 1998), *it felt empty when the heart went at first but it is alright now* (Lucy Kirkwood, 2009), and *Little on the Inside* (Alice Birch, 2014) reveal the complexity of women's pathways to crime, shredding cultural stereotypes of women who offend and drawing audiences' attention to gendered experiences of the care system, abuse, and trafficking; of the fragility of relationships tested over time and absence; and the enduring negotiation of the stigma of having a criminal record that remains long after a sentence has been spent. Over sixty productions, with all-women artistic and production teams, have been staged in an eclectic range of venues that speak to Clean Break's distinctive commitment to reach a wide range of audiences: from prisons to the Houses of Parliament; from smaller scale, fringe venues to large-scale producing theatres.

Kentish Town, North London. A warm Wednesday afternoon in July. A white prison van has pulled up in a cobbled dead-end lane, just off the bustling high street. Its engine is still running. Opaque-windows let light into the van but keep curious eyes out. Who is inside? What is happening in there?

A small group—eight of us in total—are ushered, with minimal acknowledgement from the stern prison van driver, to climb up the steep metal steps into the van. Once inside, the quality of the air is distinctly different: warmer, thicker, used. Three doors with sealed windows line one, interior side of the van. Through them, we can see the bodies of three women, locked in tiny cubicles, barely high enough to stand up in, barely wide enough to turn around in. Their profiles are outlined by the glow of sunlight that is raising the temperature of the van with each passing moment.

My breathing becomes faster, more shallow. Cells. Coffins. A meat van. A sweatbox.

The steps clang as they are folded up into the van. As the side door bangs shut, the vehicle rocks heavily from side to side. After a few moments, the engine is cut and we hear the driver's door open and slam. A woman in one of the cubicles start to shout,
"Are we here?"
Silence
"Oi! What's goin' on?"
Silence
"Can we get out now or what?"
Silence . . .

Another woman says,

> We're at HMP Bronzefield. They do this. Stop the van outside the gates then leave you sat there like battery hens. They say they're waiting for more staff to come. They *say* that. But it's about setting the tone. Letting you know who's boss.
> . . . (time passes)
> Two fucking hours we've been cooped up![14]

This is the beginning of *Sweatbox* (2015), a short play by Chloë Moss commissioned by Clean Break, performed in a decommissioned prison escort van by Eddy Emenike, Carrie Rock, and Jade Small, graduates of Clean Break's education program. Over the fifteen minutes that the play unfolds, each of the three characters in the prison van—Steph, Rachel, and Nina—offers us glimpses into the circumstances of their lives, the families they have left behind, their specific worries about their futures as they are, literally, transported from their everyday lives, from the courts where they have been sentenced, to prison. Steph, mid-twenties, is heavily pregnant. She's been in prison before and her father has been in prison while she was growing up. Nina, mid-forties, has been sentenced on a drug-related crime. It's not the first time, but she says, "this time I'm getting clean." Rachel, early thirties, is the most distressed. She's never been in prison before and only been separated from her three-year-old son for two nights before now: "My Barrister said community service. Nothing to worry about. First offence. I haven't anything with me. Didn't even bring a bag."[15] We witness Steph, Nina, and Rachel trapped in an enduring moment of consequence.

While much of Clean Break's work attends specifically to gender issues in pathways to crime, sentencing, imprisonment, and the fragile negotiation of life when released, *Sweatbox* additionally illuminates the material and economic conditions that impact on women, men, and children who are processed within the criminal justice system. Her Majesty's Inspectorate of Prisons' 2014 report *Transfers and Escorts within the Criminal Justice System* examined the use and conditions of prison vans, "sweat boxes," inspecting documentation from police, court, and secure training centers (STC), young offender institutions (YOIs) as well as the private companies that provide Prison Escort and Custody Services (PECS).[16] This report details over 820,000 escorted journeys in the year between October 2013 and September 2014 at a cost of over £130 million, paid by the British tax payers to private companies for escort and custody services. The report details shocking statistics of the conditions and treatment of people in custody, who are in the care of the state: only two-thirds of adult prisoners were told where they were being taken; over 37 percent of the journeys taken by adults take more than two hours; sometimes children and adults, men and women were transported in the same van; because there are fewer young offender institutions, special training centers, and women's prisons, children and women often have to travel longer distances; there are no seatbelts because of the risk of self-harm; there were reports of inhuman treatment with some people having no access to water, food, toilets, or air-conditioning when left for two hours over a lunch time in an airless van during the peak of summer.[17]

Steph, Rachel, and Nina's lives—interrupted and in limbo—are simultaneously specific characters and composite substitutes for other unidentified people who are both hidden and made a spectacle of as they are ferried in prison vans through towns and cities, along motorways and country roads, moved from one physical and performative manifestation of the criminal justice system to another—the police station, the court, the prison, the secure unit.

> The door of the van is opened. A security guard unfolds the steps and climbs inside. She opens each cubicle in turn and handcuffs the women. They look exhausted with anticipation of what lies ahead of them. Steph, heavily pregnant, has wet herself.

> The audience in the van leans against its walls, shifting with discomfort: heat, claustrophobia, noise, proximity, containment. This is real, this is felt. Momentarily, we, the audience are alongside the women who we can see, literally, sweat.

For the audience in *Sweatbox,* this brief experience breathes life into the documented detail of the fifty-three-page report, which concludes, "However they are organised, the escort experience is likely to be expensive and detrimental for the detainee"[18] in conditions that Peter Thatchell described as "Home Office-approved human cattle trucks."[19] The audience's applause is layered with acknowledgments: of the performances that the women have given; of the experience of being together in this moment of hiatus; of the craft of a piece of theatre that gives access and insight to the conditions of escorted custody without being voyeuristic. There is acknowledgment too of the realization that the performers, graduates of Clean Break's education program, have experience of the criminal justice system, have been transported in a sweatbox and who, in collaboration with the playwright, Chloë Moss, and director, Imogen Ashby, offer this testimony to us. During *Sweatbox*, these lives are witnessed by us, a theatre audience. Each performance is a call to the audience to be morally, politically, ethically present—to be alongside, to be face to face with those who are masked by stereotypical representations and cultural shorthand.[20] This fifteen-minute immersive experience is the manifestation of Clean Break's holistic approach to furthering public understanding of women, crime, punishment, and stigma across four decades of practice.[21]

Addressing Epistemological Injustice through Disconfirmation and Representation

Clean Break's representational disconfirmation is an important act of culture making, a practical iteration of Jill Dolan's commitment "to refocus the lens, to see from the side, as it were, where all the holes in the narrative are suddenly clear, and where all its presumptions and exclusions are most transparent."[22] Many of Clean Break's commissions expose the holes in limited narratives and representations of criminalized women, exploding "presumptions and exclusions" to reveal the material conditions and social implications of gendered experiences of poverty, racism, and abuse. However, in addition to doing this critical work, I argue that specific productions have the capacity to address what Miranda Fricker has defined as a "distinctively epistemic kind of injustice," when someone is wronged in their capacity as a knower.[23] Clean Break's practices—across all strands of work—facilitate an economy of credibility where women, too often dismissed as unreliable or untrustworthy, are re-presented as expert witnesses.

Miranda Fricker's *Epistemic Injustice: Power and the Ethics of Knowing* is provocative in considering how, through the form and the content of the plays, Clean Break disrupts, dissects, and disconfirms cultural stereotypes about women and crime. Fricker builds on the work of C.A.J. Coady, who considers the epistemological status of testimony, making the distinction between "formal testimony" offered in a legal context and "natural testimony," as a knowledge based on what others tell us, circulated in daily life.[24] For Coady, a reductive approach to testimony values evidence gathered by eyewitnesses, it is empirical—it has to be seen to be believed; an anti-reductive approach is expansive and accommodating—it is based on perception, memory, and the word of others and is how we come to know and navigate the world. In this framework, theatre and performance—its narratives and representations—act as a kind of testimony, offering new understandings and perspectives on the world. If cultural forms articulate ideological positions that negate the experience of criminalized women, or who are represented only as being other or socially deviant, then the kind of testimony offered through them is limited. For Fricker, a lack of representation about the nuanced, complex, and hidden experience of these women is an epistemic injustice, when an individual or a group of people are wronged in their capacity as "knowers." She identifies two distinct areas of injustice—testimonial and hermeneutic.[25] Fricker proposes that "testimonial injustice occurs when prejudice causes a hearer to give a deflated level of credibility to a speaker's word. . . . An example . . . might be that the police do not believe you because you are black."[26] This is aligned with but separate to what Fricker identifies as "hermeneutical injustice." This occurs, she argues, "when a gap in collective interpretative resources puts someone at an unfair disadvantage when it comes to making sense of their social experiences . . . an example . . . might be that you suffer sexual harassment in a culture that still lacks that critical concept." [27]

In the following section, I consider how, in three particular texts and productions, Clean Break addresses both the testimonial and the hermeneutic injustice faced by women whose lives are shaped by societal structures of disadvantage resources to consider the representation and understanding of women, crime, and justice, supporting a "community of knowledge" that gives credence to their testimony through theatre.[28]

While most of Clean Break's plays have a small number of characters (often two or three) bound together in the telling of a narrative of realism, Bryony Lavery's *Wicked* (1990) is an important exception. A program note introduces the play as "a wicked comedy about incarceration" in which

> Bailey, a seedy, oily, oozing showbiz entrepreneur presents his travelling show. Out of dark, bottomless boxes he pulls his unwitting performers to presents their acts. These miserable women sing, dance and play for Bailey' pleasure. Until one day, something goes wrong and the women become considerably less miserable.[29]

Three actors play twelve characters, including a trio of singing, dancing prison officers—the Screw Sisters—in a production that draws on vaudeville, cabaret, verse, and farce to critique social expectations of femininity and gendered experiences of crime and punishment. Bailey, a reference to the Old Bailey, the Central Criminal Court in England and Wales, is a showman and wordsmith who represents the criminal justice system. His collection of "freakiest," "weirdest," "shockingest" showgirls[30]— Evvie, Banshee, and Zombie—are iterations of the way in which women are treated within it. Original production photos are charged with a sense of exuberant surrealism: the Screw Sisters—Moo, Sue, and Lou—wear matching black leatherette jackets and turrets of beehive wigs; Bailey wears a quaffed hair piece and peach silk jacket with a golden shirt; and the show's finale includes a scene where Bailey is led to a man-size box and sawn into three parts by Banshee before the trio of "freaks" sing,

> Been through isolation
> Deprivation
> Self-mutilation
> Rehabilitation
> But I'm still me
> I've been through strip-searches
> Investigated
> Incarcerated
> Hated, gated
> Retaliated
> But I'm me
> I'm still SHE.[31]

Lavery's play is unusual within the Clean Break canon, not only because of its nonnaturalistic form but because, rather than focus on a single narrative about a particular woman, Lavery grabs the criminal justice system and its institutional sexism with full theatrical force to reveal the structures that additionally punish women who offend. She uses surrealism, humor, and stage-magic to expose the ways in which the supposed caring work of justice undoes society through the extraction of women from their families and infantilization through institutionalization. Lavery's ludic, acerbic text eats away at the fallacy of equitable treatment of women in the eyes of the law. This sophisticated critique—in both form and content—of women's experience of the binds of femininity and the additional stigma that adheres to criminalization women offers a living, breathing thesis that necessitates an audiences' critical engagement.

Vivienne Franzmann's *Pests* (2014) tells the story of two sisters, Rolly and Pink, who have been in and out of prison. Unlike the image of the nameless, faceless, sexualized woman in the poster for *Bad Girls* who is called upon to act as a referent for all women in prison, *Pests* gives us insight into the experience of individuals whose lives have been ravaged by neglect, poverty, drugs, and sexual abuse. Rolly, who is heavily pregnant, has just been released from prison. She is on methadone and trying, minute by minute, to steer a path through life that will enable her to keep this baby. Previously, her daughter, Tia, was removed by social services. Rolly seeks shelter with her sister, Pink. However, her home is not a place of sanctuary: the squalor and distress of Pink's life is staged in the psychotic hallucinations projected across the set of heaped, ripped, and oozing mattresses, framed by a scaffold of pipes. It is a world that is both exposed and insurmountable. Both Rolly and Pink are caught in a vice of circumstance, in a world where the past puts a stranglehold on any hope of a different future, where the phrase "social deprivation" seems inadequate to contain the repercussions of poverty inscribed across all aspects of life.[32] Franzmann found herself addressing the ethical issues of writing about the consequences of "vicious poverty" without being voyeuristic, through her use of a stylized language shared by Rolly and Pink: a London hyper slang.

> It ain't my fault, I was lyin' dere. Dey just stoled 'em. Tugged 'em off my foots. I's right sorrowed, but . . . . It weren't my fault. I couldn't done do nuttin. Dey just powered over. Right over, gotte in my face. Couldn't see proper, but dere was hordes of da buggers, conquered by dem all, all f dem all roar an' roar an' roar. Wanted dem shimmy shoes. [. . .] Don't be angryfied on me, it weren't my fault. I's on da florr. I's all crunched on da pavement, face in da glass.[33]

Pests is disturbingly explicit, detailing the layers of catastrophic, gendered disadvantage that shape pathways to crime, binding many women to the enduring stigma of a prison sentence and subsequent cycles of offending behavior.[34] For Franzmann, the play is a cry of anger at the way society treats women in prison: "When we've been into prisons, you're in a room with twenty women, and in that room it's so clear that there is mental illness, there are educational special needs, there's addiction, there's self-harm, there are women who are victims of rape, abuse, neglect, childhood trauma—it's all there."[35]

Dolan and Fricker have been explicit in identifying the political ramifications of the absence of representation of individuals who are othered by experiences marked by gender, race, class, stigma, and criminalization.

This representational gap is made explicit in *Joanne* (Soho Theatre London, 2015) by Deborah Bruce, Theresa Ikoko, Laura Lomas, Chino Odimba, and Ursula Rani Sarma. Each writer introduces us to a character played by the same actor (Tanya Moodie): Stella, a social worker who has been made redundant; Grace, a police officer; Kathleen, an Accident and Emergency receptionist who is exhausted by the limitations of a service that cannot cope with the increasing demands of the public; Alice, the hostel worker; Becky, the teacher. Each of these lives is enmeshed with Joanne, a young woman the audience never see but witness only through the testimony of the five women who encounter her at different, pivotal moments in her life. Through their reflections, we piece together fragments of Joanne's life: a girl who lost her father; who was wrecked with grief, distant from her mother; who self-harmed; who became a drug addict; who stole; who was imprisoned; who had no one but a social worker to meet her when she was released from prison; a young woman who was given the wrong medication; who asked for help from individuals in social services, the police, the National Health Service; a young woman who was suicidal; who fell time and again between the cracks of various care systems that were unable to catch, protect, or support her. Each scene details the complexity and fragility of a life that is barely visible to the public—that is made even more vulnerable in a context of cuts to services in the name of austerity. Joanne is, in Corston's terms, "troubled rather than trouble," the individual that becomes a statistic in government reports about vulnerable women. Stella, the social worker who meets Joanne on her last day of work, says of her, "And she's alright. This one. You know what I mean? Something about her makes me hope she'll make it somehow. That's all I can do now. Hope."[36] But this hope cannot prevent a series of events that lead to Joanne's death hours after her release from prison. At the end of the play, we are compelled to do more than hope—to acknowledge, to act, to do imaginative work in filling in the gaps left by the writers, director, and actor in order to allow Joanne to appear in the audience's mind's eye. However distressing this is, *Joanne* offers an invitation to the audience to construct an understanding of an individual, to attend to what we—individuals and the state—don't, or won't, see.

Conclusion

Throughout its history, Clean Break has taken radical action to address both the testimonial and the hermeneutic injustice faced by women it works with and for. It creates environments where the economy of credibility is robust, where women who face prejudice because of their race, class, gender, mental ill health, or criminal record are believed: where actions are taken in good faith rather than being tainted by societal prejudice. Critically, Clean Break's work gives authority to women with experience of the criminal justice system as "knowers," providing expanded interpretive resources to enhance public understanding of women, crime, and justice. Clean Break makes and supports a community of knowledge, giving credence to criminalized women's testimony of experience through theatre and performance by, with, and about them.

NOTES

Foreword

1. Regarding the racialized nature of American incarceration, regardless of period, see Kali Gross, *Colored Amazons: Crime, Violence, and Black Women in the City of Brotherly Love, 1880–1910* (Durham: Duke University Press, 2006); Khalil Gibran Muhammad, *The Condemnation of Blackness: Race, Crime, and the Making of Modern Urban America* (Cambridge: Harvard University Press, 2011); Nikil Singh, *Black Is a Country: Race and the Unfinished Struggle for Democracy* (Cambridge: Harvard University Press, 2005); Miroslava Chavez-Garcia, *States of Delinquency: Race and Science in the Making of California's Juvenile Justice System* (Berkeley: University of California Press, 2012); Kelly Lytle Hernandez, *City of Inmates: Conquest, Rebellion, and the Rise of Human Caging in Los Angeles, 1771–1965* (Chapel Hill: University of North Carolina Press, 2017); Patrick Wolfe, "Settler Colonialism and the Elimination of the Native." *Journal of Genocide Research* 8.4 (December 2006): 387–409; Dennis Childs, *Slaves of the State: Black Incarceration from the Chain Gang to the Penitentiary* (Minneapolis: University of Minnesota Press, 2015).

2. The Justice Policy Institute, "The Punishing Decade: Prison and Jail Estimates at the Millennium" (2000), http://www.justicepolicy.org/images/upload/00 -05_rep_punishingdecade_ac.pdf.

3. National Research Council, "The Growth of Incarceration in the United States: Exploring Causes and Consequences" (Washington DC: The National Academies Press, 2014), https://doi.org/10.17226/18613.

4. Wendy Sawyer and Peter Wagner, "Mass Incarceration: The Whole Pie," Prison Policy Initiative (March 19, 2019), https://www.prisonpolicy.org/reports/pie 2019.html.

5. Ibid.

6. Wendy Sawyer, "Youth Confinement: The Whole Pie," Prison Policy Initiative (February 27, 2018), https://www.prisonpolicy.org/reports/youth2018.html.

7. "Americans with Criminal Records," report by the Sentencing Project and Half by Ten, https://www.sentencingproject.org/wp-content/uploads/2015/11/Amer icans-with-Criminal-Records-Poverty-and-Opportunity-Profile.pdf. Also see: Rebecca Vallas and Sharon Dietrich, "One Strike and You're Out: How We Can Eliminate Barriers to Economic Security and Mobility for People with Criminal Records" (Washington: Center for American Progress, 2014).

Notes

8. For more on this established fact see National Research Council, "The Growth of Incarceration in the United States." Also see Elizabeth Kai Hinton, *From the War on Poverty to the War on Crime* (Cambridge: Harvard University Press, 2016), and Heather Ann Thompson, "Why Mass Incarceration Matters: Crisis, Decline, and Transformation in Postwar American History," *Journal of American History* 97.3 (2010): 703–34.

9. The literature on the devastating collateral consequences of mass incarceration is rich. For but a sampling of it, see Todd Clear, *Imprisoning Communities: How Mass Incarceration Makes Disadvantaged Neighborhoods Worse* (Oxford: Oxford University Press, 2009) and Bruce Western, *Homeward: Life in the Year after Prison* (New York: Russell Sage, 2018). Testimonies from those on the inside who have experienced its trauma first hand also abound. For some of the most important of these, see Shaka Senghor, *Writing My Wrongs: Life, Death, and Redemption in an American Prison* (New York: Convergent Books, 2017); Susan Burton, *Becoming Ms. Burton: From Prison to Recovery to Leading the Fight for Incarcerated Women* (New York: The New Press, 2019) and Aylelet Waldman and Robin Levi, *Inside This Place, Not of It: Narratives from Women's Prisons* (San Francisco: Verso, 2017).

Introduction

1. For more cross-gender performances in prisons, see Chapters One, Two, and Four and the Conclusion.

2. Lucy Jackson, "An Introduction to Ancient Greek Theatre," Archive of Performances of Greek and Roman Drama website, http://www.apgrd.ox.ac.uk/learning/an-introduction-to/an-introduction-to-ancient-greek-theatre, retrieved January 17, 2019.

3. K. M. Coleman, "Fatal Charades: Roman Executions Staged as Mythological Enactments," *The Journal of Roman Studies* 80 (1990): 44–73.

4. Robert Jordan, *The Convict Theatres of Early Australia 1788-1840* (Hertfordshire: University of Hertfordshire Press, 2002), 27.

5. Buzz Alexander, *Is William Martinez Not Our Brother?: Twenty Years of the Prison Creative Arts Project* (Ann Arbor: University of Michigan Press, 2010), 6.

6. Jean Trounstine, *Shakespeare Behind Bars: One Teacher's Story of the Power of Drama in a Women's Prison* (Ann Arbor: University of Michigan Press, 2001), x–xi, 3.

7. Rob Pensalfini, *Prison Shakespeare: For These Deep Shames and Great Indignities* (Hampshire: Palgrave Macmillan, 2016), 2–3.

8. Geese Theatre Company website, http://www.geese.co.uk/about/our-history/, retrieved February 2, 2019; For more on drama therapy, see John Bergman, "The Theatre of Meeting: The History of Drama and Other Experimental Therapies as Neurological Analogs," in Robert E. Longo, David S. Prescott,

John Bergman, and Kevin Creeden (eds.), *Current Perspectives & Applications in Neurobiology: Working with Young Persons Who Are Victims and Perpetrators of Sexual Abuse* (Holyoke: NEARI Press, 2013), 317–43.

9. Leonidas Cheliotis, "The Arts of Imprisonment: An Introduction," in Leonidas Cheliotis (ed.), *The Arts of Imprisonment* (Surrey: Ashgate, 2012), 2.

10. Mary Louise Pratt, *Imperial Eyes: Travel Writing and Transculturation* (Routledge: London, 1992), 4.

11. Chloé Branders, "Theater and Confinement: The Collective Creation as a Modality of the Investigation Experience in Prison," *Criminocorpus* (June 30, 2017), http://journals.openedition.org.proxy.lib.umich.edu/criminocorpus /3541, retrieved January 25, 2020.

12. Anna Deavere Smith, *Talk to Me: Travels in Media and Politics* (New York: Anchor Books, 2000), 9.

13. Natalia Kuziakina, *Theatre in the Solovki Prison Camp*, trans. Boris M. Meerovich (Luxembourg: Harwood Academic Publishers, 1995), xii.

14. Eduardo Galeano, "In Defense of the Word," trans. Bobbye S. Ortiz, in *Days and Nights of Love and War*, trans. Judith Brister (New York: Monthly Review Press, 1983), 190; emphasis in original.

15. Ashley Lucas, Natália Fiche, and Vicente Concilio, "We Move Forward Together: A Prison Theatre Exchange Program among Three Universities in the United States and Brazil," *Prison Journal* 99.4 (2019): 1–22. https://doi.org /10.1177/0032885519861061.

16. Rachel Marie-Crane Williams, "Learning to Teach by Traveling Inside: The Experience and Process of Mural-Making in a Women's Correctional Facility," in Rachel Marie-Crane Williams (ed.), *Teaching the Arts Behind Bars* (Boston: Northeastern University Press, 2003), 138–52.

17. Loïc Wacquant, "The Curious Eclipse of Prison Ethnography in the Age of Mass Incarceration," *Ethnography* 3.4 (2012): 371–97.

18. National Competition of Dramatic Art for Prison Inmates website, http://ckz amek.pl/wydarzenia/2858-v-ogolnopolski-konkurs-wieziennej-tworczosci-t eatr/, retrieved March 10, 2019.

19. Frank B. Wilderson III, "The Prison Slave as Hegemony's (Silent) Scandal," *Social Justice* 30.2 (2003): 20.

Chapter 1

1. I have been a member of the Open Hearts Open Minds Advisory Board since 2014.

2. *The Winter's Tale* 3.3.58.

3. Much to my astonishment, theatre producers Gustavo Moraes and Pia Susaeta told me that they encountered no resistance from the warden of the

Las Rosas prison in Maldonado, Uruguay, when they proposed a production of George Orwell's *Animal Farm*, despite the fact that the standard Spanish translation of the title is *Un rebelde en la granja*—literally *A Rebellion in the Barnyard*. They believe that the seemingly incendiary title and content of the novel did not trigger any censorship from the authorities because Orwell's writings are considered so canonical as to be sacrosanct. Throughout my research, this is the only instance I found of prisons declining to censor an author besides Shakespeare, based purely on the writer's accepted cultural status; Gustavo Moraes and Pia Susaeta, Skype conversation with author, July 7, 2016.

4. Johnny Stallings, interview by author, September 27, 2014.

5. Johnny Stallings, email to author, February 12, 2015.

6. Ibid.

7. Open Hearts Open Minds website, http://openheartsopenminds.net/, retrieved May 11, 2015.

8. Open Hearts Open Minds cast of *The Winter's Tale*, conversation with author, filmed by Bushra Azzouz, Umatilla, OR (September 28, 2014).

9. Shakespeare Behind Bars (SBB) is a name used by two separate and unaffiliated prison theatre organizations. Curt Tofteland's SBB that grew out of the Kentucky Shakespeare Festival has chapters in Kentucky and Michigan and is the subject of a documentary film by the same name. Jean Trounstine's SBB, which was described in her book *Shakespeare Behind Bars: The Power of Drama Inside One Women's Prison*, is no longer in existence but took place at a facility in Framingham, Massachusetts.

10. John Lonergan, *The Governor: The Life and Times of the Man Who Ran Mountjoy* (London: Penguin Books, 2010), 96.

11. Anonymous, conversation with author, South Bend, IN, November 15, 2013.

12. Open Hearts Open Minds cast, conversation.

13. Ibid.

14. Qtd. in Amy Scott-Douglas, *Shakespeare Inside: The Bard Behind Bars* (London: Continuum, 2007), 75.

15. Open Hearts Open Minds cast, conversation.

16. Ibid.

17. *Othello*, 1.3.208.

18. Open Hearts Open Minds cast, conversation.

19. Ibid.

20. Ibid.

21. Niels Herold, *Prison Shakespeare and the Purpose of Performance: Repentance Rituals and the Early Modern* (New York: Palgrave Macmillan, 2014), 12.

22. Open Hearts Open Minds cast, conversation.

23. Ibid.

24. Curt Tofteland, phone conversation with author, July 9, 2018.

25. Curt Tofteland, "The Keeper of the Keys," in Jonathan Shailor (ed.), *Performing New Lives: Prison Theatre* (London: Jessica Kingsley Publishers, 2011), 214; Tofteland, email, August 13, 2018.

26. *Shakespeare Behind Bars*, dir. Hank Rogerson (San Francisco: Philomath Films, 2005).

27. Shakespeare Behind Bars website, www.shakespearebehindbars.org, retrieved July 11, 2018.

28. I had known Berghuis for several years at this point, and she was at that time a member of the National Advisory Board for PCAP.

29. *Macbeth* 5.5.20–9.

30. Harold Bloom, *Shakespeare: The Invention of the Human* (New York: Riverhead, 1998).

31. *Richard II* 5.5.1–5.

32. Much of what we know about Shakespeare's life is speculative, and many have debated whether he might or might not have served time in prison; Mike Dash, "William Shakespeare, Gangster," Smithsonian.com, https://www.smithsonianmag.com/history/william-shakespeare-gangster-129238903/, retrieved July 17, 2018.

33. Tofteland, email, August 13, 2018.

34. Tofteland, interview.

35. Ibid.

36. Alexander, 111.

37. Tofteland, "Keeper," 213–30.

38. Pensalfini, 63–4.

39. Ibid., 35–6, 63–4, 77–8, 85–7, 102, 164–6.

40. Ibid., 13.

41. Paul Heritage, "Taking Hostages: Staging Human Rights," *The Drama Review* 48.3 (2004): 96–106.

42. Lonergan, 168.

43. The warden who succeeded Berghuis after her retirement rescinded both of these exceedingly modest privileges; Ibid.

44. Mary Berghuis, email to author, August 11, 2018.

45. Open Hearts Open Minds cast, conversation.

46. Ibid.

47. Ibid.

48. "On the street" is prison slang for things happening anywhere in the free world.

Notes

49. Open Hearts Open Minds cast, conversation.

50. Jill Dolan, *Utopia in Performance: Finding Hope at the Theatre* (Ann Arbor: University of Michigan Press, 2005), 10.

51. Ibid., 2.

52. Latin America and the Caribbean may be among the notable regional exceptions to this because these parts of the world have more populist theatre traditions that tend to reach the poor and minority ethnic groups (i.e., those most often imprisoned) more than theatre traditions in other parts of the world.

53. Open Hearts Open Minds cast, conversation.

54. Jason Berton, "When *Waiting for Godot* Played San Quentin," SF Gate website (December 23, 2008), https://www.sfgate.com/performance/article/When-Wa iting-for-Godot-played-San-Quentin-3179824.php, retrieved July 29, 2018.

55. Lance Duerfahrd, *The Work of Poverty: Samuel Beckett's Vagabonds and the Theatre of Crisis* (Columbus: The Ohio State University Press, 2013), 15.

56. Open Hearts Open Minds cast, conversation.

57. Ibid.

58. Ibid.

59. Ibid.

60. Rachel Kushner, *The Mars Room* (New York: Scribner, 2018), 126–7.

61. This moment struck me so profoundly that I used her words in the script of my play *Doin' Time: Through the Visiting Glass*.

62. Open Hearts Open Minds cast, conversation.

63. Ibid.

64. Ibid.

65. Alana Hall, "How Shakespeare is Helping Women Prisoners Help Themselves," *Huffington Post* (April 4, 2017), https://www.huffingtonpost.com /2014/04/04/shakespeare-in-prison_n_5084450.html, retrieved July 25, 2018.

66. Frannie Shepherd-Bates, email to author, July 7, 2018.

67. Ibid.

68. Frannie Shepherd-Bates, email to author, July 29, 2018.

69. Open Hearts Open Minds cast, conversation.

70. "La cárcel de Las Rosas tiene hoy 800 internos pero los servicios se cumplen adecuadamente," *Maldonado Noticias* (February 15, 2017), http://www .maldonadonoticias.com/beta/actualidad/8828-la-cárcel-de-las-rosas-tie ne-hoy-800-internos-pero-los-servicios-se-cumplen-adecuadamente.html, retrieved July 25, 2018.

71. Open Hearts Open Minds cast, conversation.

72. Ibid.

73. Ibid.

74. Sharon Lemm, phone conversation with author, July 11, 2018.

75. Ibid.

76. Open Hearts Open Minds cast, conversation.

77. Ibid.

78. Lemm, phone conversation.

79. Sharon Lemm, letter to the OHOM group, November 19, 2014.

80. Open Hearts Open Minds cast, conversation.

81. Sharon Lemm, email to author, July 20, 2019.

82. Sharon Lemm, letter to Jack Baird, February 22, 2015.

83. Lemm, email, July 20, 2019.

84. Open Hearts Open Minds cast, conversation.

85. Sharon Lemm, letter to Joshua Underhill, March 12, 2015.

86. Lemm, interview.

87. Lemm, letter to Jack Baird.

88. Sharon Lemm, letter to Rocky Hutchinson, September 20, 2017.

89. Sharon Lemm, letter to OHOM group, January 11, 2016.

90. Transforming Corrections website, http://transformingcorrections.com, retrieved July 28, 2018.

91. Tom O'Connor, email to author, August 8, 2018.

92. Tom O'Connor, phone conversation with author, July 12, 2018.

93. Randy Geer, phone conversation with author, July 24, 2018.

94. Ibid.

95. Johnny Stallings, phone conversation with author, July 9, 2018.

96. Tom O'Connor and Jeff Duncan, "The Sociology of Humanist, Spiritual, and Religious Practice in Prison: Supporting Responsivity and Desistance from Crime," *Religions* 2.4 (2011): 590–610, http://www.mdpi.com/2077-1444/2/4/590.

97. Jeff Duncan, Richard Stansfield, Steve Hall, and Tom O'Connor, "Women's Engagement with Humanist, Spiritual and Religious Meaning-Making in Prison: A Longitudinal Study of Its Impact on Recidivism," *Religions* 9.6 (2018): 171, http://www.mdpi.com/2077-1444/9/6/171.

98. Stallings, interview.

99. Pensalfini, 42–3.

100. Ibid., 43.

101. Open Hearts Open Minds cast, conversation.

102. Ibid.

Notes

103. Ibid.

104. Ibid.

105. Ibid.

106. Ibid.

107. Ibid.

108. Ibid.

109. Ibid.

110. Ibid.

111. Ibid.

112. Geer, phone conversation.

113. Open Hearts Open Minds cast, conversation; Lemm, phone conversation.

114. Open Hearts Open Minds cast, conversation.

115. Ibid.

Chapter 2

1. Lonergan, 61.

2. William Head on Stage, *Here: A Captive Odyssey* (unpublished manuscript, 2015).

3. Thana Ridha, *Exploring Prison Theatre in Canada: A Case Study on William Head on Stage (WHoS)* (unpublished dissertation, University of Ottawa, 2018), 6–7.

4. Prices have gone up. I paid $20 (Canadian) for a ticket in 2013.

5. Ingrid Hansen and Peter Balkwill, "Fractured Fables: A Prison Puppet Project," in Shauna Butterwick and Carole Roy (eds.), *Working the Margins of Community-Based Adult Learning* (Amsterdam: Sense Publishers, 2016), 139.

6. William Head is a minimum security prison in which incarcerated men have access to a woodworking shop with tools and other products that are not allowed in many other prisons.

7. All WHoS participants are referred to by pseudonyms; those who spoke to me directly chose their own. When quoting from Ridha's dissertation, I used the pseudonyms that she was using for the WHoS participants.

8. Ridha, 107.

9. *Hip Hop Hamlet*, video recording (February 26, 2015), http://prisonartsstl.org/audio-video, retrieved July 16, 2019.

10. Ibid.; Inmates at the Northeast Correctional Center, Agnes Wilcox, and Elizabeth Charlebois, *Hip Hop Hamlet* (unpublished manuscript).

11. Elizabeth Charlebois, email to author, July 14, 2019.

12. Daniel Banks, "Introduction: Hip Hop Theater's Ethic of Inclusion," in Daniel Banks (ed.), *Say Word! Voices from Hip Hop Theater: An Anthology* (Ann Arbor: University of Michigan Press, 2011), 5.

13. Inmates et al.

14. *Hip Hop Hamlet*, video; the version of the script prepared for publication changes the final lines of this scene to eliminate the reference to PPA and inserts a different joke.

15. Christopher Limber, email to author, July 8, 2019.

16. "Act V," *This American Life* (Chicago: WBEZ Radio, August 9, 2002); Prison Performing Arts website, http://prisonartsstl.org, retrieved July 16, 2019.

17. Prison Performing Arts website.

18. "Act V."

19. Ibid.

20. Christopher Limber, email to author, July 14, 2019; Christopher Limber, email to author, July 8, 2019.

21. Elizabeth Charlebois, "With Rhyme and Reason: *Hip Hop Hamlet* in Prison," in Graley Herren (ed.), *Text & Presentation, 2015* (Jefferson: McFarland & Company, Inc., 2015), 88–90.

22. Ibid., 95.

23. Charlebois, "With Rhyme," 101.

24. Ibid., 96.

25. Ibid., 95.

26. Elizabeth Charlebois, email to author, July 12, 2019.

27. Elizabeth Charlebois, Adaptation Exercises Worksheet for *Hip Hop Hamlet* (unpublished manuscript).

28. Charlebois, email, July 12, 2019.

29. Inmates et al.

30. Limber, email, July 8, 2019.

31. Banks, 6.

32. Limber, email, July 14, 2019.

33. Limber, email, July 8, 2019.

34. Ibid.; I did not get to see the Vandalia production in person, but a film of the entire play is available on the PPA website, prisonartsstl.org/ hiphophamlet2018, retrieved July 19, 2019.

35. Ridha, 133.

36. Ibid., 134.

37. Lifer Lou, letter to author, July 3, 2019.

38. Ibid.

39. Hansen and Balkwill, 143.

40. Qtd. in ibid., 134.

41. Ibid., 137.

42. Kate Rubin, interview by author, July 3, 2019.

43. Hansen and Balkwill, 140.

44. Matthew Ross, letter to author, July 3, 2019.

45. Qtd. in Ridha, 123.

46. Donald Braman, *Doing Time on the Outside: Incarceration and Family Life in Urban America* (Ann Arbor: University of Michigan Press, 2004).

47. Qtd. in Ridha, 114.

48. Christopher Limber, email to author, July 25, 2019.

49. Charlebois, email, July 14, 2019; Limber, email, July 14, 2019; Limber, email, July 15, 2019.

50. Limber, email, July 14, 2019.

51. "'Run-On Sentence' Earns Nomination for Best New Play by the St. Louis Theatre Circle," Prison Performing Arts blog, http://prisonartsstl.org/blog/runonsentenceaward, retrieved February 27, 2019.

52. Shannon Cothran, "The Prison Performing Arts Program Puts Inmates on Center Stage," Missouri Life: The Spirit of Discovery website, https://missourilife.com/prison-performing-arts/, retrieved March 25, 2019; Limber, email, June 25, 2019.

53. Limber, email, June 25, 2019.

54. Russell M. Dembin, "Nothing But Time: When 'Godot' Came to San Quentin," *American Theatre* (January 22, 2019), https://www.americantheatre.org/2019/01/22/nothing-but-time-when-godot-came-to-san-quentin/, retrieved January 22, 2019.

55. Ashley Lucas, "Prisoners on the Great White Way: *Short Eyes* and *Zoot Suit* as the First US Latina/o Plays on Broadway," *Latin American Theater Review* 43.1 (Fall 2009): 121–36.

56. Limber, email, July 8, 2019.

57. Rubin, interview.

58. Hansen and Balkwill, 140.

59. Ibid.

60. Ibid., 138.

61. Qtd. in Ridha, 81.

62. Ibid., 85.

63. Audience comments about *Crossroads: A Prison Cabaret* collected on whonstage.weebly.com (unpublished document, 2018).

64. Inmates et al.

65. Ibid.

66. *Hip Hop Hamlet*, video.

Chapter 3

1. Sarah Koenig, "A Bar Fight Walks into the Justice Center," September 20, 2018, in *Serial*, produced by Sarah Koenig, Julie Snyder, Emmanuel Dzotsi, and Ben Calhoun, podcast, mp3 audio, 53:00, https://serialpodcast.org/, retrieved December 29, 2018.

2. Achille Mbembe, *On the Postcolony* (Berkeley: University of California Press, 2001), 1.

3. Ibid., 6.

4. Miranda Young-Jahangeer, conversation with author, November 22, 2018.

5. Neal Lazarus, "The South African Ideology: The Myth of Exceptionalism, the Idea of Renaissance," *South Atlantic Quarterly* 103.4 (2004): 620.

6. Sarah Nuttall, *Entanglement: Literary and Cultural Reflections on Post-Apartheid* (Johannesburg: Wits University Press, 2009), 12.

7. Derrek Thulani and Sasha Gear, "South Africa: Prison Population," Just Detention International Prison Insider website (February 2018), https://www.prison-insider.com/countryprofile/prisonsinsouthafrica?s=la-population-carcerale#la-population-carcerale, retrieved December 30, 2018.

8. Though we both identify as being Chicana/o (people of Mexican descent and thereby members of a group that suffers discrimination in the United States), we were undoubtedly read as white in South Africa. This must have had a significant impact on how we were perceived—as bodies in danger and in need of protection. I cannot say how our experiences would have been different if we had been read as black or colored (in the South African sense) in the same contexts.

9. Norimitsu Onishi and Selam Gebrekidan, "'They Eat Money': How Graft Enriches Mandela's Political Heirs," *New York Times* CLXVII, no. 57,934 (April 16, 2018): A10.

10. Alexandra Sutherland, "'Now We Are Real Women': Playing with Gender in a Male Prison Theatre Programme in South Africa," *Research in Drama Education: The Journal of Applied Theatre and Performance* 18.2 (2013): 124.

11. Angela Y. Davis, *Are Prisons Obsolete?* (New York: Seven Stories Press, 2003), 9.

12. Stephen Peté, "A Brief History of Human Rights in the Prisons of Africa," in Jeremy Sarkin (ed.), *Human Rights in African Prisons* (Cape Town: HRSC Press, 2008), 40.

13. Ibid., 41, 43.

14. Ibid., 45.

15. Mandela spent a relatively brief period at Constitution Hill and the majority of his incarceration at Robben Island off the coast of Cape Town.

16. Human Rights Watch, "Prison Conditions in South Africa" (February 8, 1994), https://www.hrw.org/legacy/reports/1994/southafrica/, retrieved June 17, 2018.

17. Gail Super, "'Like Some Rough Beast Slouching towards Bethlehem to be Born': A Historical Perspective on the Institution of the Prison in South Africa, 1976-2004," *British Journal of Criminology* 51.1 (2011): 208.

18. Kelly Gillespie, "Moralizing Security: 'Corrections' and the Post-Apartheid Prison," *Race/Ethnicity: Multidisciplinary Global Contexts* 2.1 (Autumn 2008): 70.

19. Peté, 59.

20. Miranda Young-Jahangeer, "Bringing into Play: Investigating the Appropriation of Prison Theatre in Westville Female Prison, KwaZulu-Natal (2000-2004)," *South African Theatre Journal* 19 (2005): 143.

21. Liz McGregor, "Gibson Kente: South Africa's Father of Township Drama," *The Guardian* (November 9, 2004), https://www.theguardian.com/news/2004/nov/10/guardianobituaries.southafrica, retrieved December 30, 2018.

22. Gcina Mhlophe website, http://www.gcinamhlophe.co.za/index.html, retrieved December 30, 2018.

23. Johannes Visser, "Space and Involvement: Theatre in (a) South African Prison," *Matatu* 43.1 (2013): 167.

24. Sutherland, 122.

25. Christopher John, "Catharsis and Critical Reflection in isiZulu Prison Theatre: A Case Study from Westville Correctional Centre in Durban," in Hazel Barnes (ed.), *Arts Activism, Education, and Therapies: Transforming Communities across Africa* (Amsterdam: Rodolpi, 2013), 87.

26. Ashley Lucas, "Themba Interactive: South African Theatre and HIV/AIDS" (August 3, 2014), https://razorwirewomen.wordpress.com/2014/08/03/themba-interactive-south-african-theatre-and-hivaids/, retrieved August 8, 2019.

27. "HIV and AIDS in South Africa," AVERT website, https://www.avert.org/professionals/hiv-around-world/sub-saharan-africa/south-africa, retrieved December 30, 2018.

28. Ilham El Maerrawi and Heráclito Barbosa Carvalho, "Prevalence and Risk Factors Associated with HIV Infection, Hepatitus, and Syphilis in a State Prison of São Paolo," *International Journal of STD & AIDS* 26.2 (2014): 120.

29. Ibid., 120–7; A. M. Charles, "Indifference, Interruption, and Immunodeficiency: The Impact and Implications of Inadequate HIV/AIDS Care in US Prisons," *Boston University Law Review* 92.6 (2012): 1979–2022.

30. Young-Jahangeer, "Bringing into Play," 143; Miranda Young-Jahangeer, "Interplay: Tracing Personal and Political Transformation through Popular Participatory Theatre in Westville Correctional Centre, Durban South Africa," in Caoimhe McAvinchey (ed.), *Applied Theatre: Women and the Criminal Justice System* (London: Methuen Drama, 2020), 51 n. 3.

31. Young-Jahangeer, "Bringing into Play," 143–5; Young-Jahangeer, "Interplay," 51 n. 2.

32. Young-Jahangeer, "Interplay," 37.

33. Young-Jahangeer, "Bringing into Play," 144; Miranda Young-Jahangeer, "LIVING with the Virus Inside: Women and HIV/AIDS in Prison," *Agenda* 26.2 (2012): 93–9; Young-Jahangeer, "Interplay"; Miranda Young-Jahangeer, "Panoptic Spaces, Democratic Places? Unlocking Culture and Sexuality Through Popular Performance in Westville Female Correctional Centre, Durban, KwaZulu-Natal, South Africa," in Hazel Barnes and Marié-Heleen Coetzee (eds.), *Applied Drama/Theatre as Social Intervention in Conflict and Post-Conflict Contexts* (Newcastle upon Tyne: Cambridge Scholars Publishing, 2014), 18–32; Miranda Young-Jahangeer, "'Less Than a Dog': Interrogating Theatre for Debate in Westville Female Correctional Centre, Durban South Africa," *RiDE: The Journal of Applied Theatre and Performance* 18.2 (2013): 200–3.

34. Young-Jahangeer, "Interplay," 39.

35. Young-Jahangeer, "LIVING," 93–9.

36. Young-Jahangeer, "Interplay," 43.

37. Young-Jahangeer, "LIVING," 96.

38. Young-Jahangeer, "Interplay," 43.

39. Miranda Young-Jahangeer, interview by author and Andrew Martínez, August 2, 2014.

40. Young-Jahangeer, "Interplay," 43.

41. Miranda Young-Jahangeer, email to author, August 12, 2019.

42. Young-Jahangeer, "LIVING," 94.

43. Miranda Young-Jahangeer, interview with Lilly, February 17, 2012.

44. Young-Jahangeer, "LIVING," 97–8.

45. Young-Jahangeer, email, August 12, 2019.

46. Nesha Haniff, "Problem Posing Education as a Methodology in a Developing HIV Education for Low Literate People: Transforming Students and Communities through Paulo Freire's Praxis and the Pedagogy of Action," in Barry McGraw, Eva Baker, and Penelope L. Peterson (eds.), *International Encyclopedia of Education* (Oxford: Elsevier Ltd., 2010), 810.

47. Young-Jahangeer, interview with Lilly.

48. Young-Jahangeer, conversation with author.

49. Jorge Huerta, *Necessary Theater: Six Plays about the Chicano Experience* (Houston: Arte Público Press, 1989).

Chapter 4

1. Ngũgĩ wa Thiong'o, *Wrestling with the Devil: A Prison Memoir* (New York: The New Press, 2018), 83.

Notes

2. Ibid., 85–6.

3. Ngũgĩ wa Thiong'o, *Decolonising the Mind: The Politics of Language in African Literature* (Oxford: James Currey Ltd., 1986), 44, 57.

4. Ibid., 58; Ngũgĩ, *Wrestling*, 22–4, 27–8.

5. Ngũgĩ, *Wrestling*, 213.

6. Ibid., 214.

7. The extraordinary story of how this novel was confiscated and then recovered appears in a chapter entitled "Sherlock Holmes and the Strange Case of the Missing Novel," in Ngũgĩ, *Wrestling*, 231–6.

8. Vincent Lloyd, "'A Moral Astigmatism': King on Hope and Illusion," *Telos* 182 (Spring 2018): 128.

9. Dolan, *Utopia in Performance*, 3.

10. Lora Lempert, *Women Doing Life: Gender, Punishment, and the Struggle for Identity* (New York: New York University Press, 2016), 223–4.

11. Katie Langford, email to author, July 29, 2019.

12. Langford.

13. Somebody's Daughter Theatre Company, *I'll Be on My Way* (unpublished manuscript); emphasis in original.

14. Somebody's Daughter.

15. Ibid.

16. Ibid.

17. Ibid.

18. Seena Fazel, Martin Grann, Boo Kling, and Keith Hawton, "Prison Suicide in 12 Countries: An Ecological Study of 861 Suicides during 2003-2007," *Social Psychiatry and Psychiatric Epidemiology* 46.3 (March 2011): 191–5.

19. Curtis Dawkins, *The Graybar Hotel: Stories* (New York: Scribner, 2017), 155–6.

20. *While We Were Away* Podcast, https://lsa.umich.edu/pcap/podcast.html, retrieved August 13, 2019.

21. Kristina Perkins, "On Seeing Fireflies" (paper presented at seminar for Englehardt Social Justice Fellowship recipients, Ann Arbor, June 25, 2018).

22. Lloyd, 134.

Conclusion

1. Ngũgĩ, *Wrestling*, 133–4.

2. Galeano, 186.

3. Karlene Faith, *Unruly Women: The Politics of Confinement and Resistance* (New York: Seven Stories Press, 2011), xvii–xviii.

4. Ibid., 7.

5. Kushner, 334.

6. Eve Ensler, "The Scariest Thing about Prison Was Not the Spiked Barbed Wire," in *Insecure at Last: Losing It in Our Security-Obsessed World* (New York: Random House, 2006), 116.

7. Ibid., 119–20.

8. *What I Want My Words to Do to You*, POV television program, executive producers Eve Ensler, Carol Jenkins, and Judith Katz, written by Gary Sunshine, distributed by PBS Home Video (2004).

9. Kushner, 80.

10. Augusto Boal, *Theatre of the Oppressed*, trans. Charles A. McBride (New York: Theatre Communications Group, 1993).

11. Galeano, 150.

12. Phyllis Kornfeld, "Thirty Years Teaching Art in Prison: Into the Unknown and Why We Need to Go There" (paper presented at the "Marking Time: Prison Arts and Activism Conference," New Brunswick, October 9, 2014).

13. Prison Performing Arts website, http://prisonartsstl.org/testimonials, retrieved July 24, 2019.

14. George Lombardi, email to author, July 19, 2019.

15. Rudy Martinez, "Drama in Drag: Drama Club's Traveling Troupe Pays It Forward with a Heavy Dose of Fun on the Wards," *Angolite* 43.4 (July/August 2018): 72–4.

16. Patrick Bates, email to author, July 22, 2019.

17. Julia Barron, email to author, July 27, 2019.

18. Ibid.

19. Shannon Harper, email to author, July 26, 2019.

20. Quinn Blackledge, email to author, July 26, 2019.

21. Liv Naimi, email to author, July 26, 2019.

22. "Required Disclosure of Felony Charges and/or Felony Convictions," University of Michigan website, https://spg.umich.edu/policy/601.38, retrieved August 7, 2019.

23. "12,000 Incarcerated Students to Enroll in Postsecondary Educational and Training Programs through Education Department's New Second Change Pell Pilot Program," US Department of Education website (June 24, 2016), https://www.ed.gov/news/press-releases/12000-incarcerated-students-enroll-postsecondary-educational-and-training-programs-through-education-departments-new-second-chance-pell-pilot-program, retrieved August 7, 2019.

Notes

24. Mary Heinen McPherson, email to author, July 1, 2019.

25. Martín Vargas, email to author, July 4, 2019.

26. Lombardi.

27. Ibid.

28. Heinen McPherson.

29. At the time of her incarceration, Heinen McPherson was known as Mary Glover, and her lawsuits were filed under that name, including the most famous of her cases Glover v. Johnson; Glover v. Johnson, Civil Rights Clearinghouse website, https://www.clearinghouse.net/detail.php?id=767, retrieved July 31, 2019; Bonnie Ernst, *Women in the Age of Mass Incarceration: Punishment, Rights, and Resistance in Michigan* (Ann Arbor: ProQuest Dissertations and Theses, 2018).

30. Heinen McPherson.

31. Galeano, 189.

32. Ibid., 192.

33. Viviane Narvaes, "Teatro e resistência: figurações cênicas e dramatúrgicas da prisão" (paper presented at the Seminário Teatro e resistência: figurações cênicas e dramatúrgicas da prisão at the Universidade de São Paulo, May 15, 2019).

34. Viviane Narvaes, email to author, July 25, 2019.

35. Fernanda Pires, "Escaping with Theater: Inmates, Ill and Poverty-Stricken Find Solace," https://global.umich.edu/newsroom/escaping-with-theater/, retrieved July 25, 2019.

36. Narvaes, email, July 25, 2019.

37. Tennessee Williams, *Escape*, in Nicholas Moschovakis and David Roessel (eds.), *Mister Paradise and Other One-Act Plays* (New York: New Directions Publishing Company, 2015), 43.

38. For more on the PCAP Brazil Exchange Program, see: Lucas, Fiche, and Concilio, 1–22.

39. Williams did not date the drafts of the manuscript of *Escape*. The editors of a collection of his short plays have estimated that *Escape* was written sometime in the late 1930s or early 1940s; Nicholas Moschovakis and David Roessel, "Introduction: 'Those Rare Electrical Things Between People,'" in Tennessee Williams, *Mister Paradise and Other One-Act Plays*, eds. Nicholas Moschovakis and David Roessel (New York: New Directions Publishing Company, 2005), xvii.

40. Viviane Narvaes, email to author, July 22, 2019; translation mine.

41. Edson Sodré, "Rebelião da banana," in Viviane Narvaes, *Mostre-me a saída* (unpublished manuscript); all translations from *Mostre-me a saída* are mine.

42. Viviane Narvaes, *Mostre-me a saída* (unpublished manuscript).

43. Jaílton de Carvalho e Rafael Soares, "Carro de músico fuzilado: tenente do Exército fez 77 disparos de fuzil na ação" (May 9, 2019), https://oglobo.globo .com/rio/carro-de-musico-fuzilado-tenente-do-exercito-fez-77-disparos-de-fu zil-na-acao-23651708, retrieved August 7, 2019; Narvaes, *Mostre-me a saída*.

44. Viviane Narvaes, email to author, July 23, 2019.

Chapter 5

1. Ric Knowles, *Reading the Material Theatre* (Cambridge: Cambridge University Press, 2004).

2. National Offender Management Service, "National Security Framework. Ref: NSF 1.1. Categorisation and Recategorisation of Adult Male Prisoners" (Ministry of Justice, August 31, 2011), 6.

3. HMP************* website 2019. Prison wishes to remain anonymous.

4. Marie Hutton, "An Interpretative Evaluation of the Children's Play Project at HMP ************" (Unpublished Evaluation, 2012).

5. Ibid., n.p.

6. "2010 to 2015 Government Policy: Reoffending and Rehabilitation," Policy Paper (Ministry of Justice, 2010), https://www.gov.uk/government/publicatio ns/2010-to-2015-government-policy-reoffending-and-rehabilitation/2010-to-2015-government-policy-reoffending-and-rehabilitation.

7. Kimmett Edgar, Andreas Aresti, and Neil Cornish, "Out for Good: Taking Responsibility for Resettlement" (Prison Reform Trust, 2012), 5.

8. "2010 to 2015 Government Policy."

9. Social Exclusion Unit, "Reducing Re-Offending by Ex-Prisoners" (Office of the Deputy Prime Minister, July 2002), 7, emphasis in original.

10. Edgar, Aresti, and Cornish, 37.

11. Ibid., 38.

12. Transition to Adulthood (T2A), "Pathways from Crime: Ten Steps to a More Effective Approach for Young Adults in the Criminal Justice Process," Summary Report (Barrow Cadbury Trust, 2012).

13. HMP************* website 2019.

14. Shadd Maruna, *Making Good: How Ex-Convicts Reform and Rebuild Their Lives* (Washington DC: American Psychological Association, 2007), 1.

15. Ibid., 24.

16. Lynda Clarke et al., "Fathering behind Bars in English Prisons: Imprisoned Fathers' Identity and Contact with Their Children," *Fathering: A Journal of Theory, Research, and Practice about Men as Fathers* 3.3 (2005): 229.

Notes

17. Hutton, n.p.

18. Ibid.

19. Jenny Hughes, "Doing the Arts Justice: A Review of Research Literature, Practice and Theory," Report (The Unit for the Arts and Offenders Centre for Applied Theatre Research, 2006), 7.

20. Ibid., 9.

21. See Leon Digard, Anna Von Sponeck, and Alison Liebling, "All Together Now: The Therapeutic Potential of a Prison-Based Music Programme," *Prison Service Journal*, no. 170 (2007): 3–14; Andrew Miles and Paul Strauss, "The Academy: A Report on Outcomes for Participants (June 2006–June 2008)," Report (ESRC Centre for Research on Socio-cultural Change University of Manchester, 2009); Sara Houston, "The Touch 'Taboo' and the Art of Contact: An Exploration of Contact Improvisation for Prisoners," *Research in Dance Education* 10.2 (July 1, 2009): 97–113; Rehabilitation Services Group and Shadd Maruna, "Understanding Desistance from Crime," Report (National Offender Management Service, Ministry of Justice, 2010); Leigh Harkins et al., "Evaluation of Geese Theatre's Re-Connect Program: Addressing Resettlement Issues in Prison," *International Journal of Offender Therapy and Comparative Criminology* 55.4 (May 14, 2010): 546–66.

22. See Kirstin Anderson et al., "Inspiring Change: Final Project Report of the Evaluation Team," Report (Creative Scotland, 2011), http://www.artsevidence.o rg.uk/media/uploads/evaluation-downloads/mc-inspiring-change-april-2011.pdf.

23. See Farrall Stephen and Calverley Adam, *Understanding Desistance from Crime* (Maidenhead: Open University Press, 2005); Fergus McNeill, "A Desistance Paradigm for Offender Management," *Criminology & Criminal Justice* 6.1 (July 24, 2016): 39–62; Lyn Tett et al., "Learning, Rehabilitation and the Arts in Prisons: A Scottish Case Study," *Studies in the Education of Adults* 44.2 (September 1, 2012): 171–85.

24. See Michael Balfour, "The Politics of Intention: Looking for a Theatre of Little Changes," *Research in Drama Education: The Journal of Applied Theatre and Performance* 14.3 (August 1, 2009): 347–59.

25. Maruna, 26.

26. Ibid., 26.

27. See Balfour, "The Politics of Intention."

28. Selina Busby, "A Pedagogy of Utopia," *Research in Drama Education: The Journal of Applied Theatre and Performance* 20.3 (November 16, 2015): 413–16.

29. Paul Ricœur, *Lectures on Ideology and Utopia* (New York: Columbia University Press, 1986), 310.

30. Baz Kershaw, "Pathologies of Hope in Drama and Theatre," in Michael Balfour (ed.), *Theatre in Prison: Theory and Practice* (Bristol: Intellect Books, 2004), 36.

31. Ibid.

32. Hutton, n.p.

33. Ricœur, 310.

34. Ibid., 299.

35. Hutton, n.p.

36. Anderson et al., 56.

37. Cf. Ricœur, xxi.

Chapter 6

1. Michael Balfour, "Introduction," in Michael Balfour (ed.), *Theatre in Prison: Theory and Practice* (Bristol: Intellect Books, 2004), 16. See also Caoimhe McAvinchey, *Theatre & Prison* (New York: Palgrave Macmillan, 2011), 77: "The pioneering, radical spirit which characterized early theatre in prison has, in some cases, been compromised by the impact of private management principles embraced by government which inform the discourse and practice of both the arts and the criminal justice system." Laurence Tocci, *The Proscenium Cage: Critical Case Studies in US Prison Theatre Programs* (Youngstown and New York: Cambria Press, 2007), 5–6.

2. Larry Sharp, "A Passion for the Play," *The Angolite* 37.3 (May/June 2012): 64.

3. Robertson, "In Prison"; "On This Stage, Jesus is a Robber, The Devil's a Rapist," narrated by John Burnett, Weekend Edition, *NPR* (June 23, 2012), http://www.npr.org/2012/06/23/155535620/on-this-stage-jesus-is-a-robber-the-devils-a-rapist.

4. Jonathan Shailor, *Performing New Lives: Prison Theatre* (Philadelphia: Jessica Kingsley Publishers, 2011), 22.

5. Burl Cain, *Cast the First Stone*, dir. Jonathan Stack (New York: Highest Common Denominator Media Group, LLC, 2012).

6. Sandra Starr, *Cast the First Stone*, dir. Jonathan Stack (New York: Highest Common Denominator Media Group, LLC, 2012).

7. Qtd. in Sharp, 64; emphasis mine.

8. Qtd. in Layla Roberts, "Audio Slideshow: Prisoners at Play in 'The Life of Jesus Christ,'" *National Public Radio* (June 23, 2013), http://www.npr.org/2012/06/23/155456533/audio-slideshow-prisoners-at-play-in-the-life-of-jesus-christ.

9. Qtd. in Sharp, 64.

10. Ibid.

11. Gail Willars, "Breaking New Ground: The Passion, the Play, the Women," *The Angolite* 37.3 (May/June 2012): 61.

12. Frances Morrison, email to author, June 14, 2012.

13. Serey Kong, *Cast the First Stone*, dir. Jonathan Stack (New York: Highest Common Denominator Media Group, LLC, 2012).

Notes

14. Qtd. in "Audio Slideshow."

15. Gary Tyler, *Cast the First Stone*, dir. Jonathan Stack (New York: Highest Common Denominator Media Group, LLC, 2012).

16. Qtd. in Sharp, 65.

17. Ibid., 63.

18. Ibid., 55.

19. Floyd Webb, "Drama Club," *The Angolite* 14.3 (May/June 1989): 69–70; Lisa Frazier, "Rhythm and Sunshine—Behind Bars," *Times-Picayune* (March 10, 1989): E1.

20. Kim Cobb, "Louisiana Inmates Get their Act Together to Make a Point," *The Houston Chronicle* (March 14, 1993): 20.

21. "Drama Club Banquet," *The Angolite* 15.6 (November/December 1990): 47.

22. Willars, "Breaking New Ground," 61.

23. Sharp, 64–5.

24. Qtd. in Robertson, A18.

25. Anne Bucey, email to author, June 14, 2012.

26. Cindy Dunlop, email to author, June 14, 2012.

27. Bobby Wallace, interview by author, June 16, 2016.

28. Sharp, 59.

29. Bobby Wallace, interview by author, June 16, 2016.

Chapter 7

1. Buckfast is a caffeinated fortified wine that was originally made by monks at Buckfast Abbey in Devon, England. The alcoholic drink, which is now made under a license granted by the monastery, is distributed by J. Chandler & Company in the UK and Grants of Ireland Ltd in Ireland. It is based on a traditional recipe from France. Despite being marketed as a tonic, Buckfast has become notorious in Scotland for its association with those who are involved in antisocial behavior.

2. John Riley, "The Burden of the Sash," qtd. in Martin Travers, *Scarfed for Life* (London: Methuen Drama, 2013), vii.

Chapter 8

1. Tamsin Blanchard, "Arts: Sensation as Ink and Egg are Thrown at Hindley Portrait," *The Independent* (September 18, 1997), http://www.independent.co

.uk/news/arts-sensation-as-ink-and-egg-are-thrown-at-hindley-portrait-1239892.html, retrieved December 12, 2016.

2. Gillian McIvor, *Women Who Offend* (London and Philadelphia: Jessica Kingsley Publishers, 2004).

3. It is important to note that *Bad Girls, Monster*, and *Myra* do not just offer a single take on women and crime or on specific individuals whose lives have become notorious—each is considered and provocative—however, the choices of titles of subjects offer an immediate resonance with a wider public perception about women who offend.

4. For further consideration about the Women in Prison genre, see: Suzanne Bouclin, *Caging Women: Punishment, Judgment, Reform, and Resistance in Women in Prison Films* (unpublished thesis, University of Manitoba, 2007); Suzanne Bouclin, "Women in Prison Movies as Feminist Jurisprudence," *Canadian Journal of Women and the Law / Revue femmes et droit* 21.1 (2009): 9–34.

5. Jill Dolan, *The Feminist Spectator in Action: Feminist Criticism for the Stage and Screen* (Basingstoke: Palgrave Macmillan 2013), 1–3.

6. Sara Ahmed, "Affective Economies," *Social Text* 22.2 (2004): 117–39.

7. Dora Rickford, *Troubled Inside: Responding to the Mental Health Needs of Women in Prison. Prison Reform Trust Report* (London: Prison Reform Trust, 2011); Jill Annison, Jo Brayford, and John Deering, *Women and Criminal Justice: From the Corston Report to Transforming Rehabilitation* (Bristol: Policy Press, 2015).

8. Baroness Corston, *The Corston Report: A Report by Baroness Jean Corston of a Review of Women with Particular Vulnerabilities in the Criminal Justice System* (London: Crown Copyright, 2007), 16.

9. David Ramsbotham, *Women in Prison: A Thematic Review by Her Majesty's Chief Inspector of Prisons* (London: Home Office, 1997); Women in Prison, "Key Facts: A Round-Up and Latest Key Statistics Regarding Women Affected by the Criminal Justice System" (2016), womeninprison.org.uk, retrieved December 12, 2016; Roy Allen, "Global Prison Trends 2016" (London: Prison Reform International, 2016), http://www.penalreform.org/wp-content/uploads/2016/05/Global_prison_trends_report_2016.pdf, retrieved July 1, 2016.

10. McIvor, *Women Who Offend*.

11. Caoimhe McAvinchey, *Possible Fictions: The Testimony of Applied Performance with Women in Prison in England and Brazil* (unpublished dissertation, Queen Mary University of London, 2007), 121.

12. Interview with Jacqueline Holborough, Unfinished Histories—Clean Break (2013), http://www.unfinishedhistories.com/history/companies/clean-break/, retrieved December 12, 2016.

13. Dolan, *The Feminist Spectator in Action*, 3.

14. Chloë Moss, *Sweatbox* (unpublished script, commissioned by Clean Break, London, 2015), 1–2.

15. Ibid., 4.

16. Escort and Custody Services are currently provided by GEO Amey and Serco Wincanton and Secure Escort Services for Children and Young People (SESCYP) by Serco.

17. HMI Prisons, *Transfers and Escorts within the Criminal Justice System* (London: HM Inspectorate of Prisons, 2014), http://www.justiceinspectorate s.gov.uk/hmiprisons/inspections/transfers-and-escorts-within-the-criminal-j ustice-system/, retrieved December 12, 2016.

18. Ibid., 6.

19. Peter Thatchell, "Treating People like Cattle," *The Guardian* (January 30, 2008), http://www.theguardian.com/commentisfree/2008/jan/30/treatingpeoplelik ecattle, retrieved November 30, 2015.

20. Paul Ricœur, "The Moral, the Ethical and the Political," in Greg S. Johnson and Dan R. Stiver (eds.), *Paul Ricœur and the Task of Political Philosophy* (New York: Lexington Books, 2013).

21. Chloë Moss talks about *Sweatbox* for Clean Break, https://www.youtube.com/ watch?v=u9wdW0AVy1U, retrieved December 12, 2016.

22. Dolan, *The Feminist Spectator in Action*, 9.

23. Miranda Fricker, *Epistemic Injustice: Power and the Ethics of Knowing* (Oxford: University of Oxford Press, 2010), 1.

24. C. A. J. Coady, *Testimony: A Philosophical Study* (Oxford and New York: Clarendon Press, 1995), 26.

25. Fricker, 1.

26. Ibid.

27. Ibid.

28. Axel Gelfert, *A Critical Introduction to Testimony* (London: Bloomsbury, 2014), 227.

29. *Wicked* by Bryony Lavery, programme note (1991), Clean Break archive.

30. Bryony Lavery, *Her Aching Heart, Two Marias, Wicked* (London: Methuen Drama, 1991), 92.

31. Ibid., 144.

32. John Hills, Julian Le Grand, and David Piachaud, eds., *Understanding Social Exclusion* (Oxford: Oxford University Press, 2002).

33. Vivienne Franzmann, *Pests* (London: Nick Hern Books, 2014), 70; Ellie Kendrick and Sinéad Matthews played Pink and Rolly in the original production (Royal Court Theatre, London).

34. Tim Brennan et al., "Women's Pathways to Serious and Habitual Crime: A Person-Centered Analysis Incorporating Gender-Responsive Factors," *Criminal Justice and Behaviour* 39.11 (2012): 1481–508.

35. Amelia Gentleman, "Vivienne Franzmann's Pests: 'It's Brutal, but It's Authentic,'" *The Guardian* (March 5, 2014), https://www.theguardian.com/st age/2014/mar/05/pests-vivienne-franzmann-women-prison-drugs, retrieved November 10, 2016.

36. Deborah Bruce, Theresa Ikoko, Laura Lomas, Chino Odimba, and Ursula Rani Sarma, *Joanne* (London: Nick Hern, 2015), 5.

SELECTED BIBLIOGRAPHY
ON PRISON THEATRE

"Act V." *This American Life*. Chicago: WBEZ Radio, August 9, 2002.

Alexander, William. *Is William Martinez Not Our Brother?: Twenty Years of the Prison Creative Arts Project*. Ann Arbor: University of Michigan Press, 2010.

Balfour, Michael. *Theatre in Prison: Theory and Practice*. Bristol: Intellect, 2004.

Bates, Laura. *Shakespeare Saved My Life: Ten Years in Solitary with the Bard*. Naperville: Source, 2013.

Bernstein, Lee. *America Is the Prison: Arts and Politics in Prison in the 1970s*. Chapel Hill: U of North Carolina, 2010.

Biggs, Lisa. "Serious Fun at Sun City: Theatre for Incarcerated Women in the 'New' South Africa." *Theatre Survey* 57.1 (2016): 4–36.

Cast the First Stone. Directed by Jonathan Stack. New York: Highest Common Denominator Media Group, LLC, 2012.

Charlebois, Elizabeth. "With Rhyme and Reason: *Hip Hop Hamlet* in Prison." In *Text & Presentation, 2015*, edited by Graley Herren, 87–107. Jefferson: McFarland & Company, Inc., 2015.

Cheliotis, Leonidas K. *The Arts of Imprisonment: Control, Resistance and Empowerment*. Farnham: Ashgate, 2012.

Concilio, Vicente. *Teatro e prisão: dilemas da Liberdade artística*. São Paulo: Aderaldo & Rothschild Editores, 2007.

Ensler, Eve. "The Scariest Thing About Prison Was Not the Spiked Barbed Wire." In *Insecure at Last: Losing It in Our Security-Obsessed World*, 115–24. New York: Random House, 2006.

Fahy, Thomas Richard, and Kimball King, eds. *Captive Audience: Prison and Captivity in Contemporary Theater*. New York: Routledge, 2003.

Fraden, Rena. *Imagining Medea: Rhodessa Jones & Theater for Incarcerated Women*. Chapel Hill: University of North Carolina Press, 2001.

Hansen, Ingrid, and Peter Balkwill. "Fractured Fables: A Prison Puppet Project." In *Working the Margins of Community-Based Adult Learning*, edited by Shauna Butterwick and Carole Roy, 133–44. Amsterdam: Sense Publishers, 2016.

Hensley, Michelle. *All the Lights On: Reimagining Theater with Ten Thousand Things*. St. Paul: Minnesota Historical Society Press, 2014.

Heritage, Paul. "Staging Human Rights: Securing the Boundaries?" *Hispanic Research Journal* 7.4 (December 2006): 353–63.

Heritage, Paul. "Taking Hostages: Staging Human Rights." *TDR/The Drama Review* 48.3 (2004): 96–106.

Herold, Niels. *Prison Shakespeare and the Purpose of Performance: Repentance Rituals and the Early Modern*. New York: Palgrave Macmillan, 2014.

Hip Hop Hamlet at Northeast Correctional Center. February 26, 2015. prisonartsstl. org/audio-video.

Hip Hop Hamlet at Women's Eastern Reception, Diagnostic, & Correctional Center. September 13, 2018. prisonartsstl.org/hiphophamlet2018.

John, Christopher. "Catharsis and Critical Reflection in isiZulu Prison Theatre: A Case Study from Westville Correctional Centre in Durban." In *Arts Activism, Education, and Therapies: Transforming Communities across Africa*, edited by Hazel Barnes, 85–96. Amsterdam: Rodolpi, 2013.

Jordan, Robert. *The Convict Theatres of Early Australia 1788-1840*. Hertfordshire: University of Hertfordshire Press, 2002.

Kuziakina, Natalia. *Theatre in the Solovki Prison Camp*, trans. by Boris M. Meerovich. Luxembourg: Harwood Academic Publishers, 1995.

Lawston, Jodie Michelle, and Ashley E. Lucas. *Razor Wire Women: Prisoners, Activists, Scholars, and Artists*. Albany: SUNY Press, 2011.

Lonergan, John. *The Governor: The Life and Times of the Man Who Ran Mountjoy*. Dublin: Penguin Ireland, 2010.

Lucas, Ashley. "Prisoners on the Great White Way: *Short Eyes* and *Zoot Suit* as the First US Latina/o Plays on Broadway." *Latin American Theater Review* 43.1 (Fall 2009): 121–35.

Lucas, Ashley. "When I Run in My Bare Feet: Music, Writing, and Theatre in a North Carolina Women's Prison." *American Music* 31.2 (Summer 2013): 134–162.

Lucas, Ashley, Natália Fiche, and Vicente Concilio. "We Move Forward Together: A Prison Theatre Exchange Program among Three Universities in the United States and Brazil." *Prison Journal* 99.4 (2019): https://doi. org/10.1177/0032885519861061.

McAvinchey, Caoimhe. *Applied Theatre: Women and the Criminal Justice System*. London: Methuen Drama, 2020.

McAvinchey, Caoimhe. *Theatre & Prison*. Basingstoke: Palgrave Macmillan, 2011.

Mickey B. Directed by Tom MaGill. Educational Theatre Company LTD., 2007.

Mohler, Courtney Elkin. "How to Turn 'a Bunch of Gang-Bangin' Criminals into Big Kids Having Fun': Empowering Incarcerated and At-Risk Youth through Ensemble Theatre." *Theatre Topics* 22.1 (March 2012): 89–102.

Ngũgĩ wa Thiong'o. *Wrestling with the Devil: A Prison Memoir*. New York: The New Press, 2018.

O'Connor, Peter, and Molly Mullen. "Prison Theatre: Letting the Light in to Disciplinary Relationships." *NJ Drama Australia Journal* 35.1 (2011): 133–45.

Pensalfini, Rob. *Prison Shakespeare: For These Deep Shames and Great Indignities*. Hampshire: Palgrave Macmillan, 2016.

Pensalfini, Rob. "Shakespeare of the Oppressed." In *Teaching Shakespeare beyond the Centre: Australian Perspectives*, edited by Kate Flaherty, Penny Gay, and L. E. Semler, 225–36. Basingstoke: Palgrave Macmillan, 2013.

Ridha, Thana. *Exploring Prison Theatre in Canada: A Case Study on William Head on Stage (WHoS)*. Master's thesis, University of Ottawa, 2018.

Selected Bibliography on Prison Theatre

Shailor, Jonathan. *Performing New Lives: Prison Theatre*. London: Jessica Kingsley, 2011.

Shakespeare Behind Bars. Directed by Hank Rogerson. Shakespeare Theatre Association, 2006.

Sutherland, Alexandra. "'Now We Are Real Women': Playing with Gender in a Male Prison Theatre Programme in South Africa." *Research in Drama Education: The Journal of Applied Theatre and Performance* 18.2 (2013): 120–32.

Thompson, James, ed. *Prison Theatre: Perspectives and Practices*. London: Jessica Kingsley Publishers, 1998.

Tocci, Laurence. *The Proscenium Cage: Critical Case Studies in U.S. Prison Theatre Programs*. Youngstown: Cambria, 2007.

Trounstine, Jean R. *Shakespeare behind Bars: One Teacher's Story of the Power of Drama in a Women's Prison*. Ann Arbor: University of Michigan Press, 2004.

Van Steen, Gonda Aline Hector. *Theatre of the Condemned: Classical Tragedy on Greek Prison Islands*. Oxford: Oxford University Press, 2011.

Visser, Johannes. "Space and Involvement: Theatre in (a) South African Prison." *Matatu* 43.1 (2013): 161–283.

What I Want My Words to Do to You. Executive producers Eve Ensler, Carol Jenkins, and Judith Katz. Written by Gary Sunshine. PBS Home Video, 2004.

Wilcox, Agnes. "Denmark is a Prison, and You are There." *Journal of the Midwest Modern Language Association* 38.1 (Spring 2005): 116–22.

Williams, Rachel Marie-Crane. *Teaching the Arts behind Bars*. Boston: Northeastern University Press, 2003.

Woodland, Sarah. "'Magic Mothers and Wicked Criminals': Exploring Narrative and Role in a Drama Programme with Women Prisoners." *Applied Theatre Research* 1.1 (January 2013): 77–89.

Young-Jahangeer, Miranda. "Bringing in to Play: Investigating the Appropriation of Prison Theatre in Westville Female Prison, KwaZulu-Natal (2000–2004)." *South African Theatre Journal* 19.1 (2005): 143–56.

Young-Jahangeer, Miranda. "Interplay: Tracing Personal and Political Transformation through Popular Participatory Theatre in Westville Correctional Centre, Durban South Africa." In *Applied Theatre: Women and the Criminal Justice System*, edited by Caoimhe McAvinchey, 37–55. London: Methuen Drama, 2020 .

Young-Jahangeer, Miranda. "'Less Than a Dog': Interrogating Theatre for Debate in Westville Female Correctional Centre, Durban South Africa." *RiDE: The Journal of Applied Theatre and Performance* 18.2 (2013): 200–3.

Young-Jahangeer, Miranda. "LIVING with the Virus Inside: Women and HIV/AIDS in Prison." *Agenda* 26.2 (2012): 93–9.

Young-Jahangeer, Miranda. "Panoptic Spaces, Democratic Places? Unlocking Culture and Sexuality Through Popular Performance in Westville Female Correctional Centre, Durban, KwaZulu-Natal, South Africa." In *Applied Drama/Theatre as Social Intervention in Conflict and Post-Conflict Contexts*, edited by Hazel Barnes and Marié-Heleen Coetzee, 18–32. Newcastle upon Tyne: Cambridge Scholars Publishing, 2014.

SELECTED LIST OF PRISON THEATRE COMPANIES AND PROGRAMS

The following list includes only the prison theatre companies and programs encountered in the research for this book. It is by no means comprehensive, even for those countries that served as major research sites for this book. The list only includes theatre companies and programs that remain active at the time of this writing. The number of companies listed for each nation has far less to do with how many programs may actually exist in each country than it does with how my network of connections led me to know about these groups.

Australia

Big hART
   Burnie, Tasmania

Daughters of the Floating Brothel (Griffith University)
   Brisbane, Queensland

Queensland Shakespeare Ensemble
   Brisbane, Queensland

Somebody's Daughter Theatre
   Albert Park, Victoria

Brazil

Celas e Elas: Teatro com Mulheres em Privação de Liberdade
   Joinville, Santa Catarina

Teatro na Penetenciária Feminina de Florianópolis (Universidade do Estado de Santa Catarina)
   Florianópolis, Santa Catarina

Selected List of Prison Theatre Companies and Programs

Teatro na Prisão (Universidade Federal do Estado do Rio de Janeiro)
Rio de Janeiro, Rio de Janeiro

Canada

William Head on Stage
Victoria, British Columbia

Lebanon

Catharsis: Lebanese Center for Drama Therapy
Sarba, Mount Lebanon

New Zealand

Arts Access Aotearoa
Wellington, New Zealand

Poland

National Competition for Dramatic Art for Prison Inmates
Poznan, Wielkopolska

South Africa

University of KwaZulu-Natal Prison Theatre Projects
Durban, KwaZulu-Natal

Young in Prison
Cape Town, Western Cape

Spain

Basket Beat Orquestra
Barcelona, Catalonia

United Kingdom

Arts in Social Justice (Royal Conservetoire of Scotland)
Glasgow, Scotland

Children's Play Project
London, England

Citizens Theatre
Glasgow, Scotland

Clean Break
London, England

Educational Shakespeare Company
Belfast, Northern Ireland

Geese Theatre Company
Birmingham, England

Only Connect
London, England

TiPP (University of Manchester)
Manchester, England

United States

Acting Out Theatre Company
Lincoln, Illinois

Actor's Gang
Los Angeles, California

Angola Drama Club
Angola, Louisiana

Appalshop
Whitesburg, Kentucky

ArtsAloud (Oklahoma State University)
Stillwater, Oklahoma

Bar None Theater Company
Niantic, Connecticut

Selected List of Prison Theatre Companies and Programs

Judy Dworin Performance Project
Hartford, Connecticut

Marin Shakespeare Company
San Rafael, California

Medea Project: Theater for Incarcerated Women
San Francisco, California

Open Hearts Open Minds
Portland, Oregon

Phoenix Players Theatre Group (Cornell University)
Ithaca, New York

Prison Creative Arts Project (University of Michigan)
Ann Arbor, Michigan

Prison Performing Arts
St. Louis, Missouri

Reforming Arts
Atlanta, Georgia

Rehabilitation Through the Arts
Purchase, New York

Shakespeare & Company—Shakespeare in the Courts
Lenox, Massachusetts

Shakespeare Behind Bars
Louisville, Kentucky and Macatawa, Michigan

Shakespeare Corrected (Millikin University)
Decatur, Illinois

Shakespeare in Prison
Detroit, Michigan

Shakespeare Prison Project
Kenosha, Wisconsin

Storycatchers Theatre
Chicago, Illinois

Ten Thousand Things Theater
St. Paul, Minnesota

Theater of Witness
Philadelphia, Pennsylvania

William James Association
Santa Cruz, California

Youth Arts Alliance!
Ann Arbor, Michigan

CONTRIBUTORS

Selina Busby is an academic and theatre practitioner who makes performances with community groups and is a National Teaching Fellow. Her research and practice focus on theatre that invites the possibility of change, both in contemporary plays and in participatory performance. As a practitioner, she works in prison settings, youth theatres, and with young people living in adverse conditions both in the UK and internationally.

Stephanie Gaskill received her PhD in Religious Studies from the University of North Carolina–Chapel Hill in 2017. Through her dissertation research, she became active in movements to end mass incarceration in Louisiana. She currently serves as Education Director for Operation Restoration, a New Orleans–based nonprofit for currently and formerly incarcerated women and girls.

Elly Goodman trained at the Royal Scottish Academy of Music and Drama. She is Community Drama Artist at the Citizens Theatre and has worked in arts and criminal justice for twenty-nine years. Goodman specializes in theatre in prisons and within the broader criminal justice sector. She is a founding member and trustee of Justice and Arts Scotland and has delivered an eight-year creative theatre residency in HM Prison Barlinnie, Scotland's largest institution for male prisoners. Goodman's work places a special emphasis on women and socially excluded adults.

Caoimhe McAvinchey is Reader in Socially Engaged and Contemporary Performance at Queen Mary University of London. Prior to this, she established the MA Applied Drama program at Goldsmiths, University of London. Her publications include *Theatre & Prison* (2011), *Performance and Community: Case Studies and Commentary* (2013), *Phakama: Making Participatory Performance* (2018), with Lucy Richardson and Fabio Santos, and *Applied Theatre: Women and the Criminal Justice System* (2020). She is currently working on a monograph about Clean Break theatre company.

Neil Packham trained as an actor at Drama Centre, London. He was introduced to the world of community theatre practice during Glasgow European City of Culture 1990. He has worked at the Citizens Theatre for eighteen years as Community Drama Director, where he started working extensively with Elly Goodman particularly in the field of theatre in prisons, collaborating with her on their residency in HM Prison Barlinnie and further projects in HM Prison Low Moss.

Heather Ann Thompson is a historian at the University of Michigan. She is the Pulitzer Prize- and Bancroft Prize-winning author of *Blood in the Water: The Attica Prison Uprising of 1971 and Its Legacy* (2016), and she writes extensively on the history of policing, mass incarceration, and the US criminal justice system.

INDEX

Index

Index

CPSIA information can be obtained
at www.ICGtesting.com
Printed in the USA
LVHW021913080920
665362LV00014B/261

9 781408 185896